THE MAN IN BACK

JIMMY CAPPS

THE MAN IN BACK

JIMMY CAPPS

The Autobiography
With Scot England

ISBN 978-0-9986367-3-3

Editor: Lindsey McNealy
Cover Design/Layout: Paula Underwood Winters
Cover Photo by David Bailey
Back Cover Photo by Fred Bingaman
www.jimmycappsbook.com Website Design: Katie Vickery

Printed in the United States of America

For more info on Jimmy Capps, including his latest CDs and other merchandise, visit www.jimmycapps.com

Published by:
England Media
102 Rachels Ct Hendersonville TN 37075
(615) 804-0361
englandmedia@yahoo.com

If you enjoyed this book, you will also like these autobiographies published by England Media:

Ronnie McDowell "Bringing It to You Personally"
Johnny Lee "Still Lookin' for Love"
Moe Bandy "Lucky Me"
Lulu Roman "This is My Story, This is My Song"

CONTENTS

THE MAN IN BACK

I'm sure that, in every interview I do about this book, I will be asked, "Why is it called 'The Man in Back'?"

It's very simple: that's where I've always been. I've always been a musician who backed up the person standing up at the middle mic. It describes exactly who I am, and what I do. Most people in any kind of entertainment want to be the center of attention. They desire to always be out front, so everyone can see them. Not me. I'm the man in back.

– Jimmy Capps

FOREWORD

"I always knew of Jimmy Capps, long before I joined the Statler Brothers. He had been with the Louvin Brothers, and I was a big fan of the Louvins. I was already a big fan of Jimmy's before I'd even met him in the early 80s.

Any time the Statlers did anything, it was always first class. Our TV show had the very best musicians in Nashville, or in anywhere in the world.

Jimmy played on our TV show for its entire run, and he was always Mr. Smooth on the guitar. He always played perfect.

During our seven-year run of the show, everybody got very close, and we always liked to joke a lot. Harold signed one of his Lester Roadhog pictures for Jimmy, and on it he wrote, 'I'd hire you if you were the last guitar player on earth!'

Jimmy Capps put his whole life into his music. He had that love for music many decades ago, and that love is still there today… and he is playing as good today as he did back in the 90s on our TV show. Plus, he looks even better! He is more handsome today. Maybe that's because he is happy. You can see that. He is married to a good woman who takes care of him, and Michele believes in him.

I always like to talk about guitars with Jimmy. We both love guitars so much. Of course, he's got about 150 more than I do.

During our visits, we've become the best of friends. We like to get together and go out to eat and just talk.

He's become a really good friend, and I cherish that more than anything. Jimmy's talent speaks for itself, but his heart speaks even louder than that. He is also a great gentleman in every way. He is one of the nicest guys in the world.

When I'm with Jimmy on the Opry, or on Larry's Country Diner, or the Family Reunion, I often just look at him and I am so proud for him. I see a man who followed his heart and did what he loved. He never gave up, and all of his dreams have now come true, and I couldn't be happier for him. I love him. Jimmy's legacy is so huge. He is up there with the best of the best. I am so glad he is finally doing this book! If anyone deserves a book, it is Jimmy Capps."

– Jimmy Fortune

DEDICATION

I would like to dedicate this book to my mom and dad, Tom and Alice, and to every member of my family, past and present. I want to say Thank You from the bottom of my heart to every person who gave me the opportunity to do what I love, and that is to play guitar to the best of my ability. But most of all I want to thank God for his blessings, and for allowing me to be, THE MAN IN BACK.

BLESSED

When I look back at my life, I seem to use that word a lot. I think that one word, sums up my life. I even thought about naming the title of this book 'Blessed'.

When I was a little boy, I would lie in my bed and dream about being on the Grand Ole Opry. I would listen to the Opry every chance that I got. One day, I heard Grady Martin playing guitar with Red Foley, and I said, "Man, it would be so great to be on that stage. Just one time."

As I lay there dreaming of playing on the Opry, just one time, there was no way I could have ever imagined that I would actually go on to play on that stage more times than anyone else in the history of the Opry. It's still hard for me to believe.

When I first started on the Opry, the hot stars were Little Jimmy Dickens, Roy Acuff, and Minnie Pearl. Yes, I was one of the "men in back." I played behind all of those performers who went on to become true legends. I started on the Opry in the late 50s, and then continued on into the 60s… and then I just kept on playing through the 1970s, the 80s, the 90s, and now we're almost twenty years into the 2000s, and I'm proud to still be there today.

And throughout all those decades, I have also enjoyed a great career as a studio musician, and you'll soon read about some of the classic songs that I was blessed to be a part of. When I stop and think about how blessed I have been, it's so hard to believe. I have to ask, "Why me? Why have I been so blessed?"

– Jimmy Capps

Chapter One

A GUITAR PICKER IS BORN

Tommie and Alice Capps loved their three sons. I was their third. Since my older brothers were born seventeen and fifteen years before me, I assume that I was an unplanned mistake. My dad spelled his name in the unique way of "Tommie". I don't know why. And he didn't have a middle name. My mom's real first name was Louie, but she went by her middle name of "Alice".

My mother gave birth to my brothers, Thomas and Fred, at home. I was the first baby she had that was born in a hospital. But I never knew my brother Fred. He died when he was just ten years old, from an appendicitis attack.

I came very close to not even making it to age ten. By the time she'd gotten pregnant with me, mom was almost 40 years old. Back then, that was pretty old to be having a kid, and she developed some complications in the delivery room. My Aunt Martha was in the room with her.

As I was born, the doctor quietly told my mother, "The baby is dead." He laid me over onto a table, then he turned to a nurse and said, "We need to work on the mother or we are going to lose her, too."

A few minutes later, my aunt looked over at me and yelled, "That baby is alive! I saw his hand move!" Today, I tell everybody that when my hand moved, I was trying to make a G-chord. It was on May 25, 1939 that James Dixon Capps made that impressive debut. You can call me Jimmy.

My middle name came from my great uncle, my grandmother's brother. His name was Gideon Dixon. Before I was born, he would tell my parents, "If it's a boy, and you name him after me, I will buy him a suit of clothes when he turns six years old." And he kept his word. You can see a picture of me wearing my new suit in the photo pages of this book.

But that suit of clothes was not the only thing that Uncle Gideon gave me. He was a fiddle player. He wasn't great at it, but he could play hoedowns and stuff. And in his will, he left me his fiddle. It's now more than 125 years old, and I've still got it.

I was born in Fayetteville, North Carolina, thirty miles east of Raleigh on Interstate 40, but we lived in Benson, North Carolina. While the doctors were able to save both me and my mother, I think that the brush with death I had when I was born is the reason my family spoiled me so much all my life. I think my mother, grandma and Aunt Martha thought that, since I'd almost died, they would give me everything that I wanted.

My oldest brother was fully grown by the time I came along. And since my other brother had died before I ever got to meet him, I was basically raised as an only child. But I had the greatest parents that a person could have. I still tear up when I think about my mom and dad. My parents supported me in everything that I wanted to do. What great parents I had.

My childhood was great. I used to think we were rich. We always had everything we needed. We had plenty of food and nice clothes. It wasn't until I left home that I found out we had actually been pretty poor.

My dad was so good to me. He was a hard-working man, and one tough son of a gun. He was a lot tougher than a guitar player, I'll tell you that! Dad drove a Mack semi-truck for the Medlin and Dorman Company. And since Benson was such a small town, dad had to go to Raleigh any time he needed to get his truck worked on. He worked six days a week, driving his truck five days, and on the sixth day he would work as a clerk in the Medlin and Dorman store, where they sold everything from appliances to country hams.

When I was nine years old, I went into the Medlin and Dorman store. My dad wasn't there this day. The store had free calendars that they gave to all their customers. They were large, nice calendars, and when I saw the stack of them that said, "Free. Take a calendar", I picked one up.

Later that night, at home, my dad saw my calendar and asked me, "Whose is this?"

I said, "It's mine. I got it at the store. They said they were free."

Dad said, "Those are for customers. What did you buy?"

"Nothing," I said.

He said, "You will take that back tomorrow."

And I did. My dad wanted to make sure that his son never took anything he didn't earn. It's a lesson I never forgot.

One year later, I got another lesson that I still remember to this day… almost every time that I go to the bathroom.

My father gave me a Quarter allowance each week, as long as I did all my chores. These included mowing the grass and cleaning up the yard. Every Saturday, I took my earnings to the local movie theater. Back then, a ticket cost 14 cents. A large Root Beer was 6 cents.

I loved the B-Western movies; Roy Rogers, Gene Autry, Lash LaRue and Sunset Carson were my favorite cowboys. On this particular Saturday, I watched the movie twice. In between showings, I got my large Root Beer.

By the time I came out of the theater, it was completely dark outside. But as soon as I started walking home, that combination of spending the entire afternoon in the theater, and my big ole Root Beer, started kicking in... very fast. I had to get to the bathroom as soon as possible! And I knew I couldn't make it home in time.

Luckily, I knew that there was an outhouse behind the hardware store. We didn't have any street lights, and it was so dark, but I knew where the outhouse was, and I found it just in time. I swung the outhouse door open, and it was even darker inside. Here I was, this 10 year old little boy, and I was afraid to go into that pitch dark outhouse. I thought there might be a rat or a snake inside. So, I decided to stand outside, and aim toward where I remembered the hole was.

As I peed into the darkness, I suddenly heard a very deep voice, saying, "Boy! You're a peein' on me!"

You've heard people say the phrase, "It scared the pee out of me"? Well, I stopped peeing mid-stream! I pulled up my pants and I ran all the way home!

My dad was gone all week, out driving a semi, so I was basically raised by a bunch of women. I was spoiled by my mom, grandma, and aunt. Grandma Alice lived next door to us. My Aunt Martha was an old maid, and she lived with my grandmother.

One of the biggest blessings of my childhood was the time I spent talking with my grandmother. She had a rocking chair and swing on the front porch. She would sit in the chair, and I would sit in the swing, and we would visit for hours.

Grandma taught me a lot about life. She was one smart, very classy lady. She had long hair that would give Crystal Gayle a run for her money. And she would sit and brush her hair each afternoon. She was a sweet lady.

THE MAN IN BACK

When I was a little boy, I sat with grandma, my mom and my aunt as they listened to radio soap operas. I can still remember one called 'Portia Faces Life'! My mom would be ironing as she listened to the show. I can still smell her iron today.

Yes, I listened to the radio soap operas each day with the women in my house, but my very favorite show would come on the air each Saturday night. That's when my dad would tune the dial on our little Philco radio to 650 AM. I couldn't wait for the Grand Ole Opry broadcast over WSM!

Dad was a big Bill Monroe fan. But I liked Red Foley. I would never have believed it if youd've told me that one day I'd get to play guitar on stage for Red Foley. But sure enough, less than ten years later, I worked with Red at a county fair in Illinois. He was a heck of an entertainer. I was simply amazed at how he could have the audience laughing one minute, and then have them crying the next. We lost him way too soon. He was just 58 years old. He died in his sleep, just after he had done a show with Billy Walker and Hank Williams, Jr. The last song Red sang that night was "Peace in the Valley".

At the start of each school year, my dad would allow me to go get new jeans and shirts. I always got to buy three pairs of jeans and five shirts. Dad let me pick out all my own clothes. He trusted my judgement. And then he paid the store five dollars a week, until my clothes were paid off.

My dad was a proud man. He liked to look good. He had "Sunday clothes", and he had everyday clothes. He wore matching khakis at work. But on Sunday, when we would go to church, he would always wear a suit with a vest. He also had a pocket watch.

I think that might be the reason why, today, I still care about my clothes and appearance. I want to look my very best when I go to the Opry. The Opry band used to wear matching outfits, and even when they did away with that, I still continued wearing a suit. I feel that I owe that to the people who are in the audience.

And I also want to look good when I go anywhere. I take pride in how I look when I go out in public. I'm sure that all started with my Dad.

For a time, we lived in the same house, with my grandmother and aunt. I slept in a bed next to my mom and dad's bed. We all shared one bathroom. When the house next door became available, we moved there. It was a nice house, and our rent was $25.00 a month. That house at 216 W. Church Street is still there to this day.

Since our house had three bedrooms, mom and dad took in a man who rented the third room. His name was Ray Jones. He was a meat cutter in a grocery store. Ray also had a Gibson guitar that he kept under his bed, and when he went to work each day, I would run to his room and pull the guitar out. I was very careful as I took it out of the case. I thought it was the prettiest thing I had ever seen.

Chapter Two

MY FIRST LOVE

She was my first love. And her name was Harmony.

At age 11, I got a job working for the City Market grocery store. A short time later, I went to work at another grocery store, which was owned by a man named Jim Thornton. Mr. Thornton would soon come to play a very important role in my country music career... but first, I had one more stop in my grocery career, and that was at Langdon's Grocery.

All of these stores offered home delivery, and I rode a bicycle that had a big basket on it so that I could carry all of my orders. The stores owned the delivery bikes, and we believe the one I rode is actually now in the Benson museum!

I made $12 a week delivering groceries all around town. There were several little restaurants in my hometown. They would buy hamburger meat and hot dogs from our store, and I would deliver their order to them. Back then, all of the restaurants had jukeboxes as well, and at each stop I made, I'd always check out the record selections. Carl Smith and Lefty Frizzell were both big on the jukeboxes. They both had four or five songs each on there. They were like a "today's" Garth Brooks.

It was during one of my grocery deliveries that I fell in love for the first time. I saw her through a screen window... her name was Harmony.

Harmony was a Silvertone Guitar. It was an arch type guitar, with F holes. Sears distributed this, guitar that was made by the Harmony company. The man who owned the guitar had screens on his windows, and when I brought groceries to his house, I'd look in through the screen at that guitar sitting in the corner. I thought, "That is a real guitar, like the big boys play in Nashville, Tennessee!"

I had no idea that the Gibson sitting under the bed in our renter's room at home was worth five times what the Silvertone was!

A year later, I would get my own guitar, but just before that, I received something else very special from my dad. When I turned 12, dad took me to a jewelry store and bought me a birthstone ring. We didn't have a lot of money, but it was important for my father to buy this special ring for my 12th birthday. I kept it all my life- and a few years ago, I had a man put the birthstone into my Opry ring, which made it even more special.

I loved my ring… but I loved the gift that my parents gave me the next Christmas even more. I had asked for a guitar, and I just knew I was going to get one, especially when I saw a beautifully wrapped, guitar-sized box waiting under our Christmas tree!

But my older brother loved to pull pranks on me, and he had found this tiny, little toy guitar, that had rubber bands on it. It was only four inches long. He wrapped it up inside a huge box the size of a real guitar, and set it under the tree. That Christmas morning, I couldn't wait to tear into it to get my dream guitar. And when I opened it, I was heartbroken.

But my sadness didn't last long. Dad said, "Maybe this will work better," and handed me the guitar I had dreamed of. In all reality, it was a twelve dollar, flat top guitar: a Stella, with some sort of laminate wood. The strings were about an inch high off the fret board. It played hard. You could only play the C and G chords. F was really hard. The further up the neck you went, the more your fingers hurt. It was a cheap guitar, but I thought it was the greatest thing in the world.

During almost every waking hour, I had that guitar in my hands. And even when I was in bed, I was still holding it. I would lay in my bed at night and literally dream about being on that Opry stage. I would try to picture what it would feel like, to be there. I knew I could never be as great as those other guitar players... but I wanted to be good enough that I could earn their respect.

As luck would have it, I didn't have to go very far in order to find my first musical teacher. My uncle Lynn, who had married my mother's sister, lived next door. Uncle Lynn was a champion fiddle player. Since I didn't know how to tune my guitar, I had my uncle do it for me. Every day when he got off from work at 6:00, I would run over to his house to ask him to tune my guitar. It would only stay in tune for the night, and then I'd always have to go back the next day.

Uncle Lynn taught me how to play hoedowns. I'd accompany him as he played the fiddle. I played my guitar every day, before and after school. Every chance I got, every spare moment, I would be picking my guitar.

A couple years later, though, my dad bought me an even nicer one. It was a Gibson ES 175, and it cost $135.00. That was a huge amount of money back then, and I don't know how my dad managed to pay for it. That guitar would be worth about $20,000 today.

Over the years, people have asked me if I've saved all of my guitars, especially the first ones I had. Unfortunately, those early ones are long gone. Since we didn't have a lot of money, if I got a new guitar I would have to trade in my old one. I couldn't keep each one.

The first real country star I ever got to see perform was Little Jimmy Dickens. Jimmy was my idol. I admired him so much. I was 12 years old when I went to see him at the Capital Theater in Raleigh, and his show just knocked me out. I couldn't believe how exciting he was! I went home and started trying to learn every Little Jimmy Dickens song that I could.

Many, many years later, I was having coffee with Jimmy backstage at the Ryman. I always called him "Mr. J.D.", and I said to him, "Mr. J.D., Did you know you were my idol? I went to see you at the Capital Theater when I was just a little boy. And I just fell in love with your music. I learned all of your songs. I even tried to imitate you. And I entered every talent contest I could. But I always came in second."

As Little Jimmy listened, I said, "I think if I had gone to see Cowboy Copas instead, I would have probably come in first."

Jimmy laughed and yelled, "You get out of my life!"

He was amazing, right up to the end. He was a great entertainer.

As a boy, my real guitar hero was a man named Hayden Ivey. He was a very popular personality in our hometown of Benson. And he could play a guitar! He knew all the chords, and he could play good licks. I really looked up to him. In 1952, Hayden told me, "You need to get up every morning at 6:00 and tune into WSM radio. There is a guitar player on there, and he works with Mother Maybelle and the Carter sisters. They have a 15 minute radio show. And they have a guitar player who is the best I've ever heard."

So, I got up early the next morning and I turned on WSM. I could just barely tune it in. There was a lot of static. But I could hear well enough to immediately know that I was listening to the greatest guitar player in the world.

The first time I heard Chet Atkins on the radio, he was playing with just a guitar plugged into an amp. There was no reverb or anything. And it was the prettiest sound that I have ever heard come out of a guitar.

Hayden Ivey was part of the James and Hayden "Smile-A-While Boys" duet. And as luck would have it, Hayden's duet partner was none other than James Thornton, my boss from the grocery store! And when he found out that I could play the guitar, he asked me to be a part of their group.

"The Smile-A-While Boys" had a local radio show, and when they hired me to be a part of their show, I had landed my first professional job... at the ripe old age of 13! They would do three radio shows a day, and I performed on two of the three of those shows each day. And not only did I get to play guitar on the radio, but I also got to sing! They let me sing one song on each of the shows. I was a bad singer then. And I still am. But, I was "in Show Business!"

Carl Lamm was the announcer for the "Smile-A-While" Boys radio show in Benson. Carl went on to become a member of the North Carolina Broadcasters Hall of Fame. He is now in his 90s, and he holds the record for continuously being on the air. He's now been on the radio for more than 71 straight years!

But when he heard about my book, Carl took a few moments off the air to share some of his memories.

"I was there when Hayden Ivey was teaching Jimmy how to play the guitar. Jimmy was just a teenager. They took their chairs and turned them so they were face to face. And I happened to be there watching. I had no idea how those guitar lessons would impact Country Music in such a huge way. And today, I thank the good Lord that he allowed me to be there to see a true legend being born. That was when the guitar great Jimmy Capps was first created!

There was a young man named Jack Butler, who wrote a song called "The Ballad of Hayden Ivey". Pat Boone recorded the song, but the title was changed to "The Ballad of Hayden Carter". This song was really about Jimmy's hero Hayden Ivey. And Jimmy ended up playing on Pat Boone's session for that song!

I knew the Louvin Brothers really well. I got to talk to Charlie Louvin quite a bit. And he loved Jimmy so much. Charlie loaned Jimmy some money, so that he could buy a home. And Charlie said Jimmy was the only person he'd ever loaned money to who had paid him back.

Jimmy is one of the best guitarists in the country. I would put him on equal footing with Chet Atkins. Jimmy is so well-known and well-loved throughout North Carolina. But he is very humble. He doesn't realize how great he really is. I know his character. I know his heart, and I count him as one of my all-time best friends. People love and adore him. I sure love him, and I always will."

- Carl Lamm

When I was 16 years old, I became part of a TV show called "Saturday Night Country Style" on WNAO in Raleigh. Jim Thornton Gerald Young, Hayden Ivey and Paul Montgomery were also in the band that performed on the show. WNAO was on UHF Channel 28. It didn't reach out far.

But we eventually moved the show to WTVD in Durham North Carolina. Drummer Bob Mitchell joined the band when "Saturday Night Country Style" aired on Channel 11 each Saturday night. It became one of the most popular shows in that area. WTVD reached 150 miles and 90% of the people in that range tuned in to watch that show every Saturday night.

I was getting a little attention for my guitar playing. I will never forget the day that my hero, Hayden Ivey asked me to start playing lead in our group. I told him, "My guitar is not good enough." And Hayden said, "You can play mine." That would be like if your hero was Babe Ruth and he said, "You can use my bat."

We each made $15 every week on "Saturday Night Country Style". Jim Thornton, who had helped start the "Smile-A-While

Boys" group was the host of the TV show. And he became a very popular entertainer.

As I mentioned, I had the greatest parents in the world. My mom was such a Christian lady. What a woman she was. She had almost no education. She could barely write her own name. But she was a very smart woman, all self-taught. I only heard my mother say one curse word in her entire life. And I was the cause of it.

The county we lived in was "dry." That meant that you couldn't buy alcohol anywhere. But, when I was 16 years old, after I had gotten my driver's license, I decided to drive over to a nearby county and buy a six-pack of beer.

I will never know why I did this, but I did. I went and bought the beer, and then brought it home and I put the six-pack in my parent's refrigerator! What a complete fool!

My mom came in and started getting ready to fix supper. When she opened the refrigerator door, she asked, "Who does this belong to?"

I said, "Well, it's mine, mama."

"I bet you would like to have one right now, wouldn't you?" she said back.

And I said, "Yes ma'am, I sure would."

Mom handed me a can. The beer cans back then didn't have flip tops. You had to use a can opener, that we called a "church key." I opened it, and I'd gotten it almost up to my lips, when mom knocked that beer right out of my hand. It went everywhere. Mom yelled, "You little sh-- turd. You would drink it, wouldn't you?"

Mom took the other five cans and poured all the beer down the sink. That was the one and only time that I ever heard my mom cuss. And it was the one and only time that I ever brought a beer into my parents' house.

My life as a teenager revolved around music. I loved playing music. And I hated school. I had no interest at all in school.

I didn't play any sports. And since I was out playing music most nights, I was usually falling asleep in class the next day.

When I was in the 11th grade, the principal called me into his office. My teacher had reported that I was sleeping during class.

My principal's name was WJ Barefoot. He said, "Jimmy, your teacher tells me you have been having trouble staying awake during class."

I said, "Yes sir. These dances I've been playing at keep me out pretty late."

The principal replied, "You don't like school, do you?" to which I quietly answered, "No sir. I don't."

He said, "You like music?"

I said, "Yes sir. That's what I want to do."

And the principal gave me his blessing for me to quit school. He said, "Of course you need to talk to your father first. But with what you've got goin', and I know you love music and know what you want to do, and I would never stop you." I went straight home to talk to dad, and he let me quit school. I never went back.

With school out of the way, I turned my attention to a new group called The Tar Heels. The group worked local clubs and Army bases, and we would fill those dance halls up. We played a mixture of different music. We did everything from Pat Boone to Bill Haley's "Rock Around the Clock". All the musicians in that band were good musicians. As a member of The Tar Heels, I started making some pretty good money. I was getting $25 a night. So, if I worked three nights a week, I was bringing home

$75 a week. Heck, my dad was making $50 driving a semi-truck all week!

In 1957, Clyde Mattocks told me that I should try out for the group he was with. This group was led by a man named Slim Mims. As soon as I had landed the job, I knew it was a big step up.

We performed two shows each day, at the WJMX radio station in Florence, South Carolina. One show was held at noon, and the other was at 5:30. We also did a weekly TV show on WBTW in Florence. Slim Mims had a full band for the show. He had a fiddle player, a bass player, electric and steel guitar players, and two vocalists who played rhythm guitar. We also had a female vocalist.

Thanks to all the exposure we were getting on local radio and television, we began to garner quite a following. And that led to lots of bookings for our live music throughout that area. Slim Mims booked us for school dances, and for anyplace else we could play to a crowd. Slim had us all on salary, and it was my very first salary job as a player.

Slim also had a place called "the Dream Ranch Barn". The Barn had originally been an airplane hangar. It was a big metal building. He called us The Dream Ranch Boys. We all dressed in western outfits with cowboy hats.

Slim dressed us sharp. He bought all the nice clothes and cowboy boots for us to wear. We were a great little band.

We would play square dances at the barn every Saturday. We also did radio shows from the Dream Ranch Barn. On Wednesday nights though, they held wrestling matches at the Barn. One day a week, we had to ride all around South Carolina and put out posters advertising the matches.

Another part of our job was to clean up the place after the wrestling matches. Since Slim was paying us a weekly salary, he'd get his money's worth by having us sweep up the popcorn and soda cups. We'd come in early every Thursday morning to clean everything up... and there was always a big mess. The crowd would always get mad at the bad guy wrestlers, and some in the crowd liked to throw their popcorn and Cokes at the wrestlers as they walked to the dressing room. The wrestling ring was on rollers, and we moved it back into a corner each week. It was an experience.

Getting to know some of the wrestlers was also an experience. I found out that they were kind of like me and the band. They were performers too, who traveled in a little group, always looking for a crowd to entertain (but I was thankful no one was throwing soda pop on me when I was performing!).

It took me a little while to find out that the wrestling matches were all fixed. They knew who was going to win. I finally realized what was going on when I went back to the dressing room. We had showers there, and after I had just watched the wrestlers trying to kill each other in the ring, I'd see them go backstage. They'd take a shower and get dried off, and I'd see them all laughing and joking around as they got dressed. They were all friends!

The wrestling matches were a part of Slim's income so that he could pay us. Those wrestling matches would always sell out. He had three-hundred people each week, and they'd each pay $2.00 each to get in. That was a pretty good night, back in 1957.

But the Dream Ranch ended up turning into a nightmare for Slim. The trouble all started one night when we were playing a dance there. We were doing the song 'Red Sails in the Sunset', when I heard something that sounded like firecrackers going off. But it turned out to be gunshots. A man had been dancing with another guy's wife, and the guy had come in and shot and killed both of them.

We had been having two-to-three-hundred people paying admission to come hear us at the Barn every time we played, but the week after the shooting, we only had 85 people come. And the week after that, we only had 25 people. Word had spread that it was a dangerous place to be, since two people had been killed there. It got to the point where Slim couldn't pay us anymore, so we all started looking for other work.

As I mentioned, Clyde Mattocks is the one who suggested that I try out for Slim Mims' group. Clyde is still a dear friend today. And this is his version of some of those early days…

"I saw Jimmy when he was playing on a local TV show. I was in the other room listening, and I heard this guitar. I ran to the TV, and I saw Jimmy playing, and I could tell in an instant that he was brilliant. He looked to be the same age as me, just a teenager, but he was playing like a seasoned professional. He was just head and shoulders above the rest of the band.

When I found out Jimmy lived only about sixty miles from me, I went to find him. After I introduced myself, we played a little guitar together, and we quickly became friends.

After I graduated from high school, I went to work for Slim Mims in Florence, South Carolina. I became one of his Dream Ranch Boys. We didn't have a guitar player, so the bass player and I had to take turns on guitar. And Slim said, "I'd hire a full time guitar player if I knew a good one."

And I said, "Let me make a phone call." I called Jimmy. He was 16 years old, and was working at a grocery store in Benson. And he accepted the job right over the phone.

Jimmy and I roomed together when we were part of Slim's Dream Ranch Boys. I would watch him sit on the side of his bed, as he worked out all these intricate tunes on his guitar. Many years later, Jimmy let me sit in with him as he played on some George Jones sessions. I didn't play. I just watched them. And that was quite a thrill.

Jimmy is such a musical chameleon. He can adapt to any situation. That's why he's been so successful for so many years. As the music has changed, he's been able to change with it. He is

> a total professional. He always comes in and does his job, and has never had an attitude that he was better than anyone else.
>
> Jimmy is such a great guy to be around. I always tell him that he would be my favorite guitar player, even if I had never met him and became friends with him."
>
> – Clyde Mattocks

After a year and a half with Slim Mims, I ended up with a man named Slim Short. I worked for a lot of men named Slim! I guess that was a common nickname back then.

Slim Short did a radio show at WGTM in Wilson, North Carolina. He was a comedian, but he also wanted to put together a little band. Slim told me he would pay me $60 a week. And I was 19 years old and still living at home with my parents, so I knew I could get by on that amount.

Our band traveled all around North Carolina, working supermarket openings, schools, and just about anywhere that would pay us.

One of those nights was especially memorable. We were playing on top of the concession stand at a drive-in theater, and I had to lug my amp and guitar up a tall ladder to get on top of the building. We didn't know that the roof was rotten, and in the middle of our show, the roof gave way and my foot went right through the roof! Luckily I fell down only to my crotch, and my guitar helped to stop me from going down farther.

We were doing a date in Jacksonville, North Carolina when we heard about a guy from Wilmington who was really great. We went over to see him play in a little honky-tonk, and I met him that night for the first time. His name was Charlie Daniels. A few years later, I played behind Charlie when he was a guest on a number of the "Country Junction" TV shows in Nashville.

Charlie Daniels became a member of the Grand Ole Opry in 2008. Of course, he was a superstar long before he joined the

Opry, but I can honestly say that Charlie has not changed one bit from the person he was when I met him in that little club in North Carolina back in the 1950s.

"I have known Jimmy Capps probably longer than just about anyone. I met him 65 years ago! Jimmy remembers meeting me at the honky-tonk in Jacksonville, but I actually met him years earlier. I was a fan of Jimmy's when he was just a young teenager. He was a child prodigy. He was a hero of all of us young musicians. I was a couple years older than he was, but he was already out there doing what I was dreaming of doing.

Jimmy was playing a place called the Fun Folk Frolic in Wilmington when I went backstage into his dressing room and asked him to play a song called "Rainbow". We were both just young boys. I used to call him, 'Little Jimmy, the chewing gum boy'. He used to chew gum all the time.

When you are starting out as a musician, you don't play too good. I know I didn't. You try to learn a few chords so you can fake your way through things as you learn how to play, but Jimmy had already achieved a high degree of professionalism and excellence when he was only in his mid-teens!

When I play the Opry today and I look over and see Jimmy, I am reminded how we are both so blessed by the good Lord. We were two little boys from North Carolina, dreaming of playing music for a living, and dreaming of being on the Grand Ole Opry. And now here we are, both about 80 years old, and all of our dreams have come true many times over. But I know that neither one of us did it by ourselves. God gave us the talent, and God has allowed us to live out our dreams for so long.

Jimmy is such a fine musician. And what a fine person he is! He has never changed at all. He ended up on the Grand Ole Opry at such a young age, and he became such a successful session player. That would give many people a big head. But not him. He is the same Tar Heel Capps I met 65 years ago. He was my hero then, and he's my hero now. He just doesn't chew as much gum as he used to."

– Charlie Daniels

A big part of our band with Slim Short was the duo of Tommy Hagen and Buck Jones. Tommy and Buck sang all of the Louvin Brothers songs of the day, and they sang them perfectly, exactly the way the Louvins did them.

In the late 50s, the Louvins were the hottest duo in country music. As a young boy, and throughout my teen years, I had always dreamed of playing on the Grand Ole Opry... but from the moment I first heard the Louvins, my main goal was to get to play with them. It's really hard for me to describe how much I loved the Louvin Brothers. I admired them so much.

I thought the Louvin Brothers were the greatest duo I had ever heard (and over the years, that thought has been proven true. They are still the best duo ever. Anyone who really knows country music will tell you that).

I would have been overjoyed just to meet the Louvin Brothers. To actually work for and play with them, however, would be a dream almost too big for me to even fathom. I had no idea how close I was to seeing that dream come true.

Chapter Three

LOVIN' THE LOUVINS

I made a lot of fans in North Carolina. I could have made a living just playing music there, but I had a dream to try to make it in Nashville.

We didn't have a phone at our house, but my grandmother next door had one. So any time we got a call, they would ring at my grandma's house, and she would have to run over to get us. One day, the phone rang at Grandma's... and it was a call that would change my life.

Aunt Martha ran over and yelled, "Jimmy, Slim Short is on the phone and wants to talk to you!"

When I got to the phone, Slim asked me, "How would you like to go to work for the Louvin Brothers?"

I yelled, "Oh man, that's my dream!"

"Charlie's gonna call you tomorrow," Slim said.

The very next day, my aunt came running over to our house again, this time saying, "Charlie Louvin's on the phone!"

I was so excited to talk to Charlie. When he asked me if I might be interested in working with them, I was so thrilled that I didn't even ask how much the job paid! Charlie told me to meet them at a show in Burlington, North Carolina so that I could audition for them.

I drove to Burlington in my two-door hard top1953 Chevy Bel-Air. Of course it was 1958, so my car was five years old, but I still thought I was hot stuff. At that time, the only other band member the Louvin Brothers had was their guitar player, Paul Yandell. Before Paul, they'd had a player named Chester Reason. And Ira always called him "Chester For No Reason"!

But Paul Yandell had just been drafted to the Army, and he had recommended me to take his place with the Louvins, because of my work with the Tommy and Buck duet. Paul later worked for Chet Atkins for 25 years.

I played electric bass for the Louvins that night in Burlington. After the show, Charlie asked me to come up to their hotel room so I could officially audition. I lugged a Fender amp and a Gretsch guitar up to their room. Charlie had his guitar, and Ira had his mandolin. Paul Yandell, whose job I was auditioning for, was also there. But he would barely look at me. He just kept looking out the window, as I played with the Louvins.

This was the audition I had been preparing for my entire life! Since the duo I had played with at WGTM in Wilson had sung all Louvin Brothers songs, I knew every song the Louvins did. I knew every intro and every solo to each song! I had even been playing them in the same key. I knew all of their arrangements.

After we had done four or five songs, I could tell that Charlie and Ira seemed to be pleased. But Paul walked over from the window and said, "Jimmy, would you play us an instrumental? Why don't you play 'Malaguena'?"

It was a famous Spanish instrumental at the time, and was very, very hard to play. I said, "Man, Paul, I don't know Malaguena."

Paul made a face that told everyone that he didn't approve of me. But Charlie looked at him and announced, "Well, me and I-

Ree hardly ever sing Malaguena anymore. And we are gonna hire him!"

Since I was a member of the Musician's Union in Raleigh, North Carolina, Charlie said he would start me out at $15 a day, for each date they worked, and that they would also pay all my expenses and for any motel rooms. I thought, "5 times $15 a day... yeah, I can live on that each week." I gave my two weeks' notice to The Tar Heels.

Just before my first tour with the Louvin Brothers, I spent my first night in Nashville. I checked into the Clarkston Hotel, just across from the War Memorial Building. The Clarkston was next door to WSM and the National Life Building.

My first job with the Louvins was at The Flame Club in Minneapolis, Minnesota. And from there, we played three straight nights in Kentucky.

I thought, "We are going to be busy all the time!" But what I didn't know was that the Louvins were not working very many dates at all. They were playing only three or four days a month! And they were hardly getting any money for the few dates they were doing.

Here they were, the biggest duo in country music, and the Louvin Brothers didn't have any money. But they still tried to live up to the image of being country stars. They had a 1957 Cadillac, with a Continental kit on the back. I just knew that Charlie and Ira had to be wealthy! But they weren't.

I ended up making a grand total of $1,500 the first year I was with the Louvins. That was for the whole year! Of course one person couldn't live on just $1,500 a year... so, what did I do? I got married!

I had first met Anne when I was 15 years old. She was from Raleigh, North Carolina, and was 16. We met when I was doing the "Saturday Night Country Style" TV show. The fiddle player in our band was dating a girl who lived in a house that had three apartments, where Anne also lived, with her dad. Her parents had gotten divorced, and she lived with her dad. She had three sisters, and their dad raised all of them, basically by himself.

Anne and I started going together a year after we first met, and just a few years later, we were married on December 11, 1958. I was 19 years old, and she was 20, when we drove to Dillon, South Carolina to get married. On our wedding day, there were twelve inches of snow on the ground and it was freezing cold. For the ceremony, I was wearing an Army parka jacket and blue jeans.

Our wedding was nothing fancy. And our honeymoon was even less. As soon as we'd said our vows, we drove to Alabama so that I could join up with the Louvin Brothers on a number of shows. We stayed at the Louvins' mom and dad's house in Henagar, Alabama.

Ira and Charlie's parents were great people, but they lived way out in the woods. When we got there, I asked them where their restroom was, and they said, "Outside."

I couldn't believe the Louvin Brothers' parents didn't have indoor plumbing! But they didn't. And that's how my wife and I spent our honeymoon.

My new wife might not have felt the same, but I thought working with the Louvins was the perfect way to spend my honeymoon! We worked schools during the day, where they let the kids come see the show. After our honeymoon tour, when we came home to Nashville, my new wife and I stayed with Charlie and his family.

A few days later, Charlie Louvin cosigned so that we could get a mobile home. It was a 36' by 10' Great Lakes mobile home. Charlie had also paid for the spot, and my first month's rent there. Our trailer had no air conditioning, and in the summertime, it got mighty hot. I finally made enough money to put a window unit air conditioner in, but it just would not cool down the entire place.

A short time later, though, we moved to a more upscale trailer park on Dickerson Road. Quite a few artists and musicians called that trailer park home, including Norma Jean and Buck Trent. And at one time, Don Gibson lived there. That trailer park is still there today, but my trailer is long gone.

The trailer park might have been a little more upscale. But I sure wasn't. I still didn't even have a phone! I couldn't afford one. But the manager of the complex, Mr. Taylor, let me give out the office number as mine. And when someone called for me, he would run and get me. Can you imagine that happening today? Any time Charlie Louvin called, or someone needed me to work a show or session, they would have to call that trailer park office, and they'd come get me.

The month of December 1958 was a truly life-changing one for me. Not only did I get married, but just days later, I would make my debut on the world famous Grand Ole Opry!

For the first time since I'd joined them, the Louvin Brothers were booked to guest star on the Opry. And now I was also going to be playing on that same stage, right behind them! When I was a teenager, listening to the Opry on the radio with my dad, I always tried to picture in my mind what it was like. And once I'd actually gotten to walk in and see it in person... it was not at all like I had pictured! It was totally different. But it was amazing.

As we carried our guitar cases toward the Ryman Auditorium, I thought, "Man, I have made it."

I was trying to stay cool as Ira and Charlie walked beside me. I could already hear the music real loud, even from outside. And I was amazed that the stage door was backed up to the backside of Tootsie's, the bar that was just a few feet across an alley.

To this day, I can still remember what it sounded like when I walked into the Ryman. It was the neatest sound. When I opened the door, I knew this was as high as I could ever go. This was where any country guitar player dreamed of being.

Yes, I had dreamed of playing the Opry as a teenager. And I was still a teen! I was 19 years old when I walked onto the Grand Ole Opry stage.

I heard Hank Garland playing as I walked in. I don't remember the artist he was playing for, but Hank was such an important player. Then, all of a sudden, I saw Chet Atkins! And then I saw the fiddle player, Tommy Jackson. And I realized that all of these immensely talented guys were working the Opry.

And the talent continued. There was Floyd Cramer playing piano! Floyd wasn't an artist yet – he was a side man. Ray Edenton, a great acoustic guitar player, was there. He was the rhythm player on the Opry. They were not officially called the Opry staff band, but they were the group of players who showed up every week. And as soon as I'd seen all those great players gathered together under one roof, I knew I had found my home... if they would let me stay.

Being backstage was the most wonderful feeling I had ever had, and I got to meet my idol Little Jimmy Dickens for the very first time! And even though he stood at only 4'11", to me he was ten feet tall.

But, as the time neared for me to actually step out onto the stage, my stomach began to churn. Sixty years have now passed since that moment... but I can still remember it like it was yesterday.

I walked out with the Louvins, and I was so nervous. We had a little junction box that we plugged our instruments into, and my hands were shaking so bad that Pete Wade, another guitar player, said, "Do you need some help?"

"I sure do," I said back. And he plugged me into the box. The first song I ever played on the Opry was the Louvin's "Knoxville Girl."

THE MAN IN BACK

When we ended our spot, I was still shaking, and not just from my nerves. I was very, very sick. I knew I had a high fever, but there was no way that I was going to miss this night. I told Charlie Louvin, "I can die tomorrow. But if I do, I will at least get to say that I played the Opry one time."

That saying almost came true. The very next day, Ira's wife Faye insisted that I go to the doctor. When I finally got to Miller's clinic on Gallatin Road, I was diagnosed with double pneumonia. I didn't die, of course. But if I had kicked the bucket the day after I'd played the Opry, I would have died a happy man!

At the time I joined the Louvin Brothers, they were not official members of The Grand Ole Opry. They had been members, but for some reason they'd quit. And that's one of the main reasons for the Louvins' financial struggles. When I'd gone to work for them, I didn't know yet that they had left the Opry.

I have no idea why they quit the Opry, but they signed on with the Wheeling Jamboree in West Virginia. Even when they were working in Wheeling each weekend, however, the Louvins still chose to live in Nashville. They drove back and forth to West Virginia every week. They were getting paid very little, and they really couldn't make a living.

To make matters worse, by the time I started with them, the Louvins had even quit playing the Wheeling Jamboree. Now they weren't there, and they weren't members of the Grand Ole Opry. Thank God for Jim Denney. Mr. Denney was the manager of the Opry, and three months after I'd started working for the Louvins, he offered to re-sign them to the Opry. They jumped at the offer.

I was elated to be back on the Ryman Auditorium stage... but even though we were "Opry stars", our financial struggles continued. Most of the people sitting in the audience were making more at their "not-so-glamorous" jobs than we were. Back then, the Grand Ole Opry was paying the Louvins a total of $32 for each show. If there were two Opry performances on a

Saturday, I made $6.00 for the first show, and $4.00 for the second spot. But that ten dollars would buy me a week's worth of groceries! I shopped at a Cooper and Martin grocery store.

But my finances got a boost thanks to the local musicians union. I was not a member of the union, but I got checks from the union for each of my Opry appearances for three or four months.

George Cooper was the President of the 257 local union. I was backstage at the Opry when Mr. Cooper walked up to me and said, "Son, I need to talk to you."

He said, "I've noticed you picking up checks at the union. But I checked you out and you are not a member. Why is that?"

I said, "To be honest with you, I can't afford to be a member."

"You be in my office Monday morning," Mr. Cooper said. "You are going to become a member."

That Monday, I explained to him, "I pay my work dues when I come in to pick up my checks. But the Louvins are just not working enough. And I can't afford to pay the up-front fee and the annual dues."

Mr. Cooper asked me, "How much can you afford to pay each week?"

"Maybe five bucks," I replied.

He said, "Then here is your card. You bring me five dollars every week."

And I did.

Mr. Cooper was so kind to me. He understood people not working a lot. But he would work with you. I have now been a member of the Musician's Union since 1959. I have been on the Executive Board for many, many years. I am a living testimony that the union is a good thing. If there wasn't a union, everyone would have to negotiate for themselves. I am pro union. There are some things in the by-laws that need improving or changed, but 99% of it is good, and it is for the musicians.

The Musicians Union is totally different from other unions in other businesses or industries. I am chairman of a committee for the union called the Emergency Relief Fund, which was set up by Vic Willis. Through it, we help musicians who might have a medical emergency or be going through some kind of hard time. We currently have about 2,500 members of the Musicians Union.

I met so many great people when I moved to Nashville. One of those was a young guy named Darrell McCall. Darrell had also recently come to town with his "brother", Johnny Paycheck. They really weren't brothers, but they were being billed as a brother act called "the Young Brothers". Soon though, Darrell would join up with me and the real-life brothers Ira and Charlie Louvin. Here are a few of Darrell's memories of those days...

"I was 18 years old when I came to Nashville in late 1958. I wanted to be a guitar player, so I started hanging around O'Dell Martin, Ben Keith, Buddy Emmons, Jimmy Day, and this guy named Jimmy Capps. And we'd all end up jamming together. I got to work with Charlie Louvin a little bit, just for a month or two. And Jimmy has been a dear friend of mine since those days.

We were so hungry back in those days. We just wanted to pick and make music. And Jimmy just fascinated me. He was so nice. He tried to show me how to play, and he didn't mind that I tried to copy him and his style.

Ten years ago, Jimmy asked me to sing a song on an album he was doing. He let me choose a song I wanted to do, and I picked a song called "Always." You can hear that on Jimmy's "Old Friends Making New Memories" album.

I played with a number of acts on the road. Of course, Jimmy did too, and he and I saw the backside of a lot of artists. We saw their backsides on and off stage! Jimmy is just a super guy. I

> think the world of him. I don't think there is a finer musician, or a finer person, than Jimmy Capps. I admire him so much."
>
> – Darrell McCall

I never pretended to be a singer. But when I was working with the Louvins, they would always let me sing one song during their concerts. My favorite one to sing was Roger Miller's big hit, "Dang Me".

When the Louvins hired me, it was a dream come true. But life with them on the road was very interesting. They were brothers, of course, but they didn't room together. Instead, I shared a room with Charlie. Like any family, they had their squabbles. I saw them get into fist fights. But I could also tell that they loved each other to death.

The very first recording session I played in Nashville was with the Louvin Brothers. This session took place at The Quonset Hut, and I was amazed at the musicians who were in the studio. As soon as I walked in, I saw Hank Garland sitting there. Then Ken Nelson came in to produce, and I was in awe of him. I had read his name on so many albums. Floyd Cramer played piano on the session, Junior Husky was on bass, and Ray Edenton was also there.

Here I was, a scared 19 year old kid, who was expected to be as good as all my heroes... who were all standing right in front of me! I was so nervous. But Hank Garland was so nice. He treated me like I was an equal. All the guys did. They treated me really nice.

I have always tried to remember that day, and have tried to repay that kindness every time that I play a session. I have tried to welcome any new musician who walks into the studio. Most are nervous when they come to town... I know I sure was. And some are just scared to death. But I try to make them feel comfortable. I try to make them feel wanted, and to put them at ease. I do that because I got that same kind of treatment when I was playing my first sessions, so I try to pay that back a little.

Later, Ira and Charlie were trying to cross over into the more lucrative Pop music world. But as Owen Bradley said about The Wilburn Brothers: "They couldn't go Pop with a firecracker in their mouth!" And neither could the Louvins.

The Louvins, like a lot of others at the time, would rehearse songs ahead of time, before they ever set foot inside a studio. That way, once their recording session was ready to begin, they would know exactly what they wanted. And all of us musicians were expected to do it exactly like they had rehearsed it.

A guy named O'Dell Martin was playing a style that sounded like a steel guitar, and I asked him if he minded if I used that style too. He said he didn't care. But that style really came from him. Of course, I also patterned myself after another guy… Chet Atkins. Before I joined the Louvins, way back when I was just a fan of theirs, they had used Chet on all of their sessions. And I thought they had the prettiest guitar playing on all their records.

I just loved Chet Atkins' playing. Everyone did. But once I got up to Nashville, I heard all these other great players, like Grady Martin, Pete Wade and Sammy Pruett, who worked with Hank Williams and Carl Smith. Those were the types of people I looked up to and wanted to be like. And I wanted to honor them with my playing.

Life on the road with the Louvins was never boring. Once, we were booked to play in a small town in Illinois, and we found ourselves needing a bass player. I asked a friend of mine if he knew of anyone, and I told him the job only paid twenty-five dollars. My friend told me I should call up to Tootsies Bar. A guy who had just come to town was hanging around there, and had told everyone he was needing some work.

So I called Tootsies and asked for this guy named Willie Nelson. I explained everything to him, and Willie assured me he could play bass. Then I told him the job only paid twenty-five bucks. He said, "That's fine. I could use the money."

The next day, Willie and I were sitting in the back seat of the Louvins' 1959 Oldsmobile station wagon, headed to Illinois. Just before we got out of Nashville, Willie said, "Jimmy, see that little brick house over there? I just bought that. The payments are ninety dollars a month. Man, I sure hope I can make those payments and not lose that house."

Just a short time later, Willie Nelson would never have to worry about making that house payment!

After we had worn out our Oldsmobile station wagon, we got a Chevrolet Corvair Van. We thought we were in high cotton! The extra space in the van was great, but it had no air conditioning, and the back windows didn't roll down. Yeah, we were in the big time!

Charlie was driving the van, as Ira slept in the back and I sat in the passenger seat. Ira had been drinking the night before, and when he woke up, he told Charlie to pull over.

"We don't have time to pull over," Charlie said.

We had been in Oklahoma on a Friday night, and were trying to make it to Nashville to play the Saturday night Opry.

Ira again said, "Pull this thing over! I own half of it and I want to stop."

Charlie asked, "Do you have to go to the bathroom?"

And Ira said, "No. I have been laying here, and I've thought up some new punches, and I'm gonna whip your a$$!"

Luckily, there was no fight that day. I just started laughing at Ira, and so did Charlie… and suddenly Ira saw the humor in it too, and he started laughing. And we made it to the Opry in time, with no bruises on anyone… this time.

THE MAN IN BACK

As the 1950s came to an end, I started the new decade of the 60s off in a big way. I went on tour not only with the Louvins, but also with another Grand Ole Opry great, Jim Reeves. The Louvins were touring with Reeves when Jim's guitar player, Leo Jackson, got drafted into the Army; so I volunteered to play guitar for their show. And Jim Reeves was hot with big hits, including "He'll Have to Go", "Billy Bayou", and "Four Walls".

And a year later, I got to work with a star who was even hotter. Patsy Cline had her biggest hits of "Crazy" and "I Fall to Pieces" in 1961. And that's when I got to work with her, as we did some Pet Milk Grand Ole Opry television shows together. The black and white shows were taped at WSM TV on 12th Avenue in Nashville. I did a bunch of shows with the Louvins there. Each show featured three artists, who sang two songs each, and they hired a small band of musicians to back all the artists. That's how I got to play with Patsy.

Later, I was on a concert in Kansas with Patsy. I was with the Louvin Brothers. I didn't play for Patsy, but I watched her show. One of my regrets in life is that I never got my photo taken with her. I wish I had one now. And it's crazy that I worked with so many of my heroes back then, but I never took a picture with them. I really should have.

I don't need any photo, though, to have a clear memory of one night in Lawton, Oklahoma. It was there that Ira and Charlie got into one of their biggest fights. We played a gymnasium there, and Little Jimmy Dickens and Jimmy C. Newman were also on the show. I played guitar for all three acts.

While the Louvins were waiting to go on, Ira was drinking. And he got bad drunk. When the Louvins came on, Ira could not get his mandolin in tune. He was so drunk, he couldn't figure out how to tune it. So he took it and threw it onto the floor, sending it sliding under the curtain backdrop. And then he walked off the stage. Charlie had to finish that show all by himself.

After the show, Ira got the mandolin and smashed it up against a big radiator that was in the dressing room. His mandolin was from the 1930s, a Mandola with "THE" Gibson written in it. It would be a very valuable collector's item today. But in his rage, Ira busted the neck of that mandolin. As he was busting it, Little Jimmy Dickens said, "Let me help you destroy that fine instrument." And Ira just glared at him.

As I loaded up the car, I had all of our show clothes stored inside separate suit bags. Each bag held four or five sets of coats, shirts and pants. I had all the bags lying out on the sidewalk. I would put the instruments in, and then I'd lay the bags of clothes flat on top, so that they wouldn't get wrinkled.

But as Ira came out to the car, still very drunk, he walked right across all the clothes. My bag was on top, and everyone else's were underneath. I said, "Ira, don't step on my clothes."

"I can walk on your clothes if I want to!" he yelled. "We bought 'em."

I said, "Well you didn't buy mine. I bought my own clothes." Which I did.

Ira screamed, "By God, you work for us. And I will walk on your clothes anytime I feel like it."

Right then, Charlie came out to the car. He tried to talk some sense into Ira, but Ira took a swing at him. He missed, and Charlie knocked him down and just started beating his head against the sidewalk. Charlie had grabbed Ira's hair, and was just smashing his head into the cement.

I know that Jimmy C. Newman saved Ira's life that night. Charlie was already so mad because Ira had stormed off in the middle of the show. When he also found out that Ira had destroyed the mandolin, he was even more hurt.

So now, Ira's walking on our clothes was just the last straw for Charlie. He lost all control. He was going to beat Ira to death. But

Jimmy C. pulled him off. Jimmy yelled, "Charlie, you are gonna kill your brother!"

Right then, a big cowboy pulled up in a pickup truck. He got out and asked, "Y'all need any help?"

Little Jimmy Dickens walked over to him, and being so short, poked him in the belt buckle. Jimmy said, "You get back in your truck and go home. This is our business and we'll take care of it." The big guy got back into his truck and left.

Once things had settled down, we all got in the car, and headed back to the hotel. Ira and Charlie got into another bad argument along the way. Charlie was driving, and Ira was in the back seat right behind him. Little Jimmy was next to Ira, and I was sitting next to Little Jimmy. Jimmy C. Newman was in the front passenger seat.

As the argument got louder and louder, Ira announced "I'll show you how to break up a duet." All of our eyes got as big as saucers when he pulled out a .38 gun. Ira cocked it and pointed it at the back of Charlie's head. Dickens grabbed the gun with his left hand, and yelled, "Give me that gun! You are too drunk to have a gun."

Here I was, 20 years old, and thinkin', "Man, I need to catch the next bus out of here." It was just a miracle that no one got hurt.

After the big fight in Oklahoma, we headed toward Potlatch, Idaho. On our way there, we played a date in Colorado and then checked into an old hotel. It was always my job to load the car, so I put all the instruments behind the back seat. It was freezing cold, and we all had top coats on. And my coat looked exactly like the coat that Little Jimmy Dickens had. As I loaded everything up, I laid my coat over top of the guitars behind the seat. Jimmy was sitting in the back seat, and he saw the coat in the back. He just assumed it was his. But when we stopped, I grabbed my coat and put it on. But Jimmy's coat was not there. He asked me, "Where is my coat big boy?"

I said, "I have no idea." But he had left his coat in the lobby of our hotel in Colorado. They had to mail it to him.

On that same tour, I was sitting in the middle in the front seat. Charlie was driving, and Jimmy C. Newman was in the passenger seat. It was always very cramped. None of us had much room. When I fell asleep, my legs would flop over into Jimmy C's space, so he asked me to take off my belt and showed me how to wrap it around my legs real tight. He said, "When you are getting ready to go to sleep, you do that so your legs stay where they're supposed to."

On another tour with Roy Drusky and Skeeter Davis, I was in the back seat next to Skeeter. I fell asleep, and when I woke up, my head was on Skeeter's shoulder! I was so embarrassed, but she never said anything. And thankfully she never made me put a belt around my neck!

Another tour with the Louvins took us to Florida. It was a package show, which included Billy Walker and Cowboy Copas. We all rode together, all the way to Florida, in our same old trusty station wagon.

We left at midnight, drove all through the night, and then early the next morning, finally stopped for breakfast. Cowboy Copas was wearing a suit like the "old salt and pepper" that Barney Fife wore on The Andy Griffith Show. After we had ridden in the car all night, when Cowboy got out of the car, he noticed that the knees on his flannel suit pants had some indentions. They were poking out where his knees had been! He said, "I look like I've been smuggling coconuts."

Every time we went out to eat, Cowboy Copas always ordered his meal first, before everyone else. For some reason though, he was always the last person to get served. They always brought his food last, no matter where we were. And it became a running joke with all of us.

Copas was such a good guy. He was bald, but very few people knew it, because he always wore his cowboy hat. He always smoked a cigar, and whenever I'd go into his dressing room, it was always filled with cigar smoke.

As I look back at 1960-61, I was really having the time of my life. Who wouldn't be? There I was, with Ira and Charlie Louvin, Cowboy Copas, Jim Reeves and Patsy Cline. Who would ever believe that, just three years later, Ira, Jim, Patsy and Cowboy Copas would all be gone... Ira killed in a car wreck, Patsy and Cowboy killed in a plane crash, and Jim Reeves in a separate plane crash.

I was in the Army when the Patsy Cline's crash happened. We had been out in the field that day; returning to the barracks, as always, I turned on my little radio... and I heard them announce that Patsy Cline had died in a plane crash. And also on board the plane were my friends Cowboy Copas, Hawkshaw Hawkins, and Randy Hughes. I was also in the service when Jim Reeves' plane went down. I was playing off post in Washington, D.C., listening to the radio in my car, when I heard that sad news.

Tommy Hill was the front man for the Jim Reeves show. He would open the concerts and then bring Jim on. During the time that I filled in on the show, Tommy got to know me and my playing. About a year later, he called me and said he was going to do an album for Starday Records, and asked if I would be a part of it. Tommy explained to me that it would be an instrumental album called "Tennessee Guitar", and he wanted me to play four songs on it. Thumbs Carlisle and Billy Byrd - who was Ernest Tubb's guitar player - were also on it.

I actually played rhythm on Billy's songs, and then he played rhythm on mine. Jerry Smith played piano on it, Junior Husky played bass, and Willie Ackerman was on drums.

I told Don Pierce, the head of the Starday label, that I had three original songs and that I also wanted to do a song I'd found called "Sweet Bunch of Daisies". It was an old song, but it wasn't in public domain yet. We went into the studio and recorded everything. Tommy Hill did the engineering.

A couple days later, they called me in to sign the contracts for them to publish my original songs, and when I got there, I noticed the contracts were for all four songs.

I said, "Mr. Pierce, I didn't write 'Sweet Bunch of Daisies'." and he said, "It's not 'Sweet Bunch of Daisies' anymore. We're gonna call it 'The Natchez Trace'.

And he said, "The writer of 'The Natchez Trace' is William S. York."

It turned out that William S. York was really Don Pierce! He got all the writer's money for "The Natchez Trace", which was really "Sweet Bunch of Daisies".

But I didn't have to worry about feeling guilty about the huge amount of money that the album brought us. To this day, I have only made $41.25 on the entire album. And that album is still in print today!

In 1962, I was living my dream. I'd been with the Louvin Brothers for four years. I was playing with my heroes. I loved traveling from show to show. And it's a good thing that I loved traveling... we once did a 110-day tour! Before we left on that tour, we took a group picture on the front steps of The Ryman Auditorium. I wish we had taken another photo on the day that three-and-a-half month tour ended. I bet we looked a lot rougher when we finally got back to Nashville!

When we weren't out on tour, we were playing the Grand Ole Opry, and I was on top of the world. I was getting paid to do what I love. I never wanted it to end. And then...it ended. Or at least, it came to a screeching halt. I received my draft notice from Uncle Sam.

Chapter Four

UNCLE SAM NEEDS…
A GOOD GUITAR PICKER

I went from standing on stage in my country music outfit, to standing in my underwear as I prepared for my Army physical. Since my wife and I didn't have any children yet, I was drafted at the age of 22.

During my physical, after they'd weighed me, I was sent to a room to meet with a guy who examined my ears. He was a Navy doctor, who looked at my paperwork and said to me, "James Dixon Capps. Didn't I see you on the Opry Saturday night with the Louvin Brothers?"

I said, "You probably did."

He said back, "You don't need to be in the Army. And I'm going to help you."

I couldn't believe it when he said, "Your hearing is real bad, isn't it?" He kind of winked as he instructed, "When you go into the next room, you pretend that you can't hear anything. If they ask you anything, you just stand there and don't answer."

I asked him, "Are you kiddin'?"

He said, "No. It will keep you out of the Army."

So like a good soldier, I walked into the next room and met with a lieutenant. He read over my papers and asked, "Capps, it says you have hearing loss. Is that true?" I just stood there and acted like I didn't hear him.

Then he got right in my ear and yelled. I tried not to flinch. He said he was going to send me to a hearing specialist in downtown Nashville.

When I got there, the doctor examined me, and said that my problem was a buildup of wax in my ear. And then, much to my dismay, he announced, "Son, you are in the Army!"

Even though I didn't want to be drafted, especially right when I had just started playing music with my heroes, I decided to go into the service with a positive attitude. I made up my mind that I would not be negative. I knew that it would be just two years of my life, and so I decided to enjoy it as much as I could.

I did miss playing music. And I was afraid that my job with the Louvins would not be there when I came back two years later. But I just made up my mind that I would be a happy camper during my time in the service. I knew I could get through two years of service. And whatever Uncle Sam wanted me to do, I would do it.

So I was sent by bus to Fort Jackson, South Carolina. Then I was transferred to Fort Gordon, Georgia, where I took basic training. When we filled out our paperwork, on the question that asked, "What kind of career would you like to have in the service?" I simply wrote, "Whatever you want me to be." I figured they would put me wherever they wanted to anyway.

Then a sergeant chose me to be an MP, and they put me through military police training. It was two months of training that taught me a lot about soldiering.

Before I went into the service, I had worked with the Louvins almost five years. While I was in MP school in the Army, during one of my breaks, I was listening to the radio. Paul Harvey's network radio show was on, and I heard Paul read, "Grand Ole Opry star Ira Louvin was shot by his wife several times last night. Ira's wife was quoted as saying, "If he ain't dead, I'll shoot him again." Then Paul Harvey added, "He's still living... Paul Harvey...good day."

Ira was lucky to live through that shooting. And I was about to catch a big break myself.

They took 150 men into a huge room, and then split us up into groups. They told one group they were being sent to Korea; another group was headed to Germany. But for some reason, I was standing all by myself. I had my duffel bag full of clothes, wondering what dangerous part of the world I was headed to. I was amazed when they announced that I was the one and only person who was being sent all the way to... Fort Lee, Virginia!

I lived off base near Fort Lee in a little mobile home. I brought my wife from Nashville, and of course I brought my guitar.

We had only been at Fort Lee for a little more than a month when I caught another big break. It came as I was directing traffic on the Army base, serving as an M.P.

I was standing in the middle of the road, on top of an old, upside-down oil drum barrel we had cut in half. I had absolutely no idea what the next car would be bringing my way.

The vehicle pulled up, and the sergeant inside yelled, "Aren't you Jimmy Capps? Don't you work with the Louvins?"

I laughed, "Well, not right now. I'm a little busy in the Army."

He said, "Man, you shouldn't be directing traffic. You need to be playing music!"

"You are right Sarge!" I replied. "But you've got to move on, you've got traffic backed up."

The sergeant pulled his car over to the side of the road and waited for my shift to end. As I rolled my oil drum barrel out of the intersection, he introduced himself again. He told me he had been a bluegrass player, and that he had seen me play with the Louvin Brothers.

He said, "I've got a friend in the Pentagon who can help you. You need to be playing guitar." And I thought, "This is a bunch of bull. This man is crazy." But he kept on, saying, "My friend's name is Corey Wayne. He can help you get into Special Services."

A week later, my First Sergeant called me to his office. He asked, "Capps, who do you know? You must know somebody very powerful."

I said, "Sergeant, I have no idea what you are talking about."

"We just got orders that you are going to Fort Meade, Maryland to be in a musical show called the 2nd Army Show Mobile. Those orders came down from the Pentagon!" he said. "You have got to know somebody. You've only been an MP for a month and a half! And now they are sending you off to be a guitar player!" He couldn't believe it.

I also couldn't believe my good fortune… but I was also concerned that my assignment was listed as "TDY". That stood for "Temporary Duty", and meant that if I wasn't talented enough, they could always send me back to my old job… standing on an oil barrel, directing traffic. Luckily, my temporary duty turned out to be permanent!

But I felt bad that they had spent all that money training me for two months, only to have me serve as an MP for a month and a half. I did feel bad. But I had to follow orders that came from the Pentagon!

When I got to Fort Meade, they changed my MOS from MP to Entertainment Specialist. Yes, I had gotten into the special services, all because of that one sergeant who'd recognized me as I stood on an oil barrel!

I spent the rest of my Army career at Fort Meade. The 2nd Army Show Mobile traveled by bus and truck all over. The show included singers, musicians and dancers. We assembled our own stage every day. Before the show, we put on coveralls to unload the huge set and stage from the truck. Then, we assembled the entire thing. Just before the show, we changed into our stage clothes - and then as soon as the show ended, we'd put the coveralls back on to tear everything down.

On our show, we played a variety of music, every kind. Our band had drums, a piano, three horns, two trumpets and a slide trombone, and I had my guitar. But in all of the 2nd Army, they couldn't find a bass player. So we did the entire show without one.

Now, about 55 years later, I still remember each guy that I played with in that show. Frank Murat was the musical director. He wrote out real musical charts for us. And it was there that I learned to read music a little better. Our drummer was Ray Stracci. Ray was from Chicago, and many years later, I got him a job at Opryland.

Charlie Shaffer, my best friend in the Army, was our piano player. Before being drafted, he had been performing in clubs in Las Vegas. He actually returned to Vegas as soon as he got out of the Army, and he still performs there today, on cruise ships and in clubs. Charlie is from the same area where my wife Michele grew up, and she was a big fan of his. Michele had heard Charlie's songs on the KQUE radio in Houston, long before she ever met ol' Jimmy Capps.

One of the guys on our show was named David Birney. And he and I became real good friends. David and his wife had a trailer just across the street from us. He went on to become a great actor and a popular TV star. He later remarried to the actress Meredith Baxter.

Corey Wayne, the man from the Pentagon who'd gotten me transferred, was in charge of the show. Corey loved country music. And he loved to sing. Many years later, I produced an album on him in Nashville. From there, he went to work for Hilltop Studios, and then became a booking agent for my company; he booked one of Moe Bandy's first dates! It really is a small world.

Our 2nd Army show had a space theme. We wore silver and blue costumes that were made of this stretchy and shiny, latex kind of material. We had pointed shoulder pads, and looked like we were out of an episode of Star Trek! The outfits had a slick lining, and the material was very thin. In the winter, when we played those cold Army bases, we would freeze to death. When I look back now at pictures of our show, I think we look like a combination between Buck Owens' Buckaroos and The Space Cadets.

I not only played music with the 2nd Army Show Mobile, but I also played off base during that time. Any time I could be performing somewhere, I was. So, to be honest, I spent almost every minute of my two years in the Army, whether I was on or off duty, playing the guitar.

In 1964, as my two-year stint at Fort Meade was coming to an end, I knew that I would soon be getting a visit from Colonel Gaffney. When a soldier was about to be released, the Colonel would call them in for a "re-up talk", where he would try and talk them into re-signing up and extending their stay with the Army. It was kind of like being in a Time Share sales talk. You have to go into it with the attitude of "No matter what they say, no matter how great they make it sound, I am saying NO!"

Right on schedule, Colonel Gaffney called me into his office. As I walked in, he smiled at me and said, "Capps!" (I don't know why the Army never used your first name. I always thought using your first name would be friendlier and warmer. And I always hated that they only called you by your last name.)

Colonel Gaffney said, "Capps, you don't want to re-up, do you?"

I said, "No sir."

He said, "Well, let's go get a cup of coffee." He didn't even try to talk me into staying! He knew that my life was playing music.

Chapter Five

THE END OF THE LOUVINS

I had enjoyed my two years in the Army. They were good years for me. But they had not been good ones for my heroes, and former bosses, the Louvin Brothers.

While I was away, the Louvins had split up. They had broken up their act and gone their separate ways. After their break up, my old friend Tommy Haggen came up to work with Charlie for about a year. And Tommy sounded just like Ira, but it was just not the same. You can't recreate the all-time best.

After their split, Capitol Records kept both Charlie and Ira on their roster as solo acts. Charlie was starting to have great success on his own as a solo artist. One morning, on my way into the barracks, I'd heard a song on the radio, and I said, "I know that guy. His voice is very familiar."

And after the song had ended, the DJ said, "That is the brand new hit by Charlie Louvin." The song was "I Don't Love You Anymore". Bill Anderson had written the song, and Charlie took it to the top of the charts. I really loved Charlie's singing. It was as soulful as George Jones, in his own way. Charlie was a great singer.

A couple weeks before I got out of the Army, I decided to call Charlie. I asked him, "I know you're on your own now. Do you think there's any chance of me getting my job back?"

And he asked, "Well, when do you get out and where are you?"

"I get out October 18th," I said, "and right now I'm at Fort Meade, Maryland."

"I'm working Baltimore on October 20th! Why don't I come by and pick you up, and you can go right to work?"

And that's exactly what I did. It could not have worked out any more perfectly! Charlie Louvin picked me up just as I walked out of Fort Meade.

After our show in Baltimore, we headed to New York, where we played a show with Minnie Pearl. I had already worked five days on the road with Charlie before I ever came back home to Nashville!

I worked with Charlie for the next year and a half, but for the rest of his life, Charlie was literally like an older brother to me. I played on almost every session he ever did. Any time he worked a TV show in Nashville, he would always insist that they have me as his guitar player. He'd tell everyone, "Jimmy has got to be with me on everything I do."

I was working with Charlie when I met Loretta Lynn for the first time. It was in the 60s, when she was just starting out. Loretta and her husband Mooney were traveling all around in just a car.

We played a park in Ohio, and Loretta was on the show. I backed her up that day. Ronnie Blackwell played bass for Charlie, and me and Ronnie were Loretta's entire band. Many years later, I played on the soundtrack album for the movie "Coal Miner's Daughter", and I always worked all of Loretta Lynn's spots on the Opry.

Charlie Louvin was so good to me. He was a crusty old dude in his later years. If you didn't want to hear the truth, then you had better not ask him a question, because I guarantee he was going to tell you the truth. And sometimes the truth hurts. But he didn't care. He would speak his mind.

While I was very close to Charlie, Ira was conversely a hard person to get to know. He seemed miserable, and he drank a lot. Charlie always told me that he thought his brother was called to preach. He said the reason for Ira's sadness and drinking was that Ira had been called to preach, and had never accepted that calling. He was running from it his entire life. You can listen to some of the songs he wrote, and they'll tell that same story.

I think that Ira would have eventually wound up being a preacher. And he would have been a good one, too. But he didn't live to fulfill that. Ira was only 41 years old when he died in a terrible car accident in Missouri.

I was on the road with Charlie when the accident happened. Charlie could only afford me and a bass player; we were his entire band. We had played at a barn dance in Richmond on a Saturday night, and we were now playing at a Hillbilly Park in Virginia. The next day, we had a matinee show at the park, but when we arrived at the gate to check in, a guard told Charlie, "Mr. Louvin, you need to go to the office. You have an emergency telephone call."

We went to the office, and I waited outside while Charlie went in. I still cry all these years later, when I remember what Charlie looked like when he came back out. He told us how Ira had been killed.

Somehow, we went ahead and did the concert that day. I don't know how Charlie got through it. I don't know how any of us did. Everybody was torn up. After the show, we got back into our station wagon and I took Charlie to a local airport so he could fly home. The bass player and I made a long, quiet and sad drive back to Nashville.

Here are the details about Ira's death. The night before, Ira had played a club called the Chestnut Inn in Kansas City. He had moved back to Alabama, and a couple who were his neighbors went to the show with Ira and his wife, Ann. The four of them were in their car driving home that Sunday morning.

The interstate they were on was being expanded, and in some areas, it was just a two-lane road, but in other parts, it had four lanes, two going in either direction. They were in Ira's neighbor's car, a white 1964 Chevrolet Super Sport Impala with a red interior and all-white roof, and Ira and Ann were in the backseat.

But as their car was topping a hill, there was another car coming in the opposite direction. There were five people inside that car. The driver of that car had forgotten that the road was two lanes instead of four, and they hit Ira's car head on. It killed all four people in Ira's car, and all five of the people in the other one. Nine people lost their lives that Sunday morning.

The coroner took a photo of the scene, and all the bodies were still there. I've seen the photo, and it chills me to the bone. It shows Ira laying half in the car and half out. He was on his knees, almost like he was praying.

The sight of Ira (the man many said had been called to be a preacher) on his knees was very eerie. But something even stranger happened at that same time.

The authorities in Missouri sent Ira and Ann's bodies to the Phillips and Robinson Funeral Home on Gallatin Road in Nashville. They asked Charlie to come identify them, and Charlie said to me, "I can't do this. Will you go with me?"

I said I would.

When we went in and looked at Ira's body, he had a hole in the middle of his forehead. It was a big triangle, and I guess it was from whatever he'd hit when they'd crashed. Charlie said, "Yeah, that's my brother." And then we looked at the woman's body. And Charlie said, "That's not his wife." They had mixed the bodies up! Instead of Ira's wife, Ann, it was the other woman who had been riding with them.

After Ira's funeral, Charlie and I went to see the car that Ira had been in. It was in a salvage yard. And when we looked in the car, we saw that the roof inside, that had been totally white, was now completely red... red from all the blood that had covered it.

Ira's life was cut very short. But his brother Charlie went on to enjoy a long and very successful life. Of course, he was a member of the Grand Ole Opry for decades. Late in his career, he opened up a little Louvin Brothers Museum on Music Valley Drive in Nashville. I would drop in to visit him quite often. Michele and I surprised him on his birthday one year and took him a gift. We also got up and played and sang for him.

Charlie was always into something to make a living; he had a record shop in Franklin, Tennessee; he had a museum up on Monteagle off of Interstate 24; and he had a museum in Bell Buckle, Tennessee.

Until the day Charlie died, I'm sure he had a big void in his life because Ira wasn't there. I don't think he ever got over Ira's death, even though he went on to have a great solo career for many decades.

In the summer of 2010, Charlie was diagnosed with pancreatic cancer. When I found out, I called him and we talked on the phone. I really believe that he truly thought that he was going to beat it. He tried everything. I also went to see him in the hospital, and I told him that I loved him, and he said he loved me too.

He ended up getting a little better, and they sent him home. Charlie might have been small, but he was tough. He was a macho little guy. And it was sad to see him weaken down to nothing. That disease is so terrible.

The last thing Charlie ever did was one of the Country's Family Reunion shows. It was a salute to Bill Anderson. We all knew that he had been fighting pancreatic cancer. But we didn't know how bad he really was. He ended up getting sick as he sat in the audience during the taping, and had to leave. I was busy playing on the show, and didn't get to say any last words to him. That is something I regret.

You should never pass up the chance to tell a dear friend that you love them. You never know when it's going to be the last time. Charlie was so good to me. He is the one who first hired me. He is the reason I am here. Charlie died on January 26, 2011, six months after he was told he had cancer.

Chapter Six

FROM THE ROAD TO THE STUDIO

I loved Charlie Louvin. He was my hero. You can blame Charlie Louvin for me being here today. But in 1967, I left him for $125.

I had received a call from the great fiddle player Shorty Lavender. Shorty played with Ray Price, and his classic fiddle intro and solo can be heard on Ray's hit, "Heart Over Mind". It's one of the great country fiddle solos of all time.

Shorty lived nine houses up from me, and one day, he called me and asked if I would like to have a salary job. I told him that would be great, but I loved working with Charlie. But Shorty told me that Ferlin Husky was looking for a guitar player, and that he would hire me on the spot right then, without me even trying out for the job.

Charlie was paying me fifty bucks a day, but sometimes we were only working one or two days a week. And when Ferlin offered me a set salary of $125 a week, I gave Charlie my notice. He understood, and didn't hold it against me. But leaving him was still tough. While I was excited about the pay increase, it was not easy for me to leave Charlie. He was the reason I was in Nashville. No one would have even known me if it weren't for Charlie Louvin. Yes, he was like a brother to me.

When I joined Ferlin, he had already had huge hits like "Gone", "Wings of a Dove", and his duet with Jean Shepard, "A Dear John Letter". Ferlin called his band the Hush Puppies.

I was a Hush Puppy for a year and a half. It was a great band, and the Hush Puppies became so popular that we even did an entire album on our own without Ferlin. Neil Wilburn ran a label called Bragg Records, and he signed just the band for that album. They didn't press many copies of our album that was called "Too Much Country", however. It was never transferred to CD. And today, it's a collector's item.

Ferlin was very proud of his band, and he always cheered us on. We cheered him on too, as he entertained crowds with his music and with his alter ego he had named "Simon Crum". In fact, sometimes "Simon" was more popular than Ferlin! He was a real funny character on stage.

When I was working with Ferlin, I grew a goatee. We were on a 12-day tour with no days off, and we went all the way to the west coast. By the time we'd made it to the Pomona State Fair in California, I had started to grow a goatee. Back then, my beard was dark brown. I had been letting it grow for about six days, and it was getting pretty good.

Ferlin came to my bunk on the bus and asked me, "How much am I paying you now?"

"$125 a week," I said.

"I'll raise you to $150 a week if you'll shave that goatee off!"

I jumped up out of my bunk and went straight to the sink and shaved right then.

Ferlin might have had a problem with my goatee, but he also had a much bigger problem. He had a drinkin' problem.

Most of his drinking came before and after my year and a half with him. For almost the entire time that I was with him, he never drank any alcohol. But one night, we were working in a club in Wichita Falls, Texas. People in Texas want to dance, and they come for the music. They don't come for a show. There is a big difference. Ferlin did shows. He was a great showman. He was used to being the center of attention, with all eyes on him.

But this night in Texas, the people did not take to him, and he got into the booze.

We were on the bus headed home. The bus driver was Ike Inman - he had played bass for Ferlin in the early part of his career – and he was driving the bus in downtown Wichita Falls when he stopped at a red light. But Ferlin was drunk, and he came walking up the aisle, yelling, "Back this bus up!"

Ike looked back at him and said, "Chief, I can't do that. There's cars right behind us."

But Ferlin yelled, "I own this bus! Back it up!" Ike shifted into reverse. The cars behind us started honking and trying to move when they saw our tail lights. But just as Ike got ready to release the clutch, Ferlin changed his mind and said, "Oh, forget it."

I was watching all of this from my bunk. And as Ferlin headed to his state room at the back of the bus, he asked me, "Am I as bad as Ira Louvin?"

I said, "You ain't even close, Chief."

And Ferlin said, "Well, shucks!" That was the one and only time I ever saw Ferlin Husky drink during the time that I worked for him. He was a great boss. I loved him dearly. He was really a good person, and he and I remained friends right up to the day he died. And I was honored to play for his funeral.

Ferlin was the last person I worked the road with as a full time job, and I sure hated to leave him, but an offer to be a regular on a TV show was too good to pass up. Pete Wade is the guy who got me that job. Pete helped me so much over the years. He had worked for Ray Price, and was a great guitar player.

Pete played on the TV show "Country Junction" on Channel 5 in Nashville. Eddie Hill was the host of the show, and he was very popular. Eddie even gave Ralph Emery a run for his money, when Ralph was doing his morning show on Channel 4.

All the "Country Junction" musicians had to be at the television studio at 5:00 each morning. They rehearsed for an hour, and then the show aired from 6:00 to 7:30. Pete Wade would call me to be a sub for him when he couldn't make it there.

After I'd subbed for a while, Pete asked if I would like to do the show every day as a regular. He said he couldn't do it anymore. He was working sessions until 1:00 in the morning. He also lived in Hendersonville, and he just couldn't keep up that pace. Pete recommended me to Lightnin' Chance, who played bass for the show. Lightnin' also did all the hiring for the band.

Hal Rugg played steel on "The Country Junction", and Willie Ackerman and Buddy Rogers were the drummers. Stan Hitchcock was the featured singer, and he also played rhythm guitar. David Reece played piano. David had come from gospel music. He was a funny human being. He had a very thin mustache, and one morning, as a joke, he shaved off half of it. As he visited with the show's host on live TV, the host said, "There is something different about you."

The band busted out laughing!

Years later, David went to work for Mel Tillis, where he played piano and also sang background. Back then, Mel was doing one-nighters almost year round. He was on the road all the time.

David Reece's wife didn't like him being gone so much, and one day she told him, "You go everywhere, and I sit home by myself. You get to see the world." So she'd bought a camera, and told David that she wanted him to take pictures of everywhere he went.

After a month on the road, David already had four rolls of film to be developed. As soon as he'd gotten them back, he'd sent them all to his wife... and in each picture, David was standing in the very same spot in front of Mel's bus. On the back of each one, he had written, "Here I am in Phoenix.", "Here I am in Los Angeles.", and every photo had the same pose of him in front of that bus. Only his clothes were different in each one!

The "Country Junction" show featured upcoming artists. In fact, when her career was just taking off, Dolly Parton came on the show, and was our guest each morning for an entire week. Of course she wasn't yet the legend she would go on to be, but playing behind her was an experience I will never forget. Barbara Mandrell also guested on the show quite a few times when she was just starting out.

When Stan Hitchcock's career gained popularity, he would sometimes have weekend road dates, and wouldn't be able to get back in time for Monday's show, so in those cases they would ask Johnny Carver to fill in for Stan. Johnny had been working at the big Palomino Club in Los Angeles, but he moved to Nashville and we all fell in love with him.

Johnny Carver was a Mississippi boy. But as soon as he got out of high school, he went up to Milwaukee and started fronting a band. He did that for four years, and then he moved to Los Angeles.

Johnny was a great singer. He had a big hit with a country version of "Tie a Yellow Ribbon Round the Old Oak Tree."

Johnny and I, along with the great steel guitar player Stu Basore, started a publishing company together. Al Jolsen Jr, was also part of our publishing company. He owned Master Links Studios at the time. We had a song called "Go to Helen",, which I loved. It went "Go to Helen, don't come back to me no more." You have to read the title out loud to get the play on words!

I pitched the song to Waylon Jennings. I knew he was looking for material for his new album. I was booked to play on the album, and when he got there, he brought all his songs with him.

He had cassette tapes, and as he laid them down on the board, I could see my "Helen" song right on top!

I thought, "Wow. I'm gonna get a 'Waylon Jennings' cut for our publishing company." But as the session went on, for some reason he never got around to recording our song. It just never got done.

But Johnny Carver and I became real, real close friends. When we weren't working together, we were playing golf. We are still very close friends today. I told him I was writing my book, and he said he had some things to share. I hope they're good!

"Jimmy Capps is a no good horse thief!

I just wanted to say something different from everyone else who is always saying how great Jimmy is!

I met Jimmy Capps when I came to Nashville to be on the Eddie Hill "Country Junction" TV show. Jimmy played in the live band on that show every morning. I was a guest on the show, and then I ended up joining the show as a regular. And I got to know Jimmy during our time on the show. I also played the Opry a lot, and Jimmy was always in the staff band.

Jimmy and I became dear friends over the years. We've taken many vacations together. I went with him on his very first cruise. He didn't enjoy it very much, though.

It was a seven-day cruise, and he got vertigo as soon as he walked onto the ship. He was dizzy that whole time, and he stayed in bed for almost the entire week.

When I got busy touring, Jimmy offered to sell me his Winnebago motorhome. He didn't use it very much; just parked it in his yard most of the time. After I test drove it around Nashville, I paid his asking price. And I was pretty proud of it, since it was my first band bus.

Our first trip in my new motorhome was to a show in Chattanooga. If you've ever been there, you know that the only way to get there from Nashville is to drive up and over a very high mountain. They call the very top of it "Monteagle".

But I barely made it up to Monteagle! When that Winnebago started up that sharp mountain incline, it started going slower and slower. I had the accelerator pressed to the floor and we were barely going 30 miles an hour! It took me two and half hours to get over that mountain!

Jimmy's Winnebago would get up to full speed once we were on flat land, but it couldn't do any kind of hill. From then on, I tried not to book any shows in Chattanooga... or Montana or Wyoming or Colorado!

Jimmy played on almost all of my recordings. My songs might not have been the biggest of Jimmy's career, but my songs did lead him to some of his biggest.

Ron Chancy was the producer on my hit song, "Tie a Yellow Ribbon", and before that session, I had told Ron, "I'd like to have a friend of mine play on this record. His name is Jimmy Capps." After I'd introduced Jimmy to Ron, and after Jimmy had done such a super job on our session, Ron decided to use Jimmy on every Oak Ridge Boys album they ever did. And Jimmy never forgot that. He always told me, "I would have never gotten any of those big hit songs if you had not put in the word and recommended me."

Jimmy is a great guy. He would do anything in the world for you. Jimmy Capps is my best friend. I have met and have known lots of people, but I consider him to be my very best friend... even if he is a no good horse thief."

- Johnny Carver

Johnny Carver took over on "The Country Junction" when Stan Hitchcock left the show. Stan went on to have a number of hits, and ended up with his own syndicated TV show, which he asked me to be a part of.

During each show, he and I would sit on a little stage and play and sing. I always thought Stan was such a great singer.

One of our most memorable shows had Stan singing the hit "Early Morning Rain", and at the end of the song, I threw a full bucket of cold water right in Stan's face. Everyone was laughing so hard that none of us noticed that the shock of that cold water had also caused Stan to wet his pants!

Stan has never forgotten that. He says, "I could have been another Perry Como. But you'd never see Perry Como's friends throw water on him. And you'd never see Perry pee his pants on national television!"

Stan might not have been Perry Como, but he did become a huge success. Many years later, he started the CMT Network, and then he founded the Americana and Blue Highways Networks. He has been a dear friend for many, many years. I wouldn't have done this book without asking Stan to add his thoughts.

"I have so many memories of my time with Jimmy Capps over the past 55 years. But one of my favorites came on May 3rd, 1968. My baby boy had just been born at Nashville's St. Thomas Hospital, and as soon as we finished our morning TV show, I asked Jimmy to go with me to the hospital.

When we got to St. Thomas, I told Jimmy, "Let me show you what I bought my son!" Jimmy was pretty surprised when I opened up a huge electric train set! And he was even more surprised when I started setting the entire track and train up on the hood of my 66 Cadillac. I had the entire thing all put together when a pretty nurse walked by. I was holding the electric plug when I asked her, "Pardon me ma'am, could you tell me where to plug this in?"

Without even slowing down, she said, "Stick it in your @$$!"

As she got in her car, Jimmy looked over at me and said, "Must not like trains."

Jimmy Capps really did the impossible. He went from being a touring musician to being one of the most sought-after studio musicians in Nashville. That just never happens. Not only that, but he even got so great that he became a member of the A-Team. Those were the very best of the best studio musicians. And Jimmy was the best. He became the premiere session guitarist.

Jimmy thanks me for helping him to get going as a studio musician. When I started recording for Epic Records, since Jimmy and I had worked together on our TV shows so much, I asked my producer, Billy Sherrill, if he would hire Jimmy to play on my sessions. And when Billy saw how great Jimmy was, he started using him on everything that he did. And that led to Jimmy playing on everything from George Jones' "He Stopped Loving Her Today" to Tammy Wynette's "Stand by Your Man".

Jimmy was born with one of the sweetest personalities out of anyone I have ever met, and he brought that to work with him each day. He was so pleasant to work with. Jimmy would sweeten each recording session just by being there. He would change the whole atmosphere in the studio.

Jimmy is a legend. He is a legendary musician. And he is one of the closest friends that I have ever had. I don't think he has ever had a bad thought toward anyone in his life. He is one of the finest men I've ever met. I love Jimmy."

– Stan Hitchcock

In 1965, I worked the Porter Wagoner show with Charlie Louvin. We filmed it at WSM, Channel 4. Porter's band had amplifiers, and Don Warden told me that I could use his. Don played steel guitar for Porter and he went on to be Dolly Parton's manager.

I used Don's amp and it sounded so good, when the show was over, I jokingly told him, "Don, I want that amp. Could you put it in your will and leave it to me when you die?"

More than thirty years later, I was at the Opry house and Don was there with Dolly. When he saw me, Don yelled, "Hey Jimmy! It's in there! I put that amp in my will for you." I couldn't believe it.

I was back at the Opry a few days later, when one of the stage hands told me that Don had dropped off something for me. It was his amp, with a handwritten letter. On Dolly's stationary, he wrote, "Dear Jimmy, I don't know how long this dying is going to take, so I want to give you the amp now. Don Warden." It is one of my most cherished possessions.

Chapter Seven

THE CHOCOLATE COAT

As I mentioned, Lightnin' Chance was the band leader on the "Country Junction" show on Channel 5... but Lightnin' Chance was also so much more. He was the bass player on all of the Everly Brothers' hit songs. He was on most of the Patsy Cline and Ray Price big hits, and Lightnin' was also a bass player for the Grand Ole Opry.

But even with a resume like that, I still can't think of Lightnin' Chance without thinking of his chocolate coat. Here's the entire story...

We all wore matching outfits on the "Country Junction" show. And Lightnin' had always kept his show clothes in a little dressing room at the station. Channel 5 threw a big Christmas party for all of their employees. Of course, none of us were invited.

But they apparently served lots of booze at the party, and there was a cameraman there who had had way too much to drink. He sat down to a big Christmas meal, and the combination of all that food with all of the booze that he'd had hit him all at once.

He started running to the bathroom, but since he was so drunk, he only made it so far as to our dressing room. It was dark, and he couldn't find the light switch, so he sat down at a bench and thought that he was in a bathroom. And he threw up right there. That was bad enough... but then he dropped his pants and started to go number 2 right on the floor!

He was so drunk that when he'd finished, he started grabbing for toilet paper. But of course, since he wasn't in a bathroom, he couldn't find any! As he felt around in the dark, though, he grabbed the sleeve of Lightnin' Chance's stage coat, pulled it off the hanger, and used that coat as toilet paper!

Over the weekend, the cleaning crew came in, and cleaned up all the puke and poop that was on the floor. And they hung Lightnin's coat back on the hanger. And when we all came in on Monday morning to get ready for our show, I was visiting with Lightnin' as he was putting on his show pants and shirt.

When he got to his coat, he looked at it and said, "Jimmy, someone has gotten chocolate candy all over the sleeve of my coat." He took his index finger and flicked at the "chocolate", and he said, "This looks like s@#t!"

And then he touched it to his tongue! And he yelled, "It IS s@#t!"

I have enough Lightnin' Chance stories to fill an entire book, but here are just a couple more.

He had just bought a new 1970 Cadillac. Junior Samples was in town, taping Hee Haw, and he had been in the studio, watching us do our show. Afterwards, Lightnin' asked Junior if he'd like to go and have breakfast with us.

I let Junior sit in the passenger seat, while I got in the back. And as Lightnin' drove, Junior said, "Man, this is a purty car." Jokingly, Lightnin' replied, "Well, it's not my car. It belongs to my neighbor. I'm trying to get a loan from the bank today, and I just borrowed the car to try to impress the banker."

And Junior looked around the inside and said, "Ya reckon I could borrow it after you get through, so I can try to get some money?"

When booking talent for our show, Lightnin' liked to book a singerfor an entire week. One time, he booked Carmol Taylor, who wrote Tammy Wynette's big hits "My Man" and "He Loves Me All the Way" with Norro Wilson and Billy Sherrill. He was from Alabama, and was also a great singer in addition to being a great writer.

You have to remember that this was before the internet, and getting information was not as easy then as it is today. So Lightnin' told the show host, Eddie Hill, that he needed to promote next week's guest, Carmol Taylor.

Now Eddie had never seen Carmol, and for some reason, he just assumed that Carmol Taylor was a woman. So when it came time for Eddie to promote the next week's shows, he said, "Folks, next week we will have the lovely and talented, pretty Miss Carmol Taylor!"

And Carmol looked like a big lumberjack. He had shoulders like a football player. He was big. The next week, we all came into the studio and Eddie asked, "Where is Carmol Taylor? I can't find her."

Lightnin' just smiled as he pointed to Carmol, who was across the studio. Eddie exclaimed, "You have got to be kidding! I've been promoting 'the lovely and talented' Carmol Taylor."

"Well he's not all that lovely," Lightnin' said, "but he is talented!"

I got paid $36 a day to do "The Country Junction." Charlie Louvin was still using me on his road dates, and I was also working with Margie Bowes when she played the Opry, along with any road shows she had. One of my most memorable shows with Margie came on a cold, snowy day in upper Michigan...

Slim Whitman was the headliner of that show, and Margie and Stan Hitchcock were the opening acts. We drove through snow and ice to get there, but once we arrived, we found that the rough weather had kept most of the crowd away. Only about 50 people had showed up all in all, but all three acts did their full performances. At the end of the night, the "entire audience" gave us a standing ovation. We felt good about that. But our good feeling disappeared when it came time for us to get paid.

As Margie, Stan and I looked on, the promoter told Slim Whitman that he only had $400. And I will never forget how Slim walked over to Margie and gave her two hundred dollars. Then he gave Stan the other two hundred. And Slim, the star of the show, kept nothing. He got paid zero for that concert. You wouldn't see many stars today do something like that for their opening act.

Many years later, I did a Christmas album with Slim. He had already become a mega star in England. People here in the U.S. have no idea how big of a star he was around the world. He sold so many records. Slim sang so good.

Just a couple years later, I played on a western album for him, and that's when I really got to know him.

For some reason, Slim really took to me and Michele. We visited so much during those sessions. When his wife died, he was so devastated. He would just cry when he talked about her to us. Slim Whitman was one of my absolute favorite people.

In the early 1960s, my wife Anne and I bought a house in Hermitage. It cost us $16,900! Married life was good, especially since I was off the road. When I was touring, even though the Louvins didn't work a lot of dates, I would also work shows with Roy Drusky and a few others. Back then, especially if you were playing country music, you really had to be working all the time just to be able to make a living.

It was during my time at Channel 5 that my wife and I started trying to have a family. By this point, we had been married for nine years. But a baby never came along. We took all kinds of tests, and the doctors told us that we should be able to have a child. But for some reason, my wife couldn't get pregnant.

So we started to talk about possibly adopting a child. We were told there was a two-to-three-year waiting list to adopt, though. And then, we received some major help from an unexpected source.

THE MAN IN BACK

The man who did the farm reports every morning for Channel 5 also worked for the state of Tennessee. He found out that my wife and I were wanting to adopt a child, and he used his pull to push us to the front of the line. That farm reporter is the one we always thank for us getting our son.

We adopted a little boy who had been born on December 31, 1967. He was just seven weeks old when we got him, and we named him Jeffrey Allen. When they gave us all the paperwork, they explained how they'd matched us up with the baby. And while they didn't have the names of the parents, they told me that his dad was drummer. So, me being a musician, they thought that I would make the perfect father for the baby boy.

When we adopted Jeffrey, no one knew who his real parents were. When he was 13 years old, Jeff told me that he wanted to meet his birth parents, and I told him I would help him do that. So we started researching everything, and we found that he was born in Louisville, Kentucky. I also found out that both his mom and dad were in the military in Clarksville, Tennessee.

Our lives totally changed after we became parents. Of course, Anne's changed more than mine. She had to become an instant mom, without having much time to prepare for anything.

It's funny how life works sometimes. Just a couple months after we adopted Jeff, my wife got pregnant! When our son Mark Jason was born on December 14, 1968, we found ourselves the parents of two baby boys in less than a year!

Today, Mark is a Grammy award winning studio engineer. He works a lot with Bill Gaither and Ben Isaacs, and he also runs any projects I produce. Mark is also a great musician. My son Jeff is a fantastic musician as well.

Mark is married to a beautiful, sweet lady named Tara. She has a daughter, McKenzie, who is Roy Acuff's great granddaughter. Mark's daughter, Summer, my granddaughter, graduated high school this year.

In the late 1960s, Anne and I were enjoying our baby boys. But on April 15, 1969, I mourned the death of my father. I was so thankful my dad lived to see my sons. He loved them. My mom died ten years after dad, on June 22, 1979.

Anne and I had ups and downs in our marriage. Most of the downs came because I was always on the road. And even when I'd started playing sessions and was able to stay in town, I was still gone from the house all the time. I was in the studio morning, noon and night, almost around the clock.

So, Anne did probably 85% of the work in raising the kids. I give her credit for raising our boys, and she did a really great job. I wasn't even home on weekends, because I was playing on the Opry.

Being married to a musician is not easy. But Anne never complained. She knew what she was getting into when she started going with me. She knew what my work was, and also what my dreams and goals were. She never tried to change me into something else. It takes a special woman, or man, to be married to an entertainer or musician.

In September of 2005, Anne had a brain aneurysm. I found her on the bathroom floor. I couldn't wake her up. I yelled for Jeff, who was still living at home. We called 9-1-1 and they took her to Summit Hospital. It was the nearest hospital to where we lived in Mt. Juliet. But they said her condition was too bad for them to handle, so she was transferred to St. Thomas Hospital.

They operated on her, and were able to stop the bleeding in her brain. But there had been too much damage, and she never regained consciousness. She was in the hospital ten days before she died.

Our marriage was not perfect. Not many are. I have good memories, and I have some bad memories. But anytime you lose a spouse, especially after you have lived together with somebody for that long, it is an extremely tough thing to go through. Anne and I had been married 47 years.

Chapter Eight

THE LEGENDS

In the 1960s, during any free time I had, I'd also started hanging around the Grand Ole Opry more and more. Back then, an artist could pick any musician that was there and available, and hire them to play on their portion of the Opry. Bob Luman was really great about that. He loved to spend the Opry's money on as many musicians as he could find! He'd walk up to me and Spider Wilson as we hung around backstage and he'd say, "I want both you guys playing for me tonight."

He always said, "Turn 'em up, boys. I want it loud out there!"

I played quite a few shows with Bob Luman. I played for him until he was able to hire a full band. Most of my time with Bob was spent at a place called The Black Poodle in Nashville, where we played five nights a week from 8:00 to 1:30 in the morning.

One night, Merle Haggard came to see us. He had had a couple hits at the time, but he was traveling in one of those little pickup campers. It was a tiny camper that you'd slide onto the back of a pickup truck! I was shocked to see how he was traveling. To me, he was already a superstar.

But he ended up sitting in and singing with us.

I was a big fan of Merle's, from the time he first started. On another occasion when I was working the Opry, Merle came over and talked to me and the other band members. He just acted like a regular guy. He didn't act like a superstar.

The "freelancing" of the pickers eventually evolved into the Opry Staff Band.

Spider Wilson was part of the original band, and he worked the Opry for years. When he was a kid, Spider and his dad lived just a few blocks from the Ryman, and they would walk down there on Saturday nights. They wouldn't have a ticket to the show... but they knew the Ryman windows were always open, since it got so hot in there in the summer. Here, Spider listened to Hank Williams, Sr. perform on the Opry through that open window. He said that you could just feel the magnetism that Hank had with the audience.

Spider Wilson also played for about ten syndicated television shows. He was part of the band in all of the classic country TV shows throughout the 60s and 70s.

Marvin Hughes played piano for the Opry, and then went on to run Capitol Records. Floyd Cramer joined the band after Marvin, and Hargus "Pig" Robbins followed Floyd. Pig is the blind piano player who has played on so many huge hit records.

Leon Rhodes and Joe Edwards were two of the all-time great members of the Opry staff band. But Joe thought that Leon was really tight when it came to money. Leon never carried any cash, and Joe always had a pocket full of money.

One night, Leon wanted to buy a guitar stand from someone who had come to the Opry, so he went to Joe and asked him to loan him $20.00, but Joe said, "No. You've borrowed money from me too many times. You need to start carrying your own money."

Then Leon came to me and said, "Can you believe that Joe won't loan me $20?"

I winked at Leon and said, "Just wait."

THE MAN IN BACK

A short while later, as I visited with Joe and Leon, I said, "Joe, I've got to stop at Kroger's on my way home tonight and pick up a few things. Have you got 20 bucks you can loan me?"

He quickly said, "Oh yeah. No problem." Joe opened his billfold, and I could see all his cash. He flipped through hundred-dollar bills and then pulled out a twenty and handed it to me.

After about thirty seconds, with Joe still looking on, I said, "Leon, didn't you need $20 for that guitar stand? Man, I can go to the grocery store tomorrow. Take this twenty. And you pay Joe back!"

Joe's face turned bright red. He knew he had been had.

The great Opry steel guitar player Weldon Myrick liked to pull pranks on people, and he pulled one of his best on our staff drummer, Harold Weakley. Harold had been bragging about the brand new set of Michelin tires that he had just bought for his car. He just kept going on and on about how great those tires were, and how smooth his van drove with them.

So the next night, while Harold was inside the Opry house, Weldon Myrick moved all of the weights on each of the wheels on Harold's van.

On his way back home that night, Harold's steering wheel started shaking as he tried to hold the van on the road. The next day, he took it to the shop and told them to balance the tires again. They did.

And the next Friday at the Opry, once again, Weldon moved all those tire weights. Again, Harold took it back to the tire shop, and again they rebalanced the tires. And can you believe that the next week, Weldon moved those weights again?!

This time when Harold took the van back to the shop the third time, they gave him a brand new set of Michelin tires. He never found out that it was Weldon playing a joke on him. He never did.

Harold Weakley was not the greatest drummer in the world. But his feel and tone were so perfect. Harold was the glue in our staff band. He was the one who held everything together.

One of the funniest things that ever happened on the Opry actually took place during the Opry Live TV show. It went nationwide for the entire country to see. Billy Linneman was the bass player with the Opry Staff Band for years, and one night, Billy and I played a practical joke on our buddy Joe Edwards. Joe was the staff fiddle player, and was one of the most recognized members of the band. He also played guitar for Bill Carlisle.

And while Bill was out doing a song, me and Billy went over to Joe as he was playing and we started rolling up his pant legs. Then we took some scissors and cut his pant legs completely off! And then we shaved his legs, right there on stage! We did all of that and Joe never missed a note, as he just kept right on playing!

There was another practical joke Billy Linneman pulled that also went nationwide: it was a Saturday night, and the Opry had two shows scheduled for that night. PBS was going to air both of those shows back-to-back, but on the West Coast, because of the time zone difference, they aired the second Opry show live, but they had taped the first Opry, and aired it after the second show. So the order of the two Opry's was flipped, for viewers in California and in the western time zone.

Billy Linneman had a full beard at the time… but as a joke, in between shows he went into the bathroom and shaved his entire beard off. And when the Opry aired on PBS, viewers in California saw him with a nice, clean, freshly shaved face. But then, a couple hours later, they saw him with a full beard! He had grown that big beard while they were watching!

Billy was in the Opry staff band from 1962 to 2005. I asked him how far back our friendship went. He says it goes back a very long time.

"It's rare when a person can say they have had a lifelong friend. I was 17 years old when I met Jimmy. And we've been friends ever since. We met for the first time before he went into the Army.

We did a lot of television work together. I hired him to be part of our band for The Waking Crew. That show was on WSM each morning, and we were the last major radio show that had a live band each day. The band was a very important part of the show. We also did the show for a year on the General Jackson boat.

Jimmy and I had a company together, Hilltop Productions. We recorded albums for so many country stars, everyone, like Jean Shepard, Justin Tubb, and Ray Pillow. We had the company for about 15 years.

We still enjoy each other's company. And we both think alike. We both have the same sense of humor. We worked hard for a few decades. But we always had so much fun every day. We had a lot of fun times as we made some good music. And I think we made a little history along the way."

– Billy Linneman

Every country music artist wanted to be on the Opry. And they wanted to be Opry members, even though they didn't get paid much by the Opry. If you were an Opry member, that gave you clout, and then you could get much bigger money when you went on the road to do concerts.

The artists would make posters to promote their shows, and above their name, they would always put "Star of the Grand Ole Opry". Man that would sell you tickets.

You were really somebody if you were a member of the Opry. And if you were a musician on the Opry, people looked at you as having made it. Well, we might have "made it", but we sure weren't making a whole lot of money.

National Life, which owned the Opry, was getting a heck of a deal. They didn't pay the Opry stars hardly anything. The Grand Ole Opry was the most well-known show in the world. It still is. It's known around the world.

But back in the day, I was playing spots on the Opry for $6.00 a night! And I was glad to get that money.

But I'm happy to say that things have changed for the artists and musicians. Right now I'd like to share a few memories of some of those early Opry stars who I was blessed to work with:

Roy Acuff - When the King of Country Music walked out on stage, for his entire career, even at the end, when he walked out on the Opry stage, he was a superstar. Everybody ran down to the front of the stage to take pictures of him. The audience loved him. When Roy Acuff walked into a room, all eyes turned to him. Roy just had a magic about him. And he kept that magic up to the very end of his life.

Minnie Pearl - Minnie Pearl was pure class. She was such a wonderful representative for the state of Tennessee and for the Grand Ole Opry. Her husband Henry was the same way. I never played behind her, but I always made a point to just sit and watch her do her thing. I knew I was watching something very magical.

Bill Monroe - Mr. Monroe was a classy gentleman. He totally invented Bluegrass music. My dad loved Bill Monroe so much. I was a fan, but I was more a fan of electric instruments. I was always able to recognize, though, that there was something in Bill's music that no one else had.

One night, I was backstage at the Opry, standing at the security desk where all the artists come in. And when Bill Monroe walked in, I said, "Mr. Bill, how long have you been on the Opry?"

And he roughly said back, "I came here in 1939. You figure it out!" and he walked off. I thought, man that was rude. I was just trying to be friendly.

But a couple minutes later, he came back and he told me how many years he had been there. And he added, "When we came to the Opry, we started wearing nice clothes. No one else dressed up. They were all wearing plaid shirts." He and his band always dressed sharp in suits and ties.

George Morgan - George Morgan was almost too good. He was so smooth. He was not near as big of a star as he should have been.

I once wanted to borrow some money from the Commerce Union Bank in Nashville, and Clarence Reynolds was the man in charge of the loans there. I was wanting to buy a mini motorhome at the time, and I needed about $5,000. Before I applied for the loan, however, I asked George Morgan to contact Clarence and put in a good word for me.

A few days later, George called me and said that Clarence Reynolds said that he'd see me. When I got there, Mr. Reynolds said, "You're a friend of George Morgan right?" to which I said "Yes."

And he said, "Let me tell you what George said about you. He said, 'If Jimmy tells you it's gonna rain, get out your umbrella.' And George's good word for you is good enough for me." I got the loan.

George Morgan was very proud of his daughter. Lorrie was a young teenager when George introduced her on the Opry, and from the first song she sang, we all knew that she was very talented.

Not long after her debut, George was getting ready to go to the hospital to have heart surgery. As he was leaving the backstage area of the Opry, the manager of the Opry said, "George, if there's anything I can do, just let me know."

And George said, "If anything happens to me, the only thing I ask is that you use Lorrie on the Opry as much as you can."

Years later, Lorrie became a member of the Opry, and went on to have big, big hits. Her dad didn't live to see all of her success. But he knew she was good. He wouldn't have asked the Opry to use her if she wasn't.

Over the last few years, I've worked Lorrie's spots when she's been on the Opry. She is just a sweetheart. She is like a female version of George. She has the same personality. I told her, "Lorrie, you have the prettiest vibrato in your voice, just like your dad's."

She hugged me and said, "You'll never know what that means to me."

She'll never know what it means to me that she is a part of my book.

"Jimmy Capps is such a special person. He was friends with my dad when I was a little girl, running around backstage at the Opry. I was very intimidated by a lot of the Opry musicians, and Jimmy is one I was intimidated by, because he always looked very serious. As I got older, I realized that he was a man who really took his work very serious.

Jimmy played on my "A Moment in Time" album. We wanted to do that album the way they used to be done in Nashville. So we asked all the musicians if they would be willing to lay down their tracks, without any overdubs. We cut 17 songs in two days! The second day, Jimmy came into the control room and asked me, "Would you let me fix just one little part? I know I can play it better." I said, "Jimmy, you were perfect. We're not touching it."

When they asked me to be on Larry's Country Diner, they told me that Jimmy would be there and I said, "Then, I'll do it." If you're gonna have a one man band, it had better be Jimmy Capps! I've always looked up to him, and when he complimented me on my voice and compared me to my father, it brought me to tears.

When I heard he was going to call his book "The Man in Back", I thought it was the perfect title. I wish I had thought of it! A musician can make you or break you. He is the one who makes us sound great. He still does so many sessions in Nashville. The newer artists want him on their sessions. He is an incredible musician.

My friendship with Jimmy has grown over the years. He knows how much I respect him and how much I depend on his guitar playing. When I'm on the Opry, he is my safety net. It is such a comfort to turn around and see him playing the guitar behind me.

Jimmy is a great man. He is a joy to be around, and he's got a great sense of humor. My dad loved him and I love him too."

– Lorrie Morgan

Tex Ritter - I worked some sessions with Tex Ritter. And Tex was part of a show I was on in Arkansas. I was working the show with the Wilburn Brothers. I was traveling in a little motorhome with my wife and two boys. My sons were five and six years old at the time. And as soon as we got out of our Winnebago, we saw Tex Ritter sitting there, smoking a pipe. I took my sons up to him and I said, "Boys, this is one of my heroes, Tex Ritter." And then I said to Tex, "Mr. Ritter, this is Jeff and this is Mark."

He shook hands with both of them and said, "Jeff, it is good to meet you. And Mark, it's good to meet you too."

About three months after that, I took my sons to the Ryman, where I was playing the Opry. Sure enough, when we stepped through the back door, we met Tex Ritter again, sitting there smoking his pipe. And he said, "Hello Jim! I see you have Jeff and Mark with you."

Later that night, I went back to Tex and asked him, "How do you do that? How do you remember names like that?"

"A person's first name," he answered, "is one of the most important things to them. And I've made it a habit to always remember people's names."

He really tried hard to please the public and to make everyone he met feel important.

Marty Robbins - When Marty Robbins played the Opry, he was usually the person who closed the show. And if he was, he would sometimes run over a half hour. He just kept singing and singing. He didn't want to stop, and the fans didn't want him to stop either!

But each Saturday, the Ernest Tubb Midnite Jamboree would come on right after the Opry on WSM radio. And when Marty got to singing, he wouldn't stop at midnight, and he would run on into Ernest's time. Ernest would be waiting and waiting to start his program, but the Opry would just let Marty go on for as long as he wanted, because he was such an entertainer; and the audience would always go out knowing that they had been entertained. They would go home and talk about how great the Opry was, and that would lead to more ticket buyers in the future.

Jack Greene - Before he started having his own big hits, Jack Greene was a member of Ernest Tubb's Texas Troubadours. Most years, Ernest Tubb would end up working more than 300 road shows! Jack Greene told me, "When I was with ET, we only came home long enough to sign our divorce papers!"

Jack's hair was thinning at an early age, and his wife at the time had talked him into buying a hairpiece. I was playing acoustic guitar on the Opry for Jack when he wore that toupee for the very first time, and I could tell he was very self-conscious about it.

He stood in the dark backstage as he waited to go on. When they introduced him, the crowd applauded. But he walked out so slow, that the applause had died down by the time he got to the microphone. It was almost total quiet, and for some reason, I said, "Don't worry Jack. They can't tell it!" If looks could kill, I would be dead.

Jack Greene and Jeannie Seely were one of the first groups to have a complete stage show. They had lighting and sound that they carried on the road with them. LeRoy Van Dyke had also done it, but Jack and Jeannie were among the first.

Jack Greene was truly a musician's friend. He loved musicians. Jack had perfect timing. Even when his memory failed him, his timing never did. One time, late in his career, we kicked off the intro to his hit, "Statue of a Fool". It's a long intro, and there's no doubt what song it is. But when it came time for him to sing, Jack broke into "There Goes My Everything". And he kept singing. The band heard what he was singing and changed over... but until then he just kept on singing the totally wrong song, but at the same time on the totally correct beat. His timing was so good, he sang a waltz in 4/4 time!

George Hamilton IV - I met George Hamilton IV when I was 16. We were in North Carolina, and I was on the TV show "Saturday Night Country Style". George was currently going to college in Chapel Hill, but he had come in to do the show. He and I were friends from that time up until his death. He was a true gentleman.

I never heard a negative word about George Hamilton IV. He was solid gold in his personality and in his attitude towards others. He was never envious about other guys being more popular than him. He had a great career. He was a great human being. I only did two albums with him, but I worked all of his Opry spots, and each night, he would turn to me on stage and say, "From my home state of North Carolina, Jimmy Capps." He was so giving.

They started selling backstage tours after the Opry, and George went to the Opry management and told them he wanted to host some of the tours. Here he was, this big star, a member of the Opry... and he was asking to be a tour guide! He was the greatest one they could have ever had! He loved meeting and talking to the fans. He loved sharing the history of the Opry with everyone. He didn't use a script. He just said everything off the top of his head.

He was such a wonderful storyteller, and almost every night, when I was trying to sneak out, George would yell, "And right there, folks, is the great Jimmy Capps, from my home state of North Carolina. He is the greatest guitar player in the world!"

Grandpa Jones - Grandpa Jones went on a tour with The Louvin Brothers to Canada. Grandpa loved Chinese food. We would all go out to eat, and he'd eat Chinese food every night. He said, "Chinese food in Canada is better than it is in the States."

During Grandpa's act, he and his wife, Ramona, used cowbells to play Jingle Bells during the Christmas season. They tied different sounding cowbells to their feet and hands, and each bell had its own tone. But one night, Grandpa's bells fell off his feet. When he put them back on, he put them on the wrong feet. When he started playing the song again, it was all wrong! It was the wrong tone, and it just sounded horrible! Grandpa got so mad that he threw all those cowbells off the stage.

Probably the greatest thing Grandpa ever did was the recitation "The Christmas Guest". It was so good. Bill Walker wrote the arrangement for it. After Grandpa died and we did our first Country's Family Reunion without him, they filmed us all sitting there as we listened to Grandpa's "Christmas Guest". We all just sat and cried as we remembered him.

He was an amazing man. He respected everyone so much, and he was a good man. On stage, he wore boots that were a hundred years old. He also wore an old cap and suspenders. But off stage, he was a very neat dresser. He was very proud of his clothes. I was always impressed by that. All of his clothes were always pressed and starched.

I was there for Grandpa's last performance on the Opry. He had just performed, and was backstage, when he had a stroke. We all watched as they carried him off on a stretcher. It was a tough thing, to have to keep going on with the show after that. We all kept asking if anyone had heard how he was doing. A short time later, he passed away.

Hank Snow - Hank Snow was a great singer, and I loved his guitar playing. He was a stylist. He did two albums with Chet Atkins, and they were first class, instrumental albums.

I was asked to be on a recording for Sony of Japan. It was a karaoke record, with instrumental versions of hit songs. I was the leader for those sessions, and I helped hire all the musicians. We were supposed to record 50 songs, one of which was the Hank Snow song "It Don't Hurt Anymore". One of the men from Japan asked me if I might be able to get Hank to come in and play on the song. I said, "I will ask him."

So, one night before the Opry, I walked into his dressing room and told him about the project. After I had explained it all, I asked him, "Mr. Hank, would you consider playing on the song? They want you to do the turnaround and all the fills on acoustic guitar." Then I quietly added, "but here's the deal: all it pays is union scale."

Hank sat there and said, "Well, them S.O.B.'s! They've got all the money in the world. Why don't they pay us more?" Then he said, "But I will do it. But I'm not doin' it for them. I'm doin' it for you, Jim."

Ernest Tubb - I haven't told this to very many people... but I had the chance to be one of Ernest Tubb's Texas Troubadours, and I turned it down.

I was playing on the road with Ferlin Husky at the time, and I was also working at the Black Poodle in Nashville with Bob Luman. One night, as I played for Bob, I saw Jack Drake and

Jack Greene sitting down at the front table. I knew they were both members of Ernest's band.

When we took our first break, Jack Drake walked up and said, "We came down to hear you play. Would you like to be a Texas Troubadour?"

I said, "Jack, man, I am so happy with my job with Ferlin. You guys have a great band and I love Ernest. But you are gone all the time, and I am happy where I'm at."

Ernest Tubb played 200-300 shows a year. But while I passed on the offer, I said, "I would like to recommend a friend of mine. His name is Steve Chapman. He would do a really great job." And he did. They hired Steve on my word.

I did get to work with Mr. Tubb one night many years later, however. Steve had quit by then, and so had quite a few other guitar players. They just couldn't take that road schedule that ET kept up.

One of Mr. Tubb's last guitar players was Pete Mitchell. They had a Friday night concert in Chicago, and after the show, Pete missed the bus. Ernest was a stickler for being on time. If you weren't there when the bus was supposed to go, he would leave without you. And he had left Pete in Chicago.

The next night, Ernest was scheduled to play the Opry, and Pete Mitchell still hadn't gotten back from Chicago. So Ernest's bass player, Ronnie Blackwell, asked me to play guitar for Ernest. One of the proudest moments of my career was when my solo came up in that performance, and Ernest Tubb called out my name. When he said, "Here's Jimmy Capps!", I almost cried right there on the Opry.

I also played on an album with Ernest. It was a double album, featuring all duets with other country stars. Ernest was a very loyal person to the Opry, to his record shop, and to his Midnite Jamboree radio show. Even if they'd had concerts scheduled anywhere in the country on Monday, Tuesday and Wednesday,

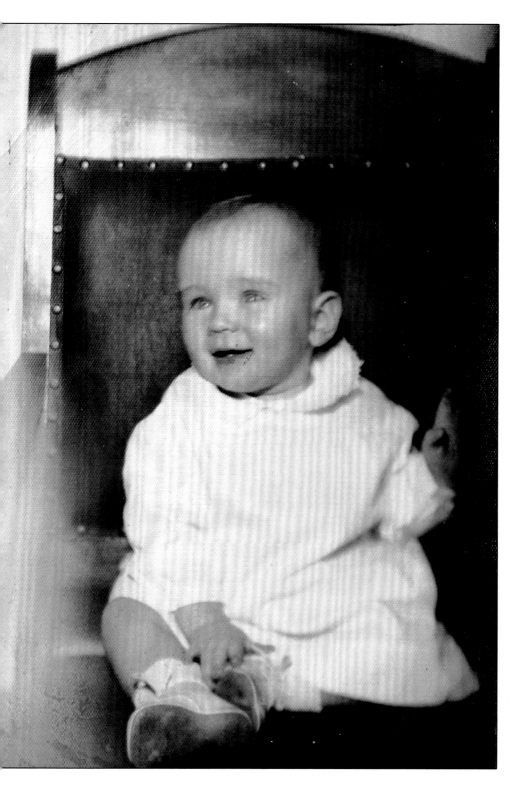

Baby James

Jimmy, 9 months old

Won't you ride in my little red wagon

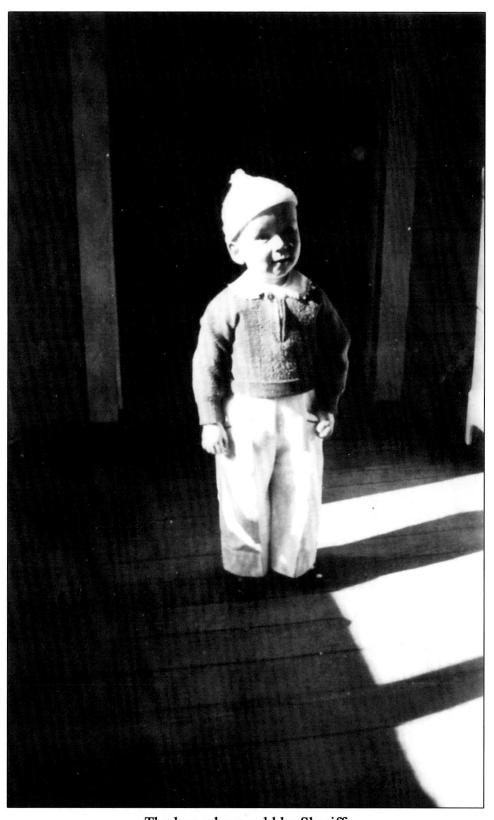

The boy who would be Sheriff

With my cousin Barbara

"Bob"   "Jim"

With my cousin Barbara.
We called her Bobbie

Bobbie Jimm
Rags + the little

In front of our house wearing the suit my great uncle bought me

Already serving

Posing on my uncle's car

Jimmy Capps, 5 years old

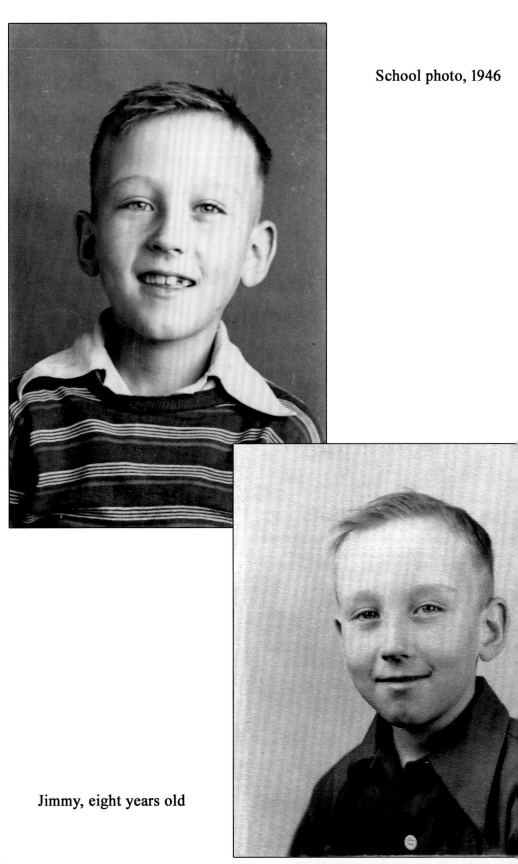

School photo, 1946

Jimmy, eight years old

With my first guitar

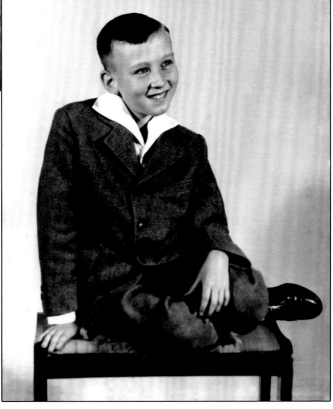

Jimmy, 10 years old

School photo, 11 years old

School photo, 11 years old

My first real guitar and my first real cowboy hat

My grandmother Alice Stephenson in front of our house in Benson N.C.

My dad, Tommie Capps

Mom and Dad

My father with
his semi truck

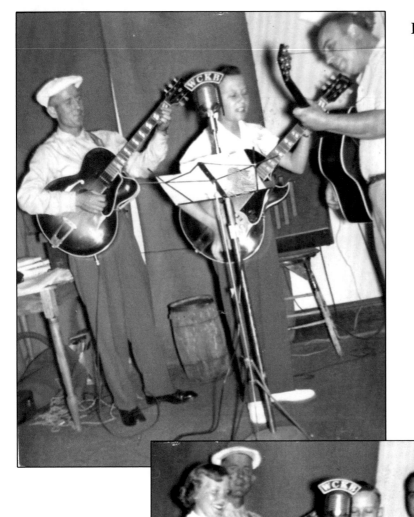

Playing with the
Smile-A-While
Boys

Playing my ES-175
Gibson on WCKB
Radio

With the
Clifton Sisters

June 1956

Age 14

The Smile-A-While Boys. Hayden Ivey
and Jim Thornton

Playing my ES-5 on a local radio
show

My 10th grade school
photo

With my parents and
my nieces Louise
and Carolyn

A great shot
of my ES-5

Slim Mims
and the
Dream
Ranch
Boys, 1956

(L-R) Jim Thornton, Unknown, Gerald Young, Mozelle
Phillips, Hayden Ivey, Jimmy Capps

Look at that crowd behind us! Smithfield NC. Jimmy Capps, Mozelle
Phillips, Jim Thornton, Gerald Young, Hayden Ivey

Playing my Chet Atkins Country Gentleman Gretsch

Hayden Ivey, Jimmy Capps, Gerald Young

With mom and dad, Aug. 1961

The Dream
Ranch Boys:
I'm on the
front right.

The Dream
Ranch Boys

Jimmy Capps,
Gerald Young at
WTVD TV

aying my Chet
Atkins 6120
Gretsch. Now
ong gone, after
meone stole it.

Meeting my fans at the Dream Ranch Barn

Gerald Young, Jimmy, Bob Mitchell, Hayden Ivey, Mozelle Phillips and Jim Thornton on the ground.

Jimmy, Paul Montgomery, Jim Thornton, Gerald Young, Hayden Ivey.
I'm sorry I don't know the little girl

On the right side, you'll see a Gibson bass guitar amp and a
Fender Pro amp. Today they are collector's items worth
$10,000 each.

The Tarheels. I'm on the far right. *Photo by Bill Norton*

I'm second from the right with The Tarheels. *Photo by Bill Norton*

With my heroes The Louvin Brothers.
Photo by Seymour Studio, Petersburg VA.

Playing a club in Minneapolis MN

With my first wife Anne

The start of a 110 day tour with the Louvin Brothers! (L-R) Hal Willis, Ginger Willis, Tommy Hill, Ira Louvin, Charlie Louvin, Jimmy Capps, Benny Martin

WSM
GRAND OLE OPRY

Plus old-Time Fiddler's Convention

And Amateur Contest

Contest Winners Will Compete For Recording -Audition
At Sylvania High School, Sylvania Alabama

——FEATURING——

Gene Woods

JUBILEE RECORDING ARTIST WHO NOW
HAS ONE OF THE NATION'S TOP RECORDS

——ALSO FEATURING——

The Louvin Sisters

Starring Ira and Charles, the Louvin Brothers,

And Featuring Jimmy Capps

Time

Admission

Fri. Nite, March 11, 1960
Asbury School, Asbury, Ala.

Making the sho[w]
poster with the
Louvins! Marc[h]
1960

Ira, Charlie,
Jimmy, 1961.
New River
Ranch, Rising
Sun Maryland.

*Photo by Leo
Kagarise*

With my hero Charlie Louvin

Playing with
the Louv[in]
1961.

*Photo
Leon
Kagari*

*With Charlie
Louvin. His
boot design
makes it look
like he's
wearing
women's shoes!*

With Charlie Louvin, showing off the Harmony guitars that were given to us by Shot Jackson

With the Louvins. Darrell McCall is on the right.

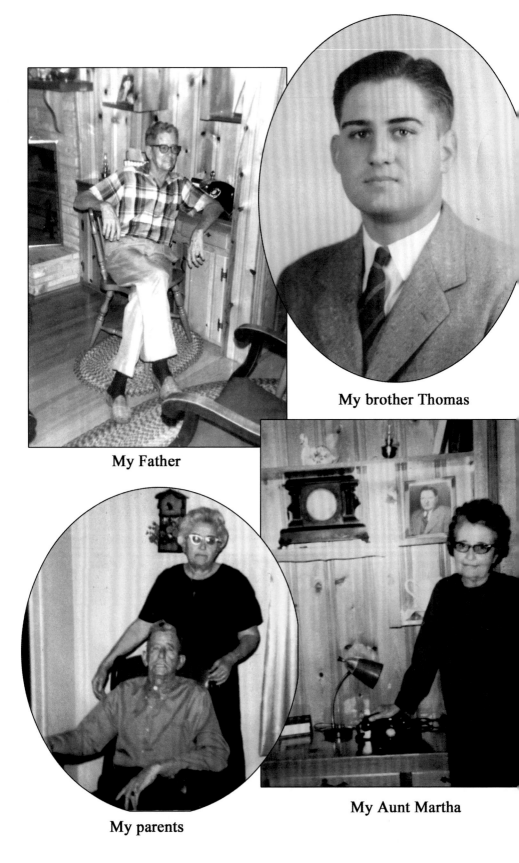

My Father

My brother Thomas

My parents

My Aunt Martha

Serving my country

A fresh hairc
I'm on the le
Charles Bole
on the righ

Proud to serve.
Fort Gordon GA

May 21, 1964. U.S. Army Photograph

On the road with the Second Army Showmobile. I'm on the far right.

Ken Luther introduces me. April 1964. *U.S. Army Photograph*

I'm in the middle. Sept. 1964. *U.S. Army Photograph*

Entertaining the troops. I'm second from the left. *U.S. Army Photograph*

I'm in the middle as the Showmobile does it's country act. Sept. 1964.
U.S. Army Photograph

I'm second from the left. Sept. 1964. *U.S Army Photograph*

Yep, this was really my Army uniform!

Playing a Gretsch guitar with a Bigsby pickup

One of the craziest Army photos you will ever see! I'm on the far left.

Trading my guitar for a banjo for a song.

Just call us the Space Cadets! I'm the cadet in the middle.

I'm the Jetson on the far right!

Jimmy Capps, second from the left. Fort Meade Maryland.
U.S. Army Photograph

Letter of appreciation as I prepared to leave the Army.

HEADQUARTERS
SECOND UNITED STATES ARMY
FORT GEORGE G. MEADE, MARYLAND 20755

IN REPLY REFER TO
AIABA-PSE

3 November 1964

Mr. Jimmy Capps
3991 Dickerson Road
Rollin Acres Trailer Park
Nashville, Tennessee

Dear Jimmy:

The accompanying document bears significant but only partial reflection of the appreciation of this office for the outstanding contribution you made to the Second United States Army Showmobile and in a broader sense to the Second United States Army Entertainment Program.

It is my most sincere wish that you should achieve every success that you seek. It is my confident expectation based upon your impeccable record that you shall do so.

You have established a formidable standard for any prospective successor. Congratulations and thank you for a job well done.

Sincerely,

CORY WAYNE
Staff Entertainment Director

1 Incl
Certificate of
Achievement

Off to another show

A Hushpuppy in action.
Playing with Ferlin Husky.

With Benny Martin. We
took this at a
carnival we were playing.

With Ronnie Blackwell during a tour with Charlie Louvin, Aug. 1965

Playing it cool as I play for the great Bob Luman

TOO MUCH COUNTRY!

MAI
music arts inc.

- **JIMMY CAPPS** - guitar
- **TERRY BETHEL** - steel guitar
- **JIMMY PEPPERS** - drums
- **ORLO THOMPSON** - bass

Album by Ferlin Husky's band The Hushpuppies. I'm on the right

Back cover of Too Much Country album

THESE ARE...
THE HUSHPUPPIES

✳

The level of musicianship in Country Music has been rising steadily during the past few years. Solo choruses that would have been startling a short time ago now become ordinary, and the listener hears new musical flights of fancy . . . both in solo and ensemble playing.

Recently four musicians gathered at Starday Studios in Nashville and laid down a collection of sounds that exhibit the compatibility of electric and steel guitar, together with bass and drums.

These sounds are made by the group that backgrounds Ferlin Husky in his numerous appearances across the country, and they're called: THE HUSHPUPPIES: JIMMY CAPPS, guitar . . . TERRY BETHEL, steel guitar . . . ORLO THOMPSON, bass . . . JIMMY PEPPERS, drums.

Jimmy Capps, 27, hails from North Carolina. Terry Bethel, 28, is from Arkansas. Orlo Thompson, 26, was born in Minnesota, and Jimmy Peppers, 26, calls Alabama home. All four are married. Thompson has two children; Bethel has five.

Produced by NEIL WILBURN, this set of songs is meant for those who dig the driving, hard-core sounds these instruments can make, when held in the hands of experts.

Outstanding cuts in the album are: "A Hard Day's Night", and "Midnight 'Til Dawn".

There's plenty more! So hasten to savor this treat for your ears, and start the grooves to spinning!

✳

JIMMY CAPPS

TERRY BETHEL

ORLO THOMPSON

JIMMY PEPPERS

- A HARD DAYS NIGHT — BMI
- EASY GOIN — BMI
- BUMP CHINK — ASCAP
- CURTAIN CALL — BMI
- RAISIN' THE DICKENS — BMI
- EL COMPANCHERO — BMI
- MIDNIGHT TILL DAWN
- NIGHT CAPP
- STEALIN' HOME
- LONESOME OUT TONIGHT
- PUNCHY
- TURN AROUND

NEIL WILBURN and the group.

Cover and back photos: BILL GRINE, NEW WORLD PHOTOGR

With Stan Hitchock filming Stan's TV show

The Stu Phillips Show. (L-R) Jimmy Capps, Hal Rugg, Jerry Arnold, Ernie Newton

Behind the scenes as we do Stu Phillips' TV show.

Filming Stu's Show. Stu is in the middle. Arlene Harden is on Stu's right.

My sons Mark and Jeff

Family Photo, early 70s

FEBRUARY 1973

S	M	T	W	T	F	S
				1	2	3
4	5	6	7	8	9	10
11	12	13	14	15	16	17
18	19	20	21	22	23	24
25	26	27	28	..	..	..

Week of **FEBRUARY 26, 1973**

57 **Monday, Feb. 26** 308

Air Conditioner
Man

2:00 Tree
Tree

Paid $68.00

58 **Tuesday, Feb. 27** 307

Star Jill

10:

Our Co.

10AM Col A Ⓜ
Tommy Overstreet
Paid Col.

Our Co.

2:00 Hilltop
Del Wood

6:00 Blue Crest
Demo -
Music City
Paid $44.00

59 **Wednesday, Feb. 28**

10 RCA - C
Jim Reeves
overdub
Paid R.C.A

2:00 Col B.
Carl Smith
Paid Col.

6:00 RCA - A
Nat Stuckey
RCA
Paid R.C.A

An average page from my 1973 appointment book

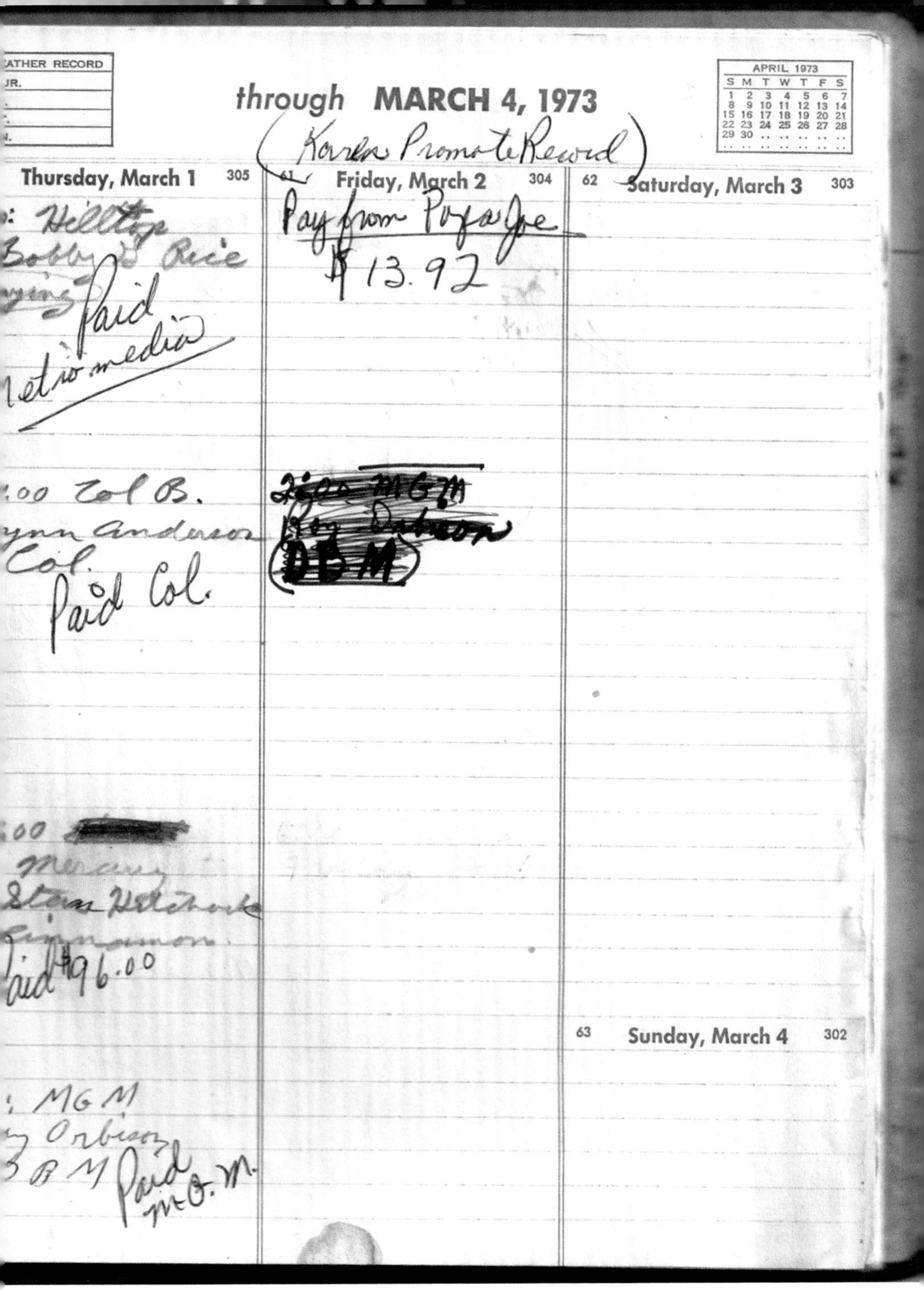

APRIL 1973

S	M	T	W	T	F	S
1	2	3	4	5	6	7
8	9	10	11	12	13	14
15	16	17	18	19	20	21
22	23	24	25	26	27	28
29	30	..	..	..	..	..
..	..	..	..	..	..	..

(Karen Promote Record)

Thursday, March 1   305

: Helltop
Bobby Rice
ying Paid
Metromedia

:00 Col B.
ynn Anderson
Col.
Paid Col.

:00
mercury
Stan Hitchcock
Cinnamon
Paid $96.00

: MGM
Orbison
B M Paid
M.G.M.

61   Friday, March 2   304

Pay from Papa Joe
$13.92

:00 MGM
Roy Orbison
DBM

62   Saturday, March 3   303

63   Sunday, March 4   302

---

ly March 1st included sessions with Bobby G. Rice, Lynn Anderson, Stan
Hitchcock and Roy Orbison

Wearing Halloween teeth for a photo with my pals Spider Wilson, Leon Rhodes and Joe Edwards

With my Denelectro 6 String Tic Tac guitar. It was stolen while I was doing a Merle Haggard session.

I'm second from left just behind President Nixon.
Photo by WSM, Les Leverett

President Nixon plays piano on the Grand Ole Opry. March 16, 1975.
I'm on the far left. *Photo by WSM, Mary Cartwright*

PAPA JOE RECORDS 70002

STEREO

TRUCK DRIVERS INSTRUMENTAL

Overdrive
What Am I Living For
One Mile North of Town
Mathilda
Keep Movin'
Road Hog
Harbor Lights
Free Wheeling
Detour
Truck Stop

Cover photo by OVERDRIVE MAGAZINE Hollywood

Can you believe they thought this photo would sell more records than my picture?

I did manage to make the back cover of my own album

ABOUT THE ARTIST

When I was asked to write the liner notes for this fine album, I was deeply honored but a little apprehensive. I kept asking myself, what could I possibly say good about Jimmy Capps that hasn't already been said, but after some deliberation and serious thinking, I have come to the conclusion that anything I have heard good is worth repeating.

Jimmy Capps is a stylist with the unusual ability to convey to you the full meaning and emotion that only the fingers of a master can do. From the beginning of *Overdrive* to the very last note in *Keep Movin'*, you will find yourself completely surrounded in the musical world of Jimmy Capps, and unlike most albums you will want to hear this one through more than just once or twice.

Jimmy hails from Benson, North Carolina, grew up pickin' country music wherever folks got together to give a listen. After playing his guitar on hundreds of hit songs over the past few years, Jimmy has justly earned the respect and admiration of his fellow musicians, and the right to be called one of the best guitar pickers of all times.

Jim Hurley
Jim Reeves Ent.

SIDE 1

1. **Overdrive**
   (Jerry Smith) Papa Joe's Music House
   —ASCAP—1:52

2. **What Am I Living For**
   (Jay-Harris) Tideland-Progressive—BMI—2:16

3. **One Mile North of Town**
   (Jerry Smith) Papa Joe's Music House
   —ASCAP—2:04

4. **Mathilda   (I Cry and Cry for You)**
   (G. Khoury, H. Thierry) Combine—BMI—2:07

5. **Keep Movin'**
   (J. Smith) Papa Joe's Music House—ASCAP—2:35

SIDE 2

1. **Road Hog**
   (Jerry Smith) Papa Joe's Music House
   —ASCAP—2:00

2. **Harbor Lights**
   (Kennedy, Williams) Chappel—ASCAP—2:35

3. **Free Wheelin'**
   (J. Capps, S. Chapman) Papa Joe's Music House
   —ASCAP—2:05

4. **Detour**
   (B. Westmorland) Hill & Range—BMI—2:10

5. **Truck Stop**
   (Jerry Smith) Papa Joe's Music House
   —ASCAP—2:22

ABOUT THE COVER

Carole Black, the beautiful girl on the beautiful Brockway, is as warm and friendly as the hot Florida sun that lights the cover picture. Glamorous as she may appear, Carole is much more than a glamour girl. Rather, she's a sincere, real person who has devoted herself to helping people who need help.

It was as a service writer for TRUX, INCORPORATED that Carole became known throughout the trucking world as "Jeannie"—the girl who really cared about truckers' problems and did something about them. Now, she works as Midwest Public Relations Representative for OVERDRIVE Magazine, writing that publication's "Dear Carole" column. Naturally, what she and her column do is help others.

Produced by Jerry and Walter Smith
Recorded at Papa Joe Studio, Box 206, Nashville, Tennessee 37202

ABOUT THE TRUCK

The cover photo shows the new Brockway Model 761 exactly as it was introduced to the trucking world at Miami in November of 1973. Representing the all-new Brockway 700 Series, this gleaming conventional model caught the fancy of truckers and truck editors alike. The superb four-color photograph was taken by Mike Parkhurst, editor and publisher of OVERDRIVE Magazine, and appeared on the December 1973 cover of that publication.

"700" denotes a carefully-planned step forward in truck engineering, incorporating all of the technical advancements found in the widely-acclaimed Brockway 300 Series that made trucking history in the mid-1960's.

As modern as an Indy race car, the 761 provides truck perfection inside and out. For example, cockpit-style wraparound instrument panels provide for quick and easy reading of the dials. The entire cab is designed for driver safety, comfort and complete control of any highway situation.

A 700 Series chassis will accept any one of three great diesel engine makes, many, many engine models as well as a range of horsepowers up to 500. A true pioneer in the manufacture of heavy-duty motor trucks, Brockway has long prided itself on custom-building trucks with all components—all elements—matched to the load and road. The company calls it Uni-Matched Construction. And the colorful chromed beauty shown here is no exception to the rule. Over 1,518 inches of radiator frontal area provides cooling for its diesel power plant. Its chassis can accommodate all truck transmissions, including automatics, and it features a fully protected air brake system. Many lightweight options are available in the 700 Series.

It's a "truck driver's truck" in an age when the nation is depending more and more on trucks to keep its economy moving. Now that energy-saving has become critical, purchasers are demanding perfectly-engineered, precisely-built trucks.

That's the only way Brockway has ever built them.

THE GRAND OLE OPRY
STAFF BAND AND CAROL LEE SINGERS

WSM GRAND OLE OPRY 650

HERMAN CAROL NORAH LEE DENNIS
GLEN HAROLD
WELDON SONNY
JERRY BILLY
SPIDER LEON JOE

WOODSMOKE RECORDS/1980
BA001
7927 Hooten Hows Road
Nashville, Tennessee 37221

Side One

1. "TURNER SPECIAL"
   Joe Edwards — Staff Band Music — BMI
   Featuring — Joe Edwards
2. "IT'S EASIER TO SAY THAN DO"
   John Patrick — Champion Music — BMI
   Featuring — Carol Lee Singers
3. "ROSE COLORED GLASSES"
   John Conlee & George Baber — Pommard Pub. Co. & House of Gold — BMI
   Featuring — Weldon Myrick
4. "A SONG HOLY ANGELS CANNOT SING"
   Gordon Jensen — Jensen Music — ASCAP
   Featuring — Carol Lee Singers
5. "SNEAKIN' TO TOOTSIES"
   Jimmy Capps & Spider Wilson — Staff Band Pub. — BMI
   Featuring — Jimmy Capps & Spider Wilson
6. "LOUISIANA MAN"
   Doug Kershaw — Acuff Rose Pub. — BMI
   Featuring — Glen Davis

Side Two

1. "GHOST RIDERS IN THE SKY"
   Stan Jones — Edwin H. Morris — ASCAP
   Featuring — Jerry Whitehurst
2. "YOU'RE A REAL GOOD FRIEND"
   Cy Coben & Charles Green — Alamo Music — ASCAP
   Featuring — Jimmy Capps & Spider Wilson
3. "LEON'S TUNE"
   Leon Rhodes — Staff Band Music — BMI
   Featuring — Leon Rhodes
4. "WILL THE CIRCLE BE UNBROKEN"
   A.P. Carter — APRS — BMI
   Featuring — Leon Rhodes
5. "IF I SAID YOU HAD A BEAUTIFUL BODY"
   David Bellamy — Bellamy Bros. Music & Famous Music — ASCAP
   Featuring — Ralph Davis, Harold Weakley, Weldon Myrick
6. "SONNY'S MEDLEY (Softly & Tenderly — What A Friend)
   Will L. Thompson — Joe Scriven — C.C. Converse — ARR — Staff Band Music — BMI
   Featuring — Sonny Burnette

The Grand Ole Opry® Staff Band Consist Of:

Jerry Whitehurst — PIANO
All songs except "Sonny's Medley"
Billy Linneman — BASS
All songs

Harold Weakley — DRUMS
Side one — cuts 4, 5, 6
Side two — cuts 2, 6, vocal on 5
Glen Davis — DRUMS
Side one — cuts 1, 2, 3, vocal on 6
Side two — cuts 1, 3, 4, 5
Sonny Burnette — STEEL
Side one — cuts 2, 6
Side two — cuts 1, 5, 6
Weldon Myrick — STEEL
Side one — cuts 1, 3, 4, 5
Side two — cuts 2, 4, vocal on 5
Jimmy Capps — LEAD
Side one — cuts 1, 2, 3(rhythm), 5(rhythm also), 6(bass guitar)
Side two — cuts 1(rhythm), 2(vocal also), 4(acoustic lead), 5 & 6(rhythm)
Spider Wilson — LEAD
Side one — cuts 1, 2, 3, 4(bass guitar),
Side two — cuts 1(bass guitar), 2 (vocal also), 4(bass guitar), 5
Joe Edwards — FIDDLE & LEAD
Side one — cuts 1, 2(rhythm), 3, 4(lead), 5, 6
Side two — cuts 2, 4, 5
Leon Rhodes — BASS GUITAR & LEAD
Side one — cuts 1, 2, 3, 5, 6(lead)
Side two — cuts 1(rhythm), 2, 3(lead, 4(vocal), 5

Ralph Davis — RHYTHM
Side one — cuts 1, 2, 3, 4, 5, 6
Side two — cuts 2, 4, 5

The Carol Lee Singers Consist Of:

Carol Lee Davis
Noral Lee Allen
Herman Harper
Dennis McCall
Featured on "It's Easier To Say Than Do" and "A Song Holy Angels Cannot Sing"
Background on: "Sonny's Medley", "Will The Circle Be Unbroken", "Louisiana Man"

Les Leverett — Cover Photograph

RECORDED: HILLTOP STUDIOS, NASHVILLE TENN.

Hard to find album recorded by the Opry staff band and Carol Lee Singers

Backcover of Opry album

The Waking Crew doing a show from atop a billboard. I'm third from the left.

WAKING CREW BILLBOARD BROADCAST, June 16, 1983

The Waking Crew

The WSM Radio Waking Crew

You can see this guitar today at the North Carolina Music Hall of Fame

ing the
, May

o
tesy,
Leverett

(L-R) Harold Weakley, Glenn Davis, Weldon Myrick, Leon Rhodes, Jim
Sonny Burnette, Joe Edwards, Spider Wilson, Jerry Whitehurst, Ralph D:
Billy Linneman. *Courtesy Libby Leberett* Crew

Opry Staff Band. (L-R) Jimmy, Joe Edwards, Weldon Myrick, Glenn Da\
Spider Wilson, Sonny Burnette, Billy Linneman, Jerry Whitehurst, Ralp
Davis, Leon Rhodes

A full page ad for Alvarez guitars

An ad for Alvarez and Crate

Having a ball with Spider Wilson on Ralph Emery's TV show.

Jimmy, Spider Wilson and Leon Rhodes on the Opry, 1996

Playing with the Boston Pops. (L-R) Hal Rugg, John Williams, Jimmy, Bruce Watkins. My tux is now in the North Carolina Music Hall of Fame.

With Charlie Louvin

Hilltop Studios. (L-R) Glen Duncan, Jimmy, Gene Chrisman, Reggie Young, Bobby Woods, Mike Leach, John Hughey

Helping Glen Campbell tune my guitar that he borrowed to play on the Opry

they would drive all the way back on Thursday so that they could be back in time to play the Opry on Friday and Saturday night. After the Saturday night Opry, he'd work the Midnite Jamboree, which aired live on WSM 650. And after that show, he'd sign autographs for every single person until two or three in the morning. Then he would get back on the bus, and head out to start the new week with another show somewhere Sunday night!

Today, many stars will say they're too tired, or need a day off, if they're home in Nashville, and they don't play the Opry. But even when Ernest Tubb was an older man, he always took time to play the Opry, even if he had just gotten back from two weeks on the road. If he was in town, he was on the Opry. He didn't miss.

Porter Wagoner - I said "no" to being a Texas Troubadour, and I also turned down Porter Wagoner. Porter called me in 1962, and he said, "Jim, our guitar player is quitting and I'd like you to go to work for us."

At that time, his band was probably the highest-paid band in country music. And Porter treated them so well. He took all of the expenses off the top, and then split the rest of the money 50/50 with his band. Nobody else ever did that. In 1962, Porter's band members were making great money. It was unheard-of for a picker.

I had never made that kind of money. But I told him, "Porter, you don't know how much I'd love to go to work for you. But I just got my draft notice. I've taken my physical, and I'm going into the Army."

Porter understood, and as we talked, I offered a suggestion that would change a number of lives: I said, "There's a guy who lives across Dickerson Road. Boy, he would sure be good for you, and he needs the money. His name is Buck Trent."

Buck and I were good friends, and as soon as I'd given Porter his number, he gave him a call. As they say, the rest is history. Buck became Porter's sound, with his electric banjo. Buck was also Norma Jean's sound. Buck was better for the job than I ever would have been. Buck was amazing back then, and he still is. He is an exciting entertainer.

They say we all touch people's lives in many ways that we don't realize at the time. But I know that Buck's life might have taken a very different turn if I hadn't suggested to Porter that he hire him. He would probably never have ended up on Porter's TV show. He might not have gotten to work with Dolly, and his very successful life in Branson, Missouri might not have happened the way it did. If I would have said yes to Porter myself, who knows the direction all our lives would have taken.

But I was just trying to help a friend. I knew that Buck could do the job, and I knew he needed the money. I'm sure there have been many, many times that a friend has put in a word for me that led to me getting hired for a job I might not have gotten otherwise.

Porter Wagoner and I never had one cross word. He was always good to me. He was a good man, and up until he died, he always paid his band members half of everything he made on the road. There were even times when he'd give them all of the money. He was getting about ten grand a show, and sometimes his band guys would get two thousand apiece.

Porter was the "ambassador" of Opryland. The theme park hired him to meet the people as they came in, and he loved walking around, talking to people and meeting with his fans.

When Michele and I got married eleven years ago, we had our reception at the Grand Ole Opry Museum. We were married in July, and it was super hot that day. We had invited all of our friends from the Opry. We knew that Porter was very sick, though, and we didn't expect him to be there.

When we went out to take photos, however, there I saw Porter, walking toward us. He was wearing a western cut, dress Nudie suit. He had been so sick, and it was so hot... but he got dressed to the hilt, just for us.

A few months later, when Porter knew he was near death, he asked for Michele and I to come and see him in the hospital. Just before we got there, the Reverend Billy Graham had prayed with Porter over the phone.

Porter was known for his perfect hair, and when we walked into his hospital room, he was sitting up in the bed, with his hair absolutely perfect. He had had Gwen, his hairstylist from the Opry, do his hair. There he was, dying, but he had his hair all fluffed up.

As we visited, I said, "Porter, we really miss you at the Opry."

And he said, "I'll be back, Jim." He died a few days later.

We were attending the Country Music Hall of Fame medallion ceremony when I found out that Porter had passed away. I was sitting next to Keith Bilbrey, and his wife, Emy Joe. Keith got a text that said that Porter had died. He showed it to me. But he said, "I don't want to ruin the ceremony. Let's keep it to ourselves." I thought that was a very noble thing for him to do.

Porter Wagoner was a very simple man. The only thing flashy about him was his Nudie suits. Every time you saw Porter though, he always looked like a star. Even if he was in hunting clothes, they were always starched and pressed. He knew how to dress. He always dressed the part of a star, and he acted the part. He was meant to be in this business.

Dottie West - The first time I ever saw Dottie West was at a show in Ohio. I was with Charlie Louvin, and Dottie was the featured female singer. I thought she was such a great singer. I was also impressed with her steel guitar player. He was such a good player, who turned out to be Dottie's husband, Bill West.

Many years later, I got to play on all the Dottie West and Kenny Rogers hit songs. I also played on Dottie's solo stuff that

Jimmy Capps

Larry Butler produced, and some of her RCA Victor records. Those were big hits, including "Lesson in Leavin'" and "You Pick Me Up and Put Me Down". Ray Edenton and I played acoustic guitars. Larry Butler always used two acoustic players, capo-ed in different positions. Ray and I played the heavy acoustic intro on "All I Ever Need is You".

Larry Butler liked to have a wall of guitars on his records, and thanks to him featuring our guitars, he made us part of the Kenny and Dottie sound.

Dottie West was amazing, and she became a superstar. She had already been a big country music star, but when she teamed up with Kenny Rogers, they crossed over, and both of them became huge stars in the Pop field.

But my friendship with Dottie ran into a little trouble, thanks to a not-so-nice comment I made on the Opry.

After Dottie's divorce from her first husband Bill, the men she had relationships with seemed to get younger and younger. The fact that I noticed that got me into trouble with Dottie.

I did a show each morning from 7 to 8 on WSM radio called The Waking Crew. We had a live band at the Opryland Hotel, and we did the show from 1983 to 1987. We had a real good band. Charlie Chase hosted the show, and he always liked to visit with the band on the air.

I had just gotten back from vacation. I had taken my kids to Disney World, and Charlie asked me, "Jim, how was your trip to Disney?"

And I said, "It was great. I ran into one of our Opry friends. As soon as we walked in, the first person we saw was Dottie West."

This was when Dottie was becoming known for her younger guys. And then, for some reason, when Charlie Chase asked me what Dottie was doing at Disney World, I said, right on the air, "She was pushing her husband around in a stroller!"

Roy Acuff happened to be listening to the radio that morning. Later that day, we had a matinee Opry show, and in the middle of Roy's portion, he called me up to the mic and then asked me to repeat my Dottie West story... right on the Opry stage! I didn't want to tell it, but I wasn't going to tell the King no... so I told it.

The next night, Dottie was at the Opry, and as soon as she saw me backstage, she jumped me about it. She chewed me out royally! She said, "Those younger men are great." We ended up laughing about it.

But there was no laughing on the night Dottie never made it to the Opry. She had been headed there, when her car started having trouble. So an elderly neighbor offered her a ride. The Opry had already gotten underway when we heard Dottie had been involved in a car accident. They had lost control on the Opryland exit ramp. The car went airborne and rolled. Dottie was critically injured, and she died five days later.

Del Reeves - Del Reeves needed a bass player. The prospective bass player came to the Opry house to meet him, and Del told him, "I need someone who can open my show for ten minutes. Can you sing?"

The guy said, "Yes, I can. I've worked lots of clubs."

"Can you play bass?"

"Yes. I play electric bass," the man said.

"Can you drive a bus?"

The guy answered, "I've got my bus license."

And then Del finally said, "Well son, all of that really doesn't matter. What I'm lookin' for is a size 40 Regular. You've got to fit into the old player's outfits!"

Bill Carlisle - Jumpin' Bill Carlisle was a character. We don't have many characters anymore in our business. Everybody's too serious. I don't know when that happened. But it seemed like we were more like a family when people weren't so serious. We really had fun with our music.

We once had a little fun at the expense of Bill Carlisle's bass player. His name was Marshall Barnes, and he tried to sing like George Jones. One day on the Opry, we had an engineer hook Marshall up with a harmonizer, a piece of equipment you can use to tune someone up and move the sound of their voice up or down. With a harmonizer, singers can hit octaves that they wouldn't be able to sing otherwise.

But as a joke, the engineers once had Marshall's mic input going through that harmonizer. He was singing the George Jones song "Tender Years", and as he heard his voice getting higher in the speakers, he started trying to follow it, and he kept singing higher and higher! It was so bad that it was just hilarious. I'm sure the people listening to the Opry on WSM wondered, what the heck is going on with this guy? And the crowd of 4,000 people in the Opry House couldn't figure it out, either.

Jean Shepard - Jean Shepard lived a very full life. She probably lived three or four lives, compared to most people. She came up in the business at a time when they didn't have female artists host segments of the Opry. When they finally changed that rule, they found out that Jean was one of the best hosts they could have ever had.

Jean Shepard was a stylist, who influenced many other female singers. Whenever she sang or said something, you always paid attention. Jean called a spade a spade. She reminded me of Charlie Louvin. If you didn't want to hear their answer, you didn't ask a question of Jean or Charlie, because they would tell you the truth. She spoke her mind.

I didn't work Jean's spots on the Opry. Her husband Benny played acoustic guitar on her spots. I did play a little for her in later years, though, because she wanted two acoustic guitars. And I also did a lot of sessions with Jean when she was recording for Larry Butler. She used me on a lot of songs.

And Jean Shepard was also involved in the most embarrassing moment of my career, which I will cover in great detail during the Country's Family Reunion chapter, later on in this book.

Jim Ed Brown - Jim Ed Brown was so warm and friendly. He could touch an audience. He had a special gift that allowed him to really connect to people.

When the Country's Family Reunion would do live road shows, Jim Ed was on a bunch of them. He rode a bus with all of us. We had about 15 people onboard. I didn't sleep in a bunk; I always slept on the front couch, and every morning, Jim Ed would walk down the aisle of that bus and he'd be whistling. Jim Ed would sit in the passenger seat next to the bus driver. He liked to visit with the driver to keep him company.

I had been working Jim Ed's spot at the Opry for a long time, and my wife, Michele, subbed for Jim Ed's regular singing partner, Christy Russell, on the Opry and on a few road shows.

Jim Ed always arrived early at the Opry, and he liked to come to the band room to visit with all of the musicians. He respected all of us. Sometimes he'd spend an hour with us, just talking to us about our lives. I really respected him very much, for his talent and as a friend.

In 2015, Jim Ed was diagnosed with lung cancer, and a short time before his death, he learned that he was going to be inducted into the Country Music Hall of Fame. In June of 2015, his steel guitar player, Daryl Hornberger, called me and said, "If you want to see Jim Ed one last time, you'd better come to the hospital right now."

So Michele and I took off. When we got there, they had just presented him with his Hall of Fame medallion. They knew he wasn't going to live to make it to the official induction ceremony, so they did his induction in his hospital room. But even at the end, he was still as sharp as a tack. His last words to me were, "Capps, don't you ever quit playin'."

Keith Whitley - I played behind Keith Whitley when he came in to guest on the Waking Crew morning show. Billy Linneman had booked that show, and he'd booked Keith Whitley and Randy Travis long before they had ever gotten record deals. They would both come in and do the show.

I also played on Keith's RCA albums and worked his spots when he played the Opry. Keith was such a great singer. Keith and Ricky Skaggs grew up together, and they both were playing bluegrass music even back then. That bluegrass background puts a lot of soul into a singer or picker. Some of the bluegrass musicians now are absolutely amazing. They play and sing so great.

It was a huge loss to our business when Keith Whitley died. I think he would have been an enormous superstar if he had lived. But he died on May 9, 1989. He was just 33.

Stringbean - David Akeman made his Stringbean character a popular fixture on both the TV show Hee Haw and at the Grand Ole Opry. Stringbean was a great comedian, and he could also play a mean banjo.

Stringbean wanted to sell me his Cadillac. He traded cars every year, and he always bought a brand new Cadillac each year. But even though he loved nice, new cars, he never got a driver's license! His wife Estelle did all the driving.

One day, Stringbean came to me and said, "My boy, you need to buy my car. I'm fixin' to trade it, but I will sell it to you."

It was a beautiful Coupe de Ville. I said, "String, I'm a mere sideman. I couldn't afford something like that."

"You can afford this," he replied. "I will finance it for you and I'll not charge any interest." He wanted $5,000 for it. But I just couldn't do it.

On November 10, 1973, Stringbean played the Saturday night Opry, then Estelle drove them both home. When they pulled into their driveway, two men attacked them. They shot and killed Stringbean. Estelle tried to run away, but the men caught her, and as she begged for her life, they shot and killed her, too.

That week, all of the Opry stars attended the funeral of their family members, Stringbean and Estelle. Everyone was in shock. We couldn't believe how these two wonderful people were gunned down.

And then we went back to work. The next weekend, the show went on. And so did we... even though our hearts were broken. How were we able to come back after their deaths, and after the deaths of all our other Opry family members over the years? How do we get up on stage and act like nothing ever happened? This is how I explain it...

I think most of us have a funny way of handling the deaths of our friends. All of the artists who play the Opry, some weeks they're there and some weeks they aren't. They'll be out playing on the road. Billy Walker, his wife and his band members, were killed in a horrible accident while they were out touring. I think some of us have a coping mechanism, a way of kind of fooling ourselves in order to go out to do the next show. We just kind of pretend that our friends are out on the road touring somewhere.

But as time passes, we start to miss them. It takes a while to sink in, and when it finally does, there is a big hurt there. By having that coping method, pretending that they were just still out on tour somewhere, that helped us get through the hurt... even when we knew that it wasn't true. But eventually, you do realize that they are really gone, and they ain't comin' back. That's when the real hurt sets in.

I have one more story about the death of one of our Opry family members.

Hoot Hester joined the Opry Staff band in 2000. Hoot also helped start the Time Jumpers group, and he played fiddle on the Opry for 14 years. He passed away from cancer on August 30, 2016.

On the Saturday night after Hoot passed away, Vince Gill did a tribute to him on the Opry, where he sang "Go Rest High on That Mountain". He has sung that at many memorials for our friends who have died, but on this particular occasion, Vince gave every musician on the stage a solo during his song. He did that all on his own, with no warning to any of us. We each took a sixteen bar solo, one after another. There were a total of thirteen solos, and all of us were in tears as we played. Thanks to Vince, a very sweet and unique thing happened in honor of our dear friend, Hoot.

Chapter Nine

SESSIONS

I have no idea how many recording sessions I have been a part of. Many players keep detailed records of each session that they are on, and they can tell you the exact day and time that they played on someone's record twenty years ago. I sure wish I had done that. It would have helped me in writing this book. I have no clue of how many songs I've played on. But to be honest, I just didn't take the time to ever keep a log or journal.

While I can't give you the exact number of sessions I've been on, I can tell you that for many years I was averaging more than 500 a year.

People talk about all the classic hits I've played on, and I have been very blessed. But if you play on that many sessions, you should be able to record a hit every now and then!

I loved playing on the road, especially with my heroes the Louvin Brothers. And of course, being on the Grand Ole Opry was a true dream come true. But my main goal was always to be in the studio as a session player.

When I started playing sessions, if you worked the road with anyone, the people who made the records in Nashville would put you in a different category than studio players. In fact, many producers didn't think the musicians who played on the road were good enough to be session players, and I knew it was a real high honor to be accepted by your peers as a recording musician.

There was a small, very elite group of musicians who were considered the very best in Nashville, called "The A-Team." And the A-Team included legends Boots Randolph, Floyd Cramer, Pete Drake, Charlie McCoy, Pig Robbins, Tommy Jackson, Grady Martin, Buddy Harman, Harold Bradley, Ray Edenton, Hank Garland, and Bob Moore.

You can look on the internet and it says that I was a member of the A-Team, but that's not true. After Ray Edenton retired, any time the A-Team did anything, Harold Bradley would hire me. But I do not consider myself to be a real member of the A-Team. But those guys have been very good to me.

Charlie McCoy is a member of the A-Team. I asked Charlie if he'd say a few words for my book…

> "I played on so many sessions with Jimmy over the years. He also played on a number of my records, and I played on his "In Time for Dinner" CD. He was also on my new album that I recorded this past July. Jimmy is so consistent. You always know it's gonna be great.
>
> Jimmy is so versatile. He is one of the most underrated guitar players in town. He gets overlooked. I know he's in the Musician's Hall of Fame, but he is still underrated. People always talk about Jerry Reed, Grady Martin, Pete Wade, and Brent Mason, and those are all all-time greats. But Jimmy is right up there with all of them. He is one of the very best there is.
>
> When me and Jimmy came up in the old days, we knew we had to do it right and do it fast. We had to learn the song in just a couple minutes, and then we had to play it perfectly. We didn't get to redo, or fix, or overdub any mistakes.
>
> I think those records that we recorded back in the 60s and 70s, when we all played together at the same time and the singer sang live with us, they still hold up. They're still being played. Those records were so much better than the stuff they're putting out today. The records that are being made today, I don't know if

you'll hear them in three years, let alone thirty years from now, like the records we made.

Jimmy was always comfortable being in the background. He didn't aspire to be in the spotlight. He let the star be the star, and he wanted to make that star shine as bright as they could."

– Charlie McCoy

When the A-Team was cutting records, they invented stuff. They were pioneers. They created a completely new kind of music, and that's why everyone wanted to come here and record.

If it had not have been for men like Harold Bradley, Grady Martin, Pete Wade, Hank Garland and Lightnin' Chance, there would be no Jimmy Capps. They cut the trail for guys like me to come to town. They cut the brush down, and I came in on asphalt. They made it easier for guys like me, and they deserve all the credit they can get.

Those guys are a big reason that I'm here. I owe them a debt of gratitude. Thanks to them, I have been able to live in Nashville all these years and make a great living.

Harold Bradley was a member of the A-Team, and is a true country music legend. Without him, Nashville would not be known as Music City. It's as simple as that. When he first started out in 1946, there were no recording studios in Nashville.

Harold and his brother Owen built the first recording studio on what would become known as Music Row. They built four studios in Nashville, and he used those studios to make the most important records that have ever been made.

Harold Bradley played guitar on every hit Patsy Cline had. He was on every hit the Everly Brothers had, and he played on almost every Roy Orbison classic. From Roy's "Only the Lonely" to Patsy's "Crazy", to Don and Phil's "Wake up Little Susie", Harold was on them all.

95

He played on country standards, including Jimmy Dean's "Big Bad John", Johnny Horton's "Battle of New Orleans", Loretta Lynn's "Coal Miner's Daughter", Conway's "Hello Darlin'", Faron young's "Hello Walls", Tammy Wynette's "Stand By Your Man", and Roger Miller's "King of the Road". And those only scratch the surface! Name a country classic, and Harold Bradley played on it.

Harold has been such a friend to me over the years. I knew I wanted to include him in my book. This year he turned 92 years old, and I was totally humbled as he spent more than an hour sharing his memories of our time together. Here are a few of those.

"Jimmy was a very good guitar player, even when he was just starting out. He has always been an exceptionally good player. No matter what you hand him to play, if it has strings on it, he can play it. He is blessed with a God-given talent.

I want to clear up something about the A-Team. There was an original list of twelve musicians that made up the A-Team. Jimmy was not one of the original twelve, but neither was Chet Atkins!

Some people thought I was the person who came up with the A-Team, but it wasn't me.

It came from two reporters from the Nashville Tennessean. They came up with the term. And if I was able, I would go to them and tell them that the A-Team should have included quite a few other people. If Chet Atkins, Buddy Emmons, Pete Wade, Lloyd Green and Jimmy Capps aren't on the team, then it doesn't even make sense! Even my brother, Owen Bradley, was not on the original A-Team list. So the whole concept really bothers me.

When Jimmy started playing sessions, he just fit like a glove in the studio. He was a wonderful player. He is a great acoustic guitar player, but he's a wonderful electric guitar player. I really admire his playing.

I hired him to play many different instruments on the sessions that I produced. I knew he would always come up with something I would like, and I knew that he would always give me his heart when he played on anyone's sessions. He understood that each session was deadly serious for each artist he was playing behind. It was their career, and their career might begin or end because of that one session.

Back when we were doing most of those classic songs, we knew we couldn't make any mistakes. And that's why the musicians like Jimmy became so great. They could play the entire song from the top to the bottom, and they could play it absolutely perfect. They had to, or we'd never get the session done!

With Jimmy being such a great guitarist, I was very surprised when I found out that he and I had something in common... neither one of us ever had any real guitar lessons! My dad had bought me a six-dollar guitar at a junk store and I'd taught myself how to play it.

When you're a studio musician, you have to park your ego at the door. And Jimmy has no ego. He was willing to try anything that was asked of him. He was like me; he'd play a set of tire chains if they made the song sound good.

And another secret to his success as a studio musician is that he was able to evolve from the style he played with the Louvin Brothers to where he could play everything. To be a studio musician, you have to be capable of playing any style of music.

Guitar Player Magazine did some research on me, and said that I was the most recorded guitar player in history, in any form of music. But all of my time came during recording sessions in the studio. I think Jimmy might actually have more recorded time than I do, when you include his sessions, along with all of the TV shows and Opry performances he was on.

One of the big songs that both Jimmy and I played on together was Freddie Hart's "Easy Loving". I will never forget that session, because I was in total agony. I had just found out I had lost $100,000 in the Florida real estate market, and I could barely keep my mind on my playing, as I thought about how many sessions I would have to work to get all of that money back.

Jimmy always credits me and some others for cutting the trail for him, but it was Jimmy's talent that got him down that trail. Jimmy is a beautiful person. He has had a great career that continues today. And I hope that his book turns out to be a great one as well."

– Harold Bradley

The session players back in the 60s and 70s were so amazing. In the mornings, they might work a bluegrass session for Jimmy Martin, and in the afternoon those very same musicians might work for Brenda Lee. Those same players would make themselves sound different for each artist. They created styles for each singer, so that they would have a unique sound from every other artist. Back then, all of the guitar players brought eight or ten guitars each day, and we tried to be prepared for any situation.

When he found out that I was wanting to start doing studio work, Lightnin' Chance got people to hire me to play on demo sessions. That gave me a lot of experience at recording. I needed as much experience as I could get, when I walked into a master session with George Jones on April 21, 1960.

George was set to record a dozen songs for an album called "George Jones Salutes Hank Williams", It was George's tribute to his hero Hank, and he sang all of Hank's biggest hits.

Buddy Killen was the band leader, and he also played bass on the album. Buddy was the one who actually hired me for the session. Pappy Daily was producing George back then, and

Pappy liked to work fast. That day, we cut twelve songs in three hours! Twelve songs! That is almost impossible.

Tommy Jackson played fiddle on the record. Jimmy Day was on steel, Willie Ackerman was the drummer, Pig Robbins played piano, and I was on electric guitar. I can't remember who played acoustic guitar.

George did all of his singing live as we played. Even now, as I look back on it, I am amazed that we recorded twelve songs in just three hours! But those Hank Williams records were so popular that we all knew them by heart. We didn't use any musical charts at all. We didn't need any practice to do them, and once we'd recorded a song, we didn't even bother to listen to a playback! We just moved on to the next one. And that album that only took us three hours to record is still in print today!

That was an amazing session, and it led to more and more studio work for me.

As I look back on my career, I almost have to pinch myself. I can't believe I was a part of all this. When I think of these superstars like George Jones, Tammy Wynette, Barbara Mandrell and Ronnie Milsap, I was there when they were just new singers, trying to find their styles in the studio. And I was there as they became these household names. I was so blessed to be able to contribute just a little bit to their careers.

The first time I played on a number one record, I thought "This is as good as it gets. It can't get any better!"

One of the first huge hits I played on was "Easy Loving" by Freddie Hart. I was on that song because of Ray Edenton.

Ray was a member of the A-Team. He'd created the style of rhythm playing that became so popular in Nashville, and he'd get so many calls that he couldn't do it all... so he'd recommend me and another guy named Bobby Thompson to work the sessions.

Ray was very busy. But he also liked to fish. One day, he called me and asked if I could play a session in his place so that he could go fishing. He explained that Freddie Hart was recording what was probably going to be his last album with Capitol Records. Capitol was getting ready to cut him, but to fulfill his contract with them, he still had to do one more album.

George Richey, who later married Tammy Wynette, was the producer on that record. I played acoustic guitar along with Harold Bradley, and during that session, we recorded what would become Freddie Hart's signature song.

After "Easy Loving" became such a huge hit, they called me to do Freddie's next session. I said, "Guys, that is Ray Edenton's account. I can't take his spot."

But they said, "Freddie ain't changin' musicians. You are the one who played on 'Easy Loving', and he's superstitious and he ain't changin' pickers."

Freddie Hart is now in his 90s, but he still remembers that day like it was yesterday, and I was honored when he shared his memories for my book:

> "We recorded 'Easy Loving' in two takes. Just two takes! I wanted to do it again for a third time, but everyone in the studio said, 'Freddie, there is no reason to do it again.' Two takes. That is truth. Can you imagine that?
>
> Billy Sanford, on electric guitar, came up with the idea to open the song the way we did. I was going to take the line 'so sexy lookin'' out. I was scared of it. Ralph Emery told me that 'Easy Loving' was the first song that had the word 'sex' in it.
>
> Of course, Jimmy played on the song, and he played on almost all of my hits from then on. We also had Harold Bradley, Pig Robbins and Charlie McCoy on the song. I am so proud of all of those people. They all worked together and came up with original ideas. They tried different things, and they weren't afraid to try something new and unique. I can't say enough good things about

them. They weren't just great musicians. You can buy great musicians.

But they were all so creative. They were the best in the world. And they helped make all of my dreams come true.

We knew that we had something magical as soon as we had recorded 'Easy Loving'. What a blessing and what a treasure that song has been to my career and to my life.

There are many great musicians, but it takes a true artist to have that creative ability to turn your talent into true magic. And Jimmy has that. Not only is he a great musician, but he is such a wonderful person. He is very down to earth. He's real. That's the kind of people I love. You can see through phony people, but Jimmy is as real as water."

– Freddie Hart

I still have to shake my head when I think that I got to be a part of that monster hit song, all because Ray Edenton wanted to go fishin'! The lesson I learned, was to never go fishing! I always stayed available to play on any session that might need me.

Ray Edenton has been a dear friend to me. He gave me a lot of work over the years. He always said that there was enough work for all of us. As I write this, Ray is now in his early 90s, and he is still sharp as a tack. He is a great friend, and I thank Ray for all of his support for me over the years.

Here are some of my memories about a few of the classic country songs I was blessed to have been a small part of:

He Stopped Loving Her Today / George Jones - I was at Pete Drakes' studio, doing a session, when George Jones came by. He had been drinking a little. He loudly announced to everyone in the studio, "I want to sing you folks a hit song!" And he started singing "He Stopped Loving Her Today."

Only a short time later, I was in the studio recording that very song with George. But by that time, George wasn't so sure that it was a hit. As a matter of fact, he made a bet with his producer Billy Sherrill that it would not be a hit. George thought it was too sad and that no one would buy it.

While we were recording the song, Billy Sherrill had to get on George, because George kept falling into the melody of "Help Me Make it Through the Night" as he sang.

Many people have said that "He Stopped Loving Her Today" is the greatest song in the history of country music. So what was our feeling in the studio after we recorded it?

Our feeling was… OK, let's move on to the next one on the list.

You've got to understand that all of us session musicians were just trying to make a living. We were going as fast and as hard as we could, as we recorded almost around the clock. We would be at a studio downtown at 9:00am, and then we'd be out at Bradley's Barn in Mt. Juliet at 2:00, and then some of us would be booked again back downtown for a 6:00pm session.

The artists and the producers got to live with the songs. They got to listen to them over and over, and tweak them and improve on them. They practiced them and maybe sang them at their concerts, to see what their crowd reactions were.

But all of us musicians would just play the song two or three times in the studio, then move on to the next song and on to the next session. We never had time to think about what songs might be a hit.

Billy Sherrill produced some of the best songs that George Jones ever did. He was also the producer for all of Tammy Wynette's classic songs. Billy was a great song man. He could find great songs. And if he couldn't find 'em, he would just write 'em.

Norro Wilson was the same way. Norro wrote "A Picture of Me Without You" for George. And Norro's co-writer on that song was George Richey, who ended up marrying Tammy Wynette six years later! I also played on that song for George. They called a special session so that he could record. And to me, that was one of the greatest songs ever.

The Gambler / Kenny Rogers - This is one of the songs I am most proud of. To know what that song has done, and then to know that I had a small role in how it sounded... "The Gambler" is one of the biggest songs in the history of country music! I was so blessed to be on it.

Larry Butler was the producer for the session, and he just knew a great song when he heard it. Don Schlitz wrote one of the all-time classics when he wrote "The Gambler".

The coolest thing about "The Gambler", at least for me, is that everyone got to hear me and Ray Edenton before you heard Kenny sing anything! We start off the song. The acoustic guitar is not like a lead instrument. When a song leans itself to acoustic, you've really got to come up with something unique that will fit the song. It's not as easy on acoustic as it is on electric instruments.

When he'd worked up the song, Larry Butler told us, "You guys play two bars up front." Then he'd say, "Make that four."

There we were, on Kenny's biggest record, and the acoustic guitars had four bars of just rhythm and finger pickin'. Ray and I were thrilled, but we were thinking, "Man, Butler is crazy to give us four bars before Kenny even opens his mouth." But it worked!

I also played on Kenny's big hit "Coward of the County". As we played that song in the studio, I said, "Them Gatlin Brothers ain't gonna like this!"

And sure enough, they didn't. Larry, Steve and Rudy were really popular, and all of a sudden one of Kenny Rogers' biggest songs has the line "The Gatlin boys came callin'" in it. And also in the song, it says they abused a woman!

I loved playing for Kenny. He was always there to work. He was a real hard worker, and we cut some very good records.

Amarillo By Morning / George Strait - I played on "Amarillo By Morning", "Let's Fall To Pieces Together", "Unwound", and a bunch of other George Strait hits. One of the first sessions I worked with George, we did at RCA studio A. And during the session I thought, "Man, this guy is gonna be a superstar. He sings great. He's got great songs, and he also looks great." I felt that he was going to be huge.

16th Avenue / Lacy J Dalton - "16th Avenue was a career record for Lacy J. It is such a great song, and I got to play the intro that kicked it off! What a blessing to be given that very recognizable lick!

"16th Avenue" describes anyone who ever came to Nashville to try to make it in country music. I'm amazed at the songwriters who are in Nashville. Without them, we wouldn't have a Music City. The songwriters, producers and engineers in Nashville do not get enough credit. People don't understand what their jobs are, and they don't realize how important they all are to the entire process. The singer and music get all the attention, that's understandable. But I wish the people who do so much work behind the scenes could get more recognition.

Somebody Should Leave / Reba McEntire - I only did one album with Reba. But it had some big hits on it. I played on "How Blue" and "Somebody Should Leave". I played harmony, and another guy was playing lead on "How Blue".

Harold Shedd produced the album, but halfway through it all, Jimmy Bowen, the head of MCA Records, took over the project. He took over everything after we had already recorded all the tracks, and Jimmy ended up taking off the lead guitar track and just left my harmony guitar part on!

Reba always sang great, and this was a great album, because it was country. But for some reason, she kinda changed her style and got away from her traditional country sound. It obviously didn't hurt her career, though. She got bigger and bigger. She has always been a sweet, nice lady. And, most importantly to me, she has always been very respectful to all of us pickers.

Somebody's Knockin' / Terri Gibbs - Terri was a great singer. She was blind and played the piano. Chet Atkins saw her playing in Georgia, and he told her she should move to Nashville.

I played electric guitar on Terri's debut single "Somebody's Knockin'". I had the intro lick on the song, and I had borrowed an amp from Paul Yandell to use on the session. "Somebody's Knockin'" was a huge hit for Terri, on both the Country and Pop charts. I also played electric guitar on a few more of Terri's sessions. But she only had two or three other hits, and then she went into gospel music.

Near You / George Jones and Tammy Wynette - As soon as I heard "Near You", I thought it was going to be a big hit record. George and Tammy were in the studio together and as usual, Billy Sherrill was the producer. "Near You" had been a big pop record. I don't know why Billy and George and Tammy picked the song to do, but it was a perfect match. The song was a perfect marriage for them, even if their real marriage was not perfect.

Stand By Your Man / Tammy Wynette - Yes, I played on Tammy Wynette's all-time classic song. Many people even say that "Stand By Your Man" is the greatest country song ever. So I know this will be hard for people to believe... but I do not actually remember a lot about that recording session!

"Stand By Your Man" was recorded on August 13, 1968, and at that time I had just started getting into doing record sessions full-time.

Pete Drake got me on that session. I probably shouldn't have been there. I didn't have the qualifications. I don't think I was worthy enough at the time. That's the truth.

Jerry Kennedy should get most of the credit for the session. He played most of the guitar on the song. He played all the licks that people remember from it. I played the Tremolo guitar on the song.

In the years to come, I would do a bunch of songs with Tammy Wynette... and THAT I do remember! I did a lot of her solo things, and I played on a bunch of her duets with George Jones, and I also did a lot of George's solo songs.

Tammy Wynette was a great songwriter, and she cut great records. Tammy was a sweet lady. She had to grow up tough, but she was so sweet. She was like quite a few of the artists back then. Many of them had been poor when they were growing up, and Tammy was one of those. They were all so thankful to be able to do what they love, and to be able to make money doing it.

Brown Eyed Handsome Man / Waylon Jennings - I played electric guitar on "Brown Eyed Handsome Man." Charlie McCoy was also on the song. He played harmonica; and my electric guitar and Charlie's harmonica played licks together. I thought it was a great record.

I did quite a bit with Waylon Jennings. He was easy to work for. He was a musician, he was a good guitar player, and he enjoyed being around other musicians.

Later on in Waylon's career, I played on one of his albums, and it had so many good songs on it. One of my favorites was called "Too Dumb for New York City and Too Ugly for L.A.". Another great one was called "Wrong".

Waylon was a sweet human being. I have found that most artists are that way. Every once in a while, you'll meet one who has a little bit of an ego, but not often. I loved Waylon. He was so different. He was the real thing.

Blanket on the Ground / Billie Jo Spears - "Blanket on the Ground" was a big hit and career song for Billie Jo Spears, and it's a good one for me, because we just vamped rhythm on the front of the song. Larry Butler produced it. When we left the studio that day, I felt like we had cut a really great record. I really believed in that song.

And I thought that Billie Jo was a great singer. She never got the credit that she should have gotten for being such a wonderful singer. Billie Jo was so easy to work with, but she was also similar to Jean Shepard in that she was very outspoken.

Billie died of cancer in 2011. She was 74 years old. She was a very sweet lady.

I Don't Know a Thing About Love / Conway Twitty - I was blessed to play on quite a few hit songs for Conway Twitty, including "The Rose", "Don't Call Him a Cowboy", and "I Don't Know a Thing About Love".

We did most of Conway's sessions at Mercury Studios, in the very small studio way in the back. They had me playing acoustic guitar, and the space we had was so tiny, they'd put me in-between two doors. One door came into the control room, and the other went into the studio, and I had to sit in a little hallway between those two doors.

"I Don't Know a Thing About Love" is one of the few songs that I just knew, as soon as we'd recorded it, was going to be a hit..

I had gotten into wanting to produce some records, and I was now listening closer to lyrics than I ever had before. I love lyrics. A lot of musicians focus on the music and instruments, but I focus a lot on song lyrics. The song is the very first ingredient in a hit.

Billy Sherrill once told me, "You can have a hit with a mediocre singer who has a great song. But you can never have a hit with a bad song sung by a great singer."

Conway Twitty was also a song man. He knew a great song when he heard it, and he always picked songs with women in mind. When he listened for songs to record, he always said that if a woman would not like a song, then he wouldn't do it. That's how he judged songs, and that sure worked for him. He had so many hits and very few misses.

I did a bunch of songs with Conway. Jimmy Bowen and Conway produced a lot of albums together, but Conway did most of the producing himself. He had a great ear for music, and he had a lot to do with the production.

My most memorable Conway Twitty session came when he was recording a Christmas album, and was going to sing "Rudolph the Red Nosed Reindeer". Gene Autry made the song famous, and sold more than 12 million copies.

We ran through it a couple times, and Conway was trying to get it all down. I was there listening with my headphones on, as Conway talked to his producer.

And on-mic, Conway said, "Would you play me that demo one more time so I can see if I've got it right?" Then he stopped, and he said, "Whoa, whoa! I'm calling Gene Autry's record a demo?! All you guys forget I ever said that!"

I said "No way!"

As a gift for us playing on his Christmas album, Conway gave us some drinking glasses from Twitty City. I've still got them.

Smokey Mountain Rain / Ronnie Milsap - Talk about a blessing. I was asked to play on every record that Ronnie Milsap recorded through 1988! And "Smokey Mountain Rain" was just one of FORTY Number 1 songs that Ronnie had during that time!

Tom Collins was producing Ronnie. Tom and I became friends, and he always had me on all of Ronnie's sessions. Tom was an excellent song man. He and Ronnie took Don Gibson's

"A Legend in My Time", and they turned it from a waltz into a 4/4 time. There ain't many songs that you can do like that. But what a great record it was.

Ronnie's records all hold up today, more than 30 years later. I listen to "Please Don't Tell Me How the Story Ends", and it is still such a super record. "The Girl Who Waits On Tables" was so cool. Back then, Ronnie would let us cut the tracks the way we wanted to. He just let us do our thing. He might have had a lot to say about the final sound after we'd left and he sat down at the board… but while we were there, he didn't say much.

When we were in the studio, I would watch as Ronnie would turn his head away from his microphone, and then bring it in as he sang different lines. He was controlling the volume just by turning his head. I was so honored when Ronnie told me that he wanted to say a few words for my book...

"I was raised in Raleigh, North Carolina, and Jimmy is from just up the road from there. Of course, I came along after him, but I loved his work with the Louvin Brothers. Charlie and Ira were incredible. They were two of my favorites.

Jimmy played on just about all of my records. Of all of those I did for RCA, probably my favorite one was a tribute album to Jim Reeves, called 'Out Where the Bright Lights are Glowing'. We did it in 1981.

One of the Jim Reeves songs I did on that was 'Am I Losing You'. It went to number one for me, and Jimmy Capps played on every song on that album.

In 1982, we were in the studio recording the song 'Any Day Now'. It turned out to be a big hit for me, but before we started laying it down, Jimmy went around the studio and wrote on the top of everybody's music sheet: 'Jimmy Day Now.'

Jimmy Day was a steel guitar legend who worked a lot with Ray Price. But I've still got one of those music sheets that Capps changed to 'Jimmy Day Now.'

They liked me to record in RCA Studio A. It's a huge studio. You could play basketball in there. After I'd had quite a few hits and made some money, I built my own studio. I bought the building from Roy Orbison, and I called it Ground Star Laboratory. And Jimmy knew that studio quite well. He was there with me for many recording sessions.

Jimmy just has perfect touch. Everything he plays is so nice and sweet. He doesn't play loud. But he sure plays good. He is a wonderful guitarist. His interpretation and style always suited me to a T.

I did a lot of my own producing. Tom Collins was the official producer, but he knew I knew a lot about studio work and what I wanted in the studio. I learned how to produce when I was in Memphis, and when I came to Nashville, I quickly learned that Jimmy Capps was truly the master guitar player.

Jimmy is one of my all-time favorite people. He is such a sweetheart. I love Jimmy Capps."

– Ronnie Milsap

Here in the Real World / Alan Jackson - I played on some of Alan Jackson's big hits, including "Wanted" and "Here in the Real World", but I only ever did one album with Alan. I don't know why they never called me to do another. I must have said the wrong thing or something! I enjoyed those sessions, because Alan was country. And in my heart, I am traditional country - and that's what he was singing.

Every Time You Touch Me, I Get High / Charlie Rich - I played on quite a few sessions with Charlie Rich. He used me a lot on acoustic guitar, and "Every Time You Touch Me, I Get High" was one of his big hits that I was on.

My Tennessee Mountain Home / Dolly Parton - I did a couple sessions with Dolly Parton when Porter was producing her. I played on her album "My Tennessee Mountain Home", released in 1973. Unfortunately, no big hits came from that album. And even more unfortunate… I don't remember anything from those sessions! Again, it was when I was so busy, running from one studio to another. I must have been mighty busy to not be able to remember being in a small room with Dolly!

Busted / John Conlee - I played on a lot of John Conlee's hit songs. I was on "Common Man" and on "Busted", on which I played the intro". And "Busted" was a big ol' record for John Conlee.

I think that John is one of the coolest singers. There is never any doubt of who is singing whenever you hear one of his songs. He has a style all of his own. His songs, and his style of singing, are so recognizable.

And once he does a song, he puts his brand on it. He's one of my favorite artists.

I love playing behind John when he is on the Opry. He ranks up there with the very best hosts that the Opry has ever had. He's got a warm appeal, and the sound of his voice is magical. And most of his band members have been with him for more than twenty years.

John still does a hundred or more shows a year. He is one of the few stars out there who drives their own bus! He has a driver, but John likes to drive too, especially right after a concert. He says it helps him wind down.

One time, as they were pulling out after a show, a fan actually waved the bus down. They had a CD with them and wanted John to sign it. John was behind the wheel, wearing a ball cap and t-shirt, when he opened the bus door and started to autograph the CD.

And the fan yelled, "I don't want the driver's autograph!" The guy couldn't believe the star was driving his own bus!

John is so laidback. If you see him off stage, he might be wearing an old t-shirt that's covered with grease or dirt. That's because he does all the maintenance on his bus, and back on his farm he's always working on his tractors.

John is happy in his own skin. He is a very religious person, and he doesn't mind sharing his faith with the public. Every time he works the Opry on a Saturday night, he always invites anyone in the audience to come to his church on Sunday morning. He is a great human being. I was so happy when John said he'd like to say a few words in my book...

"I have gotten to work with Jimmy in so many different ways over the years. He played on a lot of my early sessions. I've been able to watch him in the studio, and he is always part of our band when I play on the Opry. When I'm on the Family Reunions and Larry's Country Diner shows, Jimmy is always there. It is always a thrill to work with him in all of those different settings.

Playing on the Opry for sixty years, like Jimmy has, is such an amazing accomplishment. You won't see many people reach that milestone. And people don't know the challenge it is for someone in the staff band like Jimmy. We have so many new artists who guest on the Opry. They all have brand new songs, and Jimmy has to learn and master all of those in a very short time. He might have to learn twelve or fifteen new songs for just one Opry show, so that he can back those new artists up. There's not many people who can do that.

Jimmy is so versatile. No matter what the position is, whether he's playing lead or acoustic, he makes it work. And he does it all so quietly. He is one of the most gentle people I know. He's so humble. He calls himself 'The Man in Back', but when he comes up with those special guitar licks, he stands out. He doesn't have to be out front to outshine everyone.

I have met many, many great folks in Nashville and in the country music industry, but Jimmy is in my top five as a human being. His talent and accomplishments speak for themselves, but as a human being, he is one of those very special people. I love him and I hope he has another sixty years."

– John Conlee

Drifter / Sylvia - Sylvia is a beautiful lady. She started out as Tom Collins' secretary, and then he found out that she could sing. I played on Sylvia's hit songs, including "Drifter", "Tumbleweed", and "Like Nothing Ever Happened". Yes, I played on all of her hits... except her all-time biggest!

As she got ready to record the song "Nobody", her producer Tom Collins came to me and the other acoustic player and asked us both to lay out. And we both went to the lounge as they cut "Nobody" without any acoustic guitars.

And then, guess what... "Nobody" ended up becoming Sylvia's signature song, and it was the most played song on the radio for the entire year!

"Nobody" also sold over two million records. Since I was on the session, Tom gave me a gold record for it. But I didn't play on "Nobody".

Sylvia sings as good today as she did then, and she is still just as sweet. I'm sure she will have something nice to say in my book that will make me feel better about missing out on "Nobody".

"Jimmy was in taking a break while I was recording a million-seller... I guess we found out who the Nobody was!

I can't believe I said that! I'm just kiddin', Jimmy! I love Jimmy Capps. He is just the sweetest. He is so quiet. You would never dream that he has played on so many historic songs, and has been on the Opry for six decades. He would never brag about any of that. He is so creative. And for somebody to be that gifted and to still be so humble, that is an unusual combination.

We recorded my albums at Studio A. My producer Tom Collins chose all the musicians, and he used basically the same players and singers on all of his Barbara Mandrell, Ronnie Milsap, and Steve Wariner sessions.

Before I got my record deal, when I could, I would hang out in the studio when Barbara Mandrell recorded, and when Ronnie Milsap had a session. So when I saw all the same musicians in the studio for my recording session, I knew that I was getting the very best players.

And when we used the same players on my next three albums, that helped make me more comfortable when I went into the studio. In the 80s, I was always nervous when I recorded all my albums, but Jimmy had a way about him that made everything less stressful. And the players were all so great. They were very versatile. And as my songs progressed, and moved from very country into a more pop sound, they were all able to play any style.

Dennis Morgan played rhythm guitar along with Jimmy. Dennis was one of the writers on some of my biggest songs, including "Nobody", "Snapshot" and "Tumbleweed", but I think he left most of the guitar playing to Jimmy. And Jimmy was the anchor on those first few albums for me.

His playing was so solid, but he still had such feeling, and that is very rare.

When I did the Larry's Country Diner TV show, I was so happy to see Jimmy again. It had been a number of years since we had worked together. And he reminded me again that he did not get to play on the "Nobody" record. He's been on so many huge hit songs. But I guess that was the one that got away."

— Sylvia

Kansas City Lights / Steve Wariner - Steve Wariner is one of the most talented people I've ever met. He is also one of the nicest. I was honored to play on so many of his early hits such as "Kansas City Lights", "Your Memory", and "All Roads Lead to You". I was also honored when Steve said he'd like to be a part of my book...

"I met Jimmy for the first time when I was 18 years old. I was playing bass for Dottie West. But I knew of him long before I met him. I had watched him on TV, playing on different shows. I loved watching him and Hal Rugg and Buddy Spicher on the Wilburn Brothers show. As a young kid, I watched all those guys.

The Wilburn Brothers, and The Glen Campbell Goodtime Hour, really had an impact on me. And when other people would be watching the star sing, I was watching Jimmy and Hal in the back, where they'd be laughing and having so much fun.

Here I was, a young boy in Indiana, and that played a major role in me deciding that I wanted to get to Nashville as quickly as I could! I knew by watching them that this was what I wanted to do.

When I got to meet Jimmy in person, I was just in awe. I knew his history, and I knew he'd played on so many hit records. He was a monster studio guy and was an Opry icon. I met him and he was so nice to me. And I remember saying, "Man, this is a cool day."

A couple years later, Jimmy heard me singing with Dottie, and he called me up and asked me to sing a demo for him. I had just started playing bass for Bob Luman. This was long before I'd recorded any songs myself. And it was Jimmy who saw some of my talent for singing. I told him I would love to sing on his demo, so I went out to his house and recorded a couple songs. We've been best friends ever since those days.

Being a guitar player myself, I always looked forward to seeing him walk in the studio. I always wondered what kind of guitar he was gonna bring. And when he'd start playing, I would just try to soak it all up and try to learn everything I could from him.

I watched him all the time. A lot of his magic is just in his hands. He is so good. I like his electric guitar playing, too. He gets pigeonholed sometimes because his acoustic playing is so good, but he is also a great electric player. Today, I am still in awe of all the hit records that he played on. He would play with the artists on their records, and then he'd play with them again when they came to the Opry.

When the movie 'Nashville' came out in the 70s, you could see Jimmy throughout the entire film. They shot a lot of the movie at the Opry, which had just moved into the new Opry house. I sat in the theater and spent most of that movie looking for Jimmy Capps and the rest of the Opry band.

I played on an album he did a few years ago. It thrilled me that he'd asked me to be on it. I said, 'Are you serious?' I love Jimmy. He is one of the good ones. He is a dear, dear friend, and an unbelievable musician. I was so happy when he went into the Musicians Hall of Fame. He is one of my favorite guitarists ever. And he is one of my favorite people in the world."

– Steve Wariner

Mississippi Cotton Pickin' Delta Town / Charley Pride - I worked a lot with Charley Pride. I was on many of his hits, including "Mississippi Cotton Pickin' Delta Town" and "Honky Tonk Blue"s. I played on a bunch of Charley's RCA record sessions, and I got some awards for playing on his songs.

I played on Charley's Tribute to Hank Williams album. David Briggs told me they hired me because they thought I would play kind of simple, and he was surprised when I started playing "hot licks", as he called them. He said, "We didn't know you knew ''hot licks', but keep on playin' 'em!"

But Billy Grammer played guitar on most of Charley's early stuff, and Billy was the one who played on Charley's career song "Kiss An Angel Good Morning". Billy was a good session player, in addition to being a great artist on his own.

I play on all of Charley's Opry spots any time he's on. He loves that real traditional country music. He also likes to guess people's astrological sign. And he was right on, when he guessed mine and Michele's sign. We actually share the same birthday, May 25th, and Charley always asks, "How's Gem-in-I?!'"

Charley is a unique human being, and he's a superstar. When he hits the stage on the Opry, it's like Elvis has come back. He's a good guy, too. He's had some of the same band members for more than thirty years, and that says a lot about a performer. That doesn't happen very much. And it also doesn't happen too often that someone of Charley's stature offers to add something to your book!

> "One of the many reasons I love coming to the Grand Ole Opry is seeing Jimmy Capps' smiling face behind me on stage. I always know he's going to play exactly the right thing at exactly the right time.
>
> Jimmy is respected by his musical peers, as well as his friends and fans. He is known for the unselfish way he shares his musical knowledge, and he's been an inspiration to the many young musicians who have made their way onto the Opry stage.
>
> Jimmy has been an important part of many of my recordings, and he's also been a wonderful friend all these years."
>
> – Charley Pride

Elvira / The Oak Ridge Boys - Hit songs don't come any bigger than "Elvira". I was so blessed to play on that classic! I also played on many other huge songs for the Oak Ridge Boys, like "Bobbie Sue", "American Made", "Sail Away", "Fancy Free", and "One in a Million".

We cut "Elvira" at Woodland Street Studios. Ron Chancy produced it, and I thought it had a different, Rock-style flavor to it. The key to it was the difference between Richard Sterban singing the low part, and Joe Bonsall singing that high part. Of course, it was Richard's low part and the catchy "Giddy Up A Oom Popa Mow Mow" that got everybody all stirred up.

The Oak Ridge Boys have been really good to me over the years. I was blessed to play on a lot of the Oaks' gospel albums. And when they made their transition over to country, I was so thankful that they kept asking me to play on their sessions. While "Elvira" is always the song that people talk about, my favorite Oaks song is still "One in a Million". I had the intro on it, and it is a very recognizable lick. Vic Jordan and I both had the intro.

"Bobbie Sue" and "Elvira" both leaned more toward heavy electric instruments, so while my acoustic guitar was in there, it wasn't out front as much. But on songs like "Fancy Free" and "One in a Million", you can hear my acoustic more clearly.

All of the Oak Ridge Boys, William Lee, Duane, Richard and Joe, have been dear friends of mine for such a long time. I am honored, any time the Oaks ask me to be a part of anything that they are doing. And I was totally humbled when Duane Allen told me he would like to share some of his memories in my book...

"I met Jimmy Capps way back in 1965, when I was with the gospel group The Prophets. A year later, I joined the Oak Ridge Boys, and we had Jimmy Capps play on my first sessions with the group. He was already one of the top pickers in town, and we always tried to hire the best musicians for our albums.

Jimmy could play anything, but he was the best rhythm guitar player in the world. When Jimmy plays rhythm, the tones he gets out of that guitar is just perfection. He has such a feel.

Over the last 52 years, on every album the Oak Ridge Boys have done, if the producer asks me, 'Who do you want playing on your album?', the first guitarist I always mention is Jimmy Capps. If the producer wants someone else to play lead guitar, I say, "OK, put Capps on rhythm guitar."

'One in a Million' was our second hit record in country music, and Jimmy Capps was the one who was playing that hit lick, that intro that kicks off the song. That was a million dollar lick! And he came up with that lick himself.

When I go back and listen to any of the Oak Ridge Boys albums, I can hear Jimmy Capps all over our music. He was there during our Gospel days, he was playing on our songs when we moved over to Country, and he continued to play on all of our hits throughout our career. When he was inducted into the Musician's Hall of Fame, Jimmy asked for us to be there, and we wouldn't have missed it for anything. Jimmy is a part of the soundtrack of the Oak Ridge Boys music. He has been for over 50 years!

I recently visited the Musician's Hall of Fame in Nashville, and the first guitar that I saw there was Jimmy Capps'. I read the description, and it said, 'This is the guitar that I played when the Oak Ridge Boys recorded "Elvira".' I got chills up and down my body, just looking at that guitar that Jimmy had played on the biggest record we ever had. I was so thrilled to see it that I had my photo taken in front of the display.

Jimmy has played on as many or more gold albums and hit records than anybody else in Nashville. And every time the Oaks earned a gold record, we always made sure to present Jimmy and all the other musicians who had played on the record with their own gold album award.

Jimmy is such a positive force. When he is sitting in the studio, you know you are going to have an A-plus cut. He just records great tracks all the time. He never makes a mistake. He is always perfect. He is so gifted. He can play things that are beyond anything I can imagine.

In the studio, he doesn't say much. He just smiles and is always positive. And when you throw the ball to him, he always comes through for you. You tell him what you want and give him an idea of what you'd like to hear, and he will give you exactly what you ask for.

When we've done the 'Larry's Country Diner' TV show, I've called Jimmy our one-man orchestra. On the show, he is our entire band, just him playing the guitar, and he gives us all the rhythmic and chord support that we need. Plus he plays the licks on the intro and turnaround. He does it all at the same time! We are totally comfortable with Jimmy being our band. We've never taken anybody else on 'Larry's Country Diner'. We don't need anyone else, Jimmy Capps is there!

Very few people can do on the guitar what he can do. He's got so much feeling and soul. He doesn't have an outgoing personality. He doesn't seek attention. And he's the easiest guy to get along with in the whole world.

I love Jimmy Capps. Jimmy and his wife, Michele, are two of the best friends that I have. My wife, Norah Lee, is a backup singer on the Opry, and on most nights, Jimmy and Michele will come by our house and pick up Norah Lee, and she rides to the Opry with them. When I'm out on the road, and I know that my wife is carpooling with Jimmy and Michele, that always gives me a comforting feeling. I know that Norah is always safe on the road and doesn't have to come home by herself.

Jimmy Capps is one of the greatest guitar pickers in the whole world. And he is one of my dearest friends."

        – Duane Allen, The Oak Ridge Boys

Duane mentioned that The Oaks have always given me a gold record for each one that I played on for them. I've always been grateful to them for that. Not all the acts do that.

I got a gold record for Kenny Rogers' "The Gambler". Larry Butler was another producer who gave me gold records for every one I played on that went gold. And I'm thankful for each award I've received. But if you come over to my house, you probably won't see any. I've got them all in storage. I'm not one to hang much on the wall. I probably should display them. I'm very proud to have them, but I don't like to seem like I'm showing off, if people come over to visit.

"I Was Country When Country Wasn't Cool" / Barbara Mandrell - I played on almost all of Barbara Mandrell's hit songs, and she sure had a bunch of them! "I Was Country When Country Wasn't Cool" sounds like it was all recorded live in concert, but Barbara's producer, Tom Collins, had asked me to come in and overdub on it. I added an acoustic guitar to it, and you can't tell that I wasn't right there on stage next to Barbara.

I started working with Barbara when Billy Sherrill was producing her first sessions. He'd asked me to play on them, and I continued to play on most of her sessions throughout her entire career.

One of her hit songs where my acoustic really stands out is "Years". Pete Bordonali and I did the intro and solo on "Years", and she loved Mike Leech's bass playing. He was on all of her records. Barbara was like one of the boys. She admired all the musicians, because she was such a great musician herself.

She and I were inducted into the Musicians Hall of Fame together, and I was so honored to share that special day with her. She could play sax, steel guitar and a lot of other instruments.

Barbara Mandrell is such a sweet human being. I've been friends with she and her husband Ken for many years. Ken is a jewel. Barbara's parents were both wonderful people. And what I really loved about Barbara and her sisters was that they never dropped their dad. Their father was their manager, right up to the day he died. Barbara never left Irby behind to try and go on to bigger and better things. And I'm sure she got offers from many big names who wanted to manage her. But she always stayed with her dad. And that tells you what kind of people the Mandrells are. They let their dad direct them, and keep them on the right path. And it worked.

Barbara retired years ago, and when she did, she basically stopped giving any interviews. She is a very, very private person. That's why I actually cried when she agreed to be a part of my book.

"I came to Nashville in the summer of 1969. I was on some of the local television shows. They were always early in the morning. And Jimmy was always there. And from then on, Jimmy was always there, throughout my entire career.

Already right after we'd first met, I felt like I'd known Jimmy for a long time. He's not boisterous. He's not flamboyant and loud. He doesn't seek attention. Jimmy is genuine, and sincere, and kind.

I was so thrilled when I found out that I was going to be inducted into the Musician's Hall of Fame at the same time that Jimmy was. That made the day so much more special for me. Everyone knew that he was so deserving of that honor. He has truly earned the wonderful reputation that he has.

He is so versatile as a musician. He can play any form of music. He can do hard, classic country, or he can play the new country style. He can do pop music, or classic standards. He plays so beautifully.

I picked the musicians who played on my records. Tom Collins produced most of my sessions, and he also picked the players; but he always knew that I wanted Jimmy there, because Jimmy was always rock solid. He played right on the money. But, more importantly, he helped to create an atmosphere in the studio that made each session a true joy to be a part of.

When I was recording, I knew that I could turn around and see Jimmy playing, and I always felt very comfortable because of that. I was always comfortable, and I felt wonderful whenever I was around Jimmy. That is a major compliment to him that I can't say about very many other people.

Jimmy is a fascinating human being... as you are about to find out. He is so gifted and talented, but he is also such a kind and wonderful person. He is so deserving of this book.

Jimmy Capps is the real deal, and a real friend."

– Barbara Mandrell

I was so blessed to be allowed to make music with so many fabulous artists. There was one, however, I didn't get to record with... Elvis. I never met Elvis. But I came close.

I was 16 years old in 1955, playing in a group with Jim Thornton, and we were booked for a show at the Municipal Auditorium in Raleigh, North Carolina. We were the opening act for a big package show. Hank Snow was the headliner, but Ferlin Husky, Bill Carlisle and some others were also on the bill. Colonel Tom Parker had booked this big show. He was Hank Snow's manager, and the Colonel had just started booking a new guy named Elvis Presley.

After we'd done our part of the show, I took my girlfriend and we went and sat out in the audience to watch everyone else. After Hank Snow's portion of the show, the curtain came down and the crowd began to file out.

But the announcer got on the mic and said, "Folks, we have one more act if anyone would like to stick around and hear them." And then about 3/4s of the crowd sat back down.

The curtain came up, and it was Elvis. He just had Scotty Moore and Bill Black as his entire band. But that's all he needed. The next morning in the Raleigh newspaper, the headline read, "Elvis Presley Steals Show". And he did.

I never played for Elvis. But one of my dear friends did. Reggie Young was the lead guitarist for the American Sound Studios Band in Memphis, and he played on so many historic Elvis songs. He played guitar on "Suspicious Minds", "Kentucky

Rain", "In the Ghetto", "Don't Cry Daddy"… and those are just a few that he did!

Reggie then moved to Nashville, where he continued to play on some of the all-time greatest country songs. He played on Willie Nelson's "Always On My Mind", Billy Swan's "I Can Help", BJ Thomas' "Hooked On a Feeling", Billy Joe Royal's "Down in the Boondocks", and Neil Diamond's "Sweet Caroline".

Reggie Young's resume makes me look like a total slacker. That's why I was so shocked when he told me that I was his hero! He is definitely mine!

"I moved to Nashville in 1972. Buddy Killen called and asked me to play on a session he was producing at the Sound Shop. I honestly don't remember the artist. But I do remember the first person I saw when I walked into the studio. It was Jimmy Capps; and I got so scared! I knew he was so great. But when he saw that I was a little nervous, he went out of his way to make me feel comfortable.

I was from Memphis, and I was a big fan of Jimmy from the work he did with the Louvin Brothers. But we became good friends, and we did a lot of sessions together. And I got over any fear when I was around him. Instead of fear, every time I came to the studio and saw that Jimmy was there, I always knew that it was going to be a good day.

Jimmy is a really good player, one of the finest players I know. But he is also a good person. He is one of the few people I worked with whom I really felt comfortable with. He had a calming effect. I always enjoyed working with him. And when we weren't playing together, I just liked to hang out with him.

Jimmy is very inspiring to me. He is one of the few guys who've achieved this level of success and level of greatness, and never let it go to his head. I'm honored that he would even mention me in this book. God bless Jimmy Capps."

– Reggie Young

I have another friend whose musical accomplishments make mine look like nothing. His name is Eddie Bayers. He joined the Opry band as a drummer fifteen years ago. And when I look at his body of work, I have no idea how he even found the time to play for the Opry.

Eddie has played on 300 gold and platinum records! He was named Drummer of the Year by the Academy of Country Music fourteen times. He is still one of the most in-demand drummers in any form of music. And he somehow had time to say a few words about his pal Jimmy Capps...

"I met Jimmy in the late 1970s. I had started playing sessions, and I worked on several sessions with him. We helped make some really great records. We played on hits for artists ranging from John Conlee to John Denver, and I always felt comfortable with Jimmy in the studio. As the drummer, I know that the acoustic guitar player and I have to be connected. His playing is always in the center of the beat, and he always gives an incredible performance.

As the style of music changes over the years, if you are a session player, you can only survive if you are able to adapt to these changes. And Jimmy has. He can play with the legends, but he can also play with any new performer who might want to do country hip hop stuff.

I loved being in the studio with Jimmy. But I got to know him much better when I joined the Opry in 2003. It's been a real blessing to have been with him on the Opry for the past 15 years. He's our musical patriarch.

Jimmy's longevity is so amazing. And what is even more amazing is the fact that even though he's been on the Opry for six decades, his performance has not deteriorated. He's as great now as he ever was. He is an incredible talent and a true gentleman."

– Eddie Bayers

Eddie mentioned that session players have to be willing and able to change with the times. I guess that is what has helped me have a long career. At my age, it's hard to imagine that anyone would call me to work for them. But, thank God, they do.

I think one reason they keep calling is, I didn't get stuck back in the era that I started in. I kept playing for different artists, through the current music of today. I never stopped in one era or in one decade. I kept growing. And I always kept my interest in the latest new guitars or gear or products. I still like to go to the music store to see the newest stuff.

Not only has the music changed over the years, but as we've gotten older, the musicians themselves have changed, too. Quite a few years back, I was playing on a week-long session. All of the regular musicians were a part of it. Ray Edenton was playing rhythm guitar. Pig Robbins was on piano.

Ray said, "No one bring anything to eat tomorrow night. My wife Polly and I will fix some Firehouse cabbage."

Someone asked, "What's Firehouse cabbage?" and Ray said "Oh it's great! It's a soup with lots of ingredients. I got the recipe from a friend who's a fireman."

And then Pig Robbins remarked, "Ya know, I can remember the time when we'd spend our session breaks talking about women. And now it's come to this... now we're exchanging recipes!"

In the 1970s, I was very busy doing sessions. I was playing on two or three sessions every day, and then even sometimes four. I didn't have much free time, so many people were quite surprised when I decided to go to college! Of course, I hadn't even finished high school.

And people were really surprised when I told them the reason I wanted to go... so I could learn to read music better.

I was playing a lot with the Bill Walker Orchestra, doing all the big network TV shows, where all of the orchestra's music was written out like it should be. But I could never read music very well, so Bill always gave me cassette tapes, and I'd take them home and memorize the songs. I could read just enough music so that I could barely keep up with everyone. So I went to Belmont University, to learn musical time evaluation.

My teacher was John Pell. He was a great guitarist, and a good teacher. He taught me and one-on-one, and he did the best he could to teach me. But I was a challenge, because I would always be worn out by the time I got to his class. I was still working sessions around the clock. But John taught me for about six months.

One of the biggest changes in country music recording sessions came from something called The Nashville Number System. Neil Matthews invented it, but the Jordanaires and Charlie McCoy are really the ones who showed everyone how great and how helpful it could be.

Back when I started, we weren't using the number system. To learn a song, we had to have the artist play and sing it for us, and all the musicians would then try to put that in our memory banks. Sometimes the artists had to play it three or four times for us to remember it.

Songs were more simple back then. Today's music is much more complicated. I don't know if that's a good thing or not. And I don't know that the more complicated music of today is better than the songs that were being done back in the 50s and 60s. The songs you remember from Nashville, whether they were traditional country or bluegrass… the most memorable songs are the ones that were simple. And it was the lyrics that got you.

The Nashville Number System is kind of hard to explain, but it is essentially a system that lets us transcribe any song based on the musical scale. We can lower a key from D to C or B without us having to change anything on our charts. It's much more versatile than sheet music. Our charts don't have every note like sheet music does, but the number system lets us improvise.

If an artist comes into the recording studio and brings a musical arrangement that an arranger from L.A. or New York has written everything out, then we have to play it precisely like it is written, or it doesn't work. If they change the keys, since they are written in letters, then you have to rewrite it all, or try to transpose it all in your mind. You have to change all the chords and put them into the correct key. We can do that, but it really makes it hard, and is very time-consuming. But the number system makes it so easy.

The number system began in the recording studio, but we also use it for live performances. Kerry Marx, who plays guitar in the Opry staff band, and Larry Paxton, who plays bass, write most of our charts. But everyone in the staff band writes charts as needed. All the main information that we need, all the "ID" licks, the licks that the public remembers from the record, those are all on our charts too. But if a song just has a fill for a guitar player or steel guitar player, not an "ID" fill, then we don't write it out. The musician is allowed to play whatever they feel.

Chapter Ten

SOME DAYS ARE DIAMONDS

While I'm known for the country music I've made, I am also proud of the success I've had in playing other styles of music. I've been blessed to work with many huge stars who were not necessarily country music singers. Those have ranged from Ray Charles to Andy Williams. Here are a few memories of some of my more unique recording sessions.

Dean Martin - Dean Martin came to record in Nashville in 1983. I was so excited to play on his album "The Nashville Sessions", and Dean was just a joy to work with. Dean Martin was such a legend. But when you met him in person, he was just a regular guy. I was really impressed with the way he treated us, and how kind he was to everyone he met.

We recorded for about a week, doing three sessions a day, and we even worked through the weekend. Dean was very laidback, but he came here to work and get the job done.

They brought in Merle Haggard to do a duet with Dean. During their session, Dean went into the control room and Merle stayed in the studio in front of the mic. And Merle said, "Guys, we need to find out where Dean gets all those pretty shirts he wears. I love those shirts that have the high collars."

Dean heard him in the booth and just smiled.

Dean recorded the song "Hangin' Around" that The Whites had had a big hit with in 1982... but Dean didn't know it had been a hit until he got back home to California. When he heard The Whites singing "Hangin' Around" on the radio, he called up Jim Bowen, his producer in Nashville and said, "Hey Jim! Some kids have cut our song!"

Jim said, "Dean, it's not OUR song. It's their song. The Whites had a big hit with that song."

Dean also did a duet with Conway Twitty, called "My First Country Song". It was a fun little tune. Ironically, that album turned out to be the very last one that Dean Martin ever did.

Julie Andrews - In 1982, Julie Andrews recorded a beautiful album in Nashville. We did it over at Sound Emporium B. Of course we all knew Julie Andrews from "The Sound of Music". She was an international star. But she was a real lady in the studio. She was a class act.

Julie's album included favorites like "Love Me Tender", "Crazy", and "When I Dream". During our sessions, Julie hardly spoke at all. She let Larry Butler do all the producing. She didn't want very much input. She let all of us play what we wanted, and how we thought was best. And it turned out to be a great album.

She was married to Blake Edwards, who was the director for all of the Peter Sellers "Pink Panther" movies. Julie asked all of us musicians for our coat sizes, and then, a short time later, she gave us all "Pink Panther" jackets. I've still got mine. It's a special jacket from a very special person.

Tom Jones - Tom Jones recorded a great country album in Nashville in 1981. The title cut, "Darlin'", turned out to be a pretty big hit for Tom. Of course, Tom was very comfortable singing country music. One of his early big hits was "Green Green Grass of Home".

Tom Jones was a superstar when I recorded with him in 1981. That's why what I'm about to say is so embarrassing. And you might find it hard to believe, but I cannot remember anything about the session! Not one thing. I know that sounds awful. But I was so busy during that time. We were all running from studio to studio, all day and all night. We were constantly loading and unloading all of our gear and instruments, and then heading to the next session. I'm sorry Tom! (He probably doesn't remember me either.)

John Denver - "Some Days Are Diamonds". That was a big record. And I do remember playing on it! It was a great song. Larry Butler produced a great record on John.

When he walked into the studio, John was taller than I thought he was going to be. John Denver was very unique, and so was his voice. John was a very gracious man, and he was very appreciative of all of the musicians. Every time we'd get done with one of the tracks, he'd go around the room to each one of us and he'd shake our hands and tell each one, "Thank you so much."

The people loved John. And I loved being a part of one of his greatest records.

Ray Charles - Steel guitar legend Buddy Emmons booked me to play acoustic guitar on quite a few sessions with Ray Charles. Ray had a lot of input on his work. In fact, on most of the sessions I did with him, Ray was his own producer, and Buddy Emmons was leader. One time, Ray asked me to play two acoustic guitars. He knew the sound he was wanting. And while I did my thing, Ray played rhythm on piano as he sang.

Ray Charles always sang great, and he always played great. But on one of our sessions, Ray's vocals were real loud in our headphones. This was before they had invented "More of Me" boxes. We use those today so we can hear more of ourselves in our headphones. You can turn yourself up and turn the singer down.

But we didn't have those back then. So I finally just went to Ray and said, "Ray, I have one question to ask."

Ray said, "You can ask two questions!"

"No sir," I said, "I've just got one, and I hate to even ask it. But can we turn your vocals down? I'm having trouble hearing the drums in my headphones."

Ray smiled his big smile and said, "Well sure you can! We'll turn it down." He was very nice about it. I'm sure I was one of the few who ever told Ray Charles that I wanted to hear less of his singing!

Andy Williams - Once again, Larry Butler was the producer on this session. Larry's the one responsible for getting me on so many amazing sessions. We did Andy Williams' album over at Sound Emporium B.

Talk about a real legit singer. Andy was it. And he was just the nicest guy. During our session, Andy was very quiet. He had very little to say. He just worked hard.

Whenever these huge stars like Andy Williams, Julie Andrews and Dean Martin would come to Nashville, it always seemed like they were a little in awe of the town. They knew that Nashville was the place to record. They knew we had the very best musicians and studio people, and they were as thrilled to be working with us as we were to be working with them.

Wayne Newton - We recorded an album with Wayne Newton at 1111 Studio, next door to Waylon Jennings' office. Wayne is such a big, stout guy. He's tall; he's 6'2". And when he walked into the studio, every head turned to him. He looked like a superstar, which he was.

During our session, Wayne told Larry Butler, "I'm looking to hire a guitar player to go on the road with me. I need them to work Vegas and Branson with me."

And Larry immediately said, "Dale Sellers is your man! You will love his playing."

Dale wasn't playing on our session that day, so someone called him in, and Wayne hired him on the spot. He ended up traveling with Wayne for more than ten years.

Wayne had flown into Nashville on his private plane, and while we were in the studio, he asked his pilot to fly back to Branson so that he could get Wayne Newton jackets for all of us musicians. His pilot flew to Branson, got the jackets and flew right back, and we got those jackets before we ever left the studio! They were very nice.

The Chipmunks - Yes, I can honestly say that I played with The Chipmunks! I played on the album "Urban Chipmunk". It was The Chipmunks' version of "Urban Cowboy". The movie was so huge that someone had decided to try to cash in by having The Chipmunks sing the popular country songs of the day.

The album included The Chipmunks versions of songs like "On the Road Again", "I Love a Rainy Night", "The Gambler", and "Mamas Don't Let Your Babies Grow Up To Be Cowboy Chipmunks"!

I don't remember a lot about that session. I just know we played the songs as we normally would. The music tracks were recorded like always, and then The Chipmunks overdubbed their voices. They were not live in the studio.

Pat Boone - I played on a number of sessions in Nashville for Pat Boone, and I also helped produce three albums for him at Hilltop Studios. Johnny Gimble played on most of those. Pat was always an absolute jewel to work with.

We had a budget of $5,500 for each album, and after the record label was able to make some money on each of those albums, they asked if we could do an instrumental album of gospel standards. We used all the same musicians, but we added David Reece on piano, calling ourselves the First Nashville Jesus Band.

The Hinsons - I played on the original recording of "The Lighthouse". The song went on to become a gospel standard, but the original version was done by The Hinsons.

We cut the song in Madisonville, Kentucky. Rusty Goodman of the Happy Goodman Family produced "The Lighthouse". He could recognize a hit gospel song when he heard one. And here's a little trivia for you: it was Rusty Goodman who sang on Johnny Horton's "North to Alaska"! He sang the deep bass part of "Way Up North…"

I loved playing with The Hinsons. They were kind of a country, gospel act. Kenny Henson sang like Merle Haggard. Ronnie Hinson wrote the song.

Later on, I produced an album for the Wilburn Brothers called "Gaither and Hinson", on which they sang half Bill Gaither songs and half Hinson songs. They did a record on "The Lighthouse", and it was great. It was a real, real country version.

I played on quite a few gospel and southern gospel songs, and my work with the southern gospel group The McKameys helped get me a very special fan. His name is Chris Janson, and he's one of the newest members of the Grand Ole Opry. Chris' career is very hot right now, but he says that I was one of his inspirations. At first I thought he was joking. But then I realized that he was being serious.

I knew Chris was being honest about his admiration for me when he said that his favorite thing I had ever done was a show I'd done with The McKameys. We filmed that show at TBN in Hendersonville, and he even remembered what color shirt I was wearing and what color my guitar was.

Chris Janson is quite a showman. I know he tries to copy me, because when I watch him jumping up and down on stage as he plays harmonica, I can see a lot of me in him! Ha! Ha! He's quite an entertainer. But seriously, I know he loves me. And I love him. He's a great guy.

"Yes, Jimmy taught me all of my moves! I studied Jimmy Capps long before he had ever heard of me. I grew up a big southern gospel fan. I was raised on that kind of music. I was a huge fan of the McKameys. I followed them around. And when I saw Jimmy playing behind the McKameys, I started following him.

Jimmy is a living piece of history. He's played for generation after generation of great records and great stars. When I got to meet Jimmy when I played the Opry, he was very nice and accommodating. First impressions are everything, and during that first meeting, he treated me with great respect, and he instantly started becoming an awesome mentor.

When I started playing the Opry as a guest, before I'd become a member, it was a really big deal for me to get to play with him. And now, even when I get to bring my own band, I still invite all of the Opry band to play as well. They are all world-class musicians.

When Jimmy plays behind me, it is such a huge deal for me. But a bigger deal is the fact that we have become really good friends. I am proud to know him. I love you Jimmy Capps."

– Chris Janson

Chapter Eleven

THE OPRY

I was so busy playing sessions through the 1960s and 70s, my schedule was packed. I was making a very good living, and at that point, I really didn't need to keep playing on the Grand Ole Opry. But I did. Most of the other session players were always surprised when I kept the Opry as my main priority.

If we had a Friday afternoon recording session, I'd tell everyone that I had to be finished by no later than 5:30, because I had to get to the Opry. The other guys would ask, "Man, why do you keep doing that?"

And I'd always respond, "Well that's where a lot of my friends are. It's really like a family. It's like being a member of a country club, where we get together to tell stories and laugh and play good music every weekend. Why wouldn't I want to go there? As long as they'll let me, I'll be there."

I was saying that in 1970… and 1980… and 1990… and 2000. And I still say the same thing today, as we get ready to move into the 2020s!

A lot of the session players couldn't understand it. They kept telling me, "You need some time off." But now, maybe some of them wish they had listened to me, as sessions can be few and far between. And today, I am truly busier than I have ever been in my life. The Opry has always been so good to me.

In 1966, Ray Pillow was invited to become a member of the Grand Ole Opry. He was one of the few who were offered membership even before he had even had a hit song! But only a few months after he joined the Opry, he had a top ten song, with a duet with Jean Shepard, called "I'll Take the Dog".

When Ray joined the Opry, he also joined Jimmy Capps in a friendship that lasts to this day. Ray is one of my dearest friends. I sure hope he can say something nice about me!

"I met Jimmy at the Old Dominion Barn Dance in Richmond, Virginia, when he was working with Charlie Louvin. I had a guitar player who asked me to go with him to the Barn Dance. My friend was just in awe of Jimmy's playing, and when we got to meet Jimmy after the show, he was so nice to both of us.

A few years later, I played the Opry in 1966, and Jimmy had already been there for quite a few years. When I became an official member of the Opry, I always used the Opry staff band, and Jimmy always played for me. After we got to know each other, I never wanted to go into the recording studio unless I had Jimmy playing on my session. He played on everything I ever recorded.

The Opry staff band was so awesome, and for some reason, it always seemed to me that the band really gave everything they had for me, and we always had so much fun. We gave each other nicknames. I always called Jimmy, 'Jimmy James'. And my nickname was 'The French Cowboy'! Harold Weakley is the one who started calling me that, and I said, 'Why in the hell did you start calling me the French Cowboy?'

Harold laughed and said, 'You just look like a French cowboy to me.'

Jimmy was always honest with me. One time, I asked him, 'Jimmy, do you think I should go ahead and really learn to play the guitar, ya know, try to get where I'm pretty good at it?'

He looked at me and said, 'No. I think it's too late,' and laughed!

Back in the early 70s, I was booked on a show in Amsterdam, Holland. It was just one date. Can you imagine going all that way for a one night stand? But we did it. And I asked Jimmy to go with me. At the time, Jimmy was on a diet, trying to lose some weight. He stuck to his diet all the time we were gone, but on the night we came back, we stopped for dinner at a big buffet.

And Jimmy had his tray completely full. It was heaped up, just about overflowing! And when he went to pay for the meal, the cashier asked, 'What kind of drink?', and Jimmy said, 'I'll have a Tab.'

He thought that diet Tab would balance out the huge tray of food he was eating!

When they inducted Jimmy into the North Carolina Music Hall of Fame, I drove over from Nashville and surprised him. He was so shocked that I had made the effort to be there for him. I was also there when they made a joint resolution for him at the Tennessee State Capitol. Moe Bandy and Jan Howard also came along.

We didn't do what we did for the money. We did it for the music. And we did it for all the fun we had making music and traveling everywhere with our friends. We have had a true friendship over the years. Jimmy is a true friend. He has been there for me through good times and through bad times. I treasure my friendship with Jimmy James."

— Ray Pillow

Ray Pillow is just one of so many Opry artists who became like family to me over the years. Ricky Skaggs is another. Ricky is one talented guy. There are not a lot of people who are in Ricky Skaggs' league. He can play country, and he can play bluegrass.

He'd made a promise to Bill Monroe that, after Bill was gone, he would carry on the bluegrass music… and Ricky has kept that promise. He can jump right from bluegrass to playing the fire out of an electric guitar.

Ricky Skaggs, Vince Gill and Marty Stuart… all of those guys are so talented. The good Lord gave them a triple-helping when he was handing out talent. I think Ricky really changed country music. He is amazing as a country singer, and as a musician, he can play any style that he wants to.

A few years ago, I was producing an album for Moe Bandy. There was a real pretty song on it, and I thought it would be so great if Ricky Skaggs would sing harmony on that song.

I called and asked him, and he said, "I can't sing as high as I used to, but I'll do my best."

And he sang it so beautiful. It's a straight-ahead country song. And he also played mandolin on it.

For a couple of years, Ricky Skaggs and his wife, Sharon, hosted Bible studies, and we'd go over to their house for them. I was very impressed with their lifestyle, and the way they lived what they believed. They welcomed absolutely everybody, and would have thirty or more people in their den. Ricky and Sharon would lead the service. It was so nice. It was real. I went especially for the fellowship and the food!

Another Opry member who is real is Larry Gatlin. I played on his first demo when he was just starting out, at Bradley's Barn. While I remember that session, I was surprised that Larry did too…

> "Jimmy played on my very first demo. It was called 'You're the Other Half of Me'. We recorded it at Bradley's Barn. He had played on a lot of Dottie West's records, and since she was the one who helped me get my start in Nashville, she knew he would be great on my demo.

140

Jimmy recorded a song on his CD called 'Smoky Mountain Time'. It is such a beautiful melody, and when I heard it, I told him, 'If you will allow me, I'd like to write some words, something to go with that.' But I misplaced his CD, and kind of forgot about it. But I hope to finish that song sometime in the next year.

Jimmy is a great player, he's a great human being and a great friend. He's solid. You can depend on him. He's pretty quiet, but when he straps that guitar on, he lets it do the talkin'. I love the Sheriff."

– Larry Gatlin

Larry Gatlin is a good M.C. when he hosts the Opry Country Classics show at the Ryman, and it is the best Opry we do. The songs are all great. Even if the show has a brand new artist on, the Opry asks them to sing traditional country music. And those songs are special. And when Larry Gatlin hosts, the show is absolutely great.

The Gatlin boys, Larry, Steve and Rudy, have always been nice to me. They're good guys. They were all raised right. I work all their spots at the Opry, and I know that if I called any of them in the middle of the night and told them that I needed help, I guarantee you that they would be right there. I'd bet money on that.

The Opry has gone through so many changes over the years. When Ernest Tubb came into the Opry with an electric guitar, playing his honky-tonk music, I'm sure that there were those who thought he was going to kill the Opry. And we have had those same conversations with many new artists who've had new styles of country music ever since then. But the Opry still survives.

Ernest Tubb and Hank Williams were a couple of the very first artists to use electric instruments at the Ryman. Before that, I don't think the Opry managers allowed them.

When I started at the Opry, they didn't allow a full drum set. Lightnin' Chance had had a drum head built onto the side of his bass, and he'd played a brush on it. I think Buddy Harman, Willie Ackerman, Don Light and Harold Weakley were the first real drummers at the Opry, but they were only allowed to have a snare drum and a stick and brush.

It took a long time for them to have an entire drum set on the Opry stage. I think it was Bob Wills who finally ended that rule.

Bob was such a huge star that they had to go along with him when he brought in a full drum set. But even then, they still made him set the drums up behind the backdrop. So the audience couldn't see the drums… but they could hear them!

When we were in the original Ryman, we had no room to rehearse, practice or run over any songs. We just talked things over behind the curtain.

And even today, we only do very minimal rehearsal for the Opry. If there's a new artist coming on, and they want to use the staff band, then we'll rehearse with them. We do most of that in the band room. But there's no rehearsal for the entire Opry show. There is no other live show that goes on the air with no rehearsal like the Opry does.

Back in the 40s and 50s, there were a number of live radio shows that were similar to the Opry. Chicago had one. Cincinnati had one. The Louisiana Hay Ride was a similar show. Wheeling, West Virginia also had a radio show. But those are all long gone. The Grand Ole Opry has been running continuously since 1925.

One of the few people who's been on the Opry for more than 50 years is Jeannie Seely. Jeannie was great when she first joined the Opry in 1967, and she is even better today. I was so happy when Jeannie said she wanted to share a few of her memories of our friendship over the years.

"Jimmy is one of the very few who was there when I got to the Opry, and he's still there. What a rock he is for everyone at the

Opry. He always puts everybody at ease. He works with each artist. Whatever they need to make them feel more comfortable, Jimmy will find a way to do it.

We have worked together so much over the years. Of course, he plays on the Opry for me, but we also work together on the Country's Family Reunion shows, when I'm on Larry's Country Diner, and then we take that show on the road to Branson too. We also spend a lot of time together even when we're not working.

Before Jimmy and Michele got married, Michele was my neighbor. She lived just down the street, and we spent a lot of time together, even back then. We have a lot of mutual friends, and we all just like to be together. We truly enjoy each other's friendship.

I've been with the Opry more than 51 years. Jimmy's been there more than 60 years. We love the Opry, and we both love the history of the Opry. I know he's the same way I am: both of us can't wait to get to the Opry to see our other family members. I always say our Opry family is there to support us in the bad times, and they are also there to celebrate the good times of our lives.

Jimmy is a mainstay of Music City. He has played on so many hit records. He is so creative, and when I go into the studio to record, I want Jimmy Capps in there with me.

If you don't have a friend like Jimmy Capps, I hope you can find one. On stage and off stage, he's always got your back. He is always there."

– Jeannie Seely

When the Opry moved from the Ryman Auditorium to the new Opry house, I had a conversation with Justin Tubb. Justin was Ernest Tubb's son, and he and I were real good friends; I worked all his spots on the Opry. When we were getting ready to move to Opryland, Justin told me, "The new place is going to be great! We've got big dressing rooms. It's air conditioned and heated. I can't wait to move." He was so excited. But I was much more leery. I didn't know what to expect.

It was like we were leaving home. It was bittersweet. We were headed to a strange building. The new house had lots better parking for us. It had so many dressing rooms, and easy access to restrooms. I knew all of that was true. But I had serious doubts that the new place could ever match the feel of the Ryman. I knew things would never be the same again... I just hoped the show would be as successful at the new location as it had been back at the Ryman.

While the Ryman Auditorium was located in downtown Nashville, the new Opry House was located nine miles out of town, at the then-Opryland USA. The first Grand Ole Opry performance in the new 4,000+ seat Opry House was held on March 16, 1974. I thought the new place was great. But I also have to admit that when we started playing there, it felt more like we were doing a concert instead of the Opry.

The debut Opry in our new building may have been the most exciting one in the history of the Grand Ole Opry. To make things even more special, we were joined by the President of the United States, Richard Nixon!

When we drove up, there was so much security. As we stopped at the canopy backstage, the Secret Service took our car and went through it. President Nixon helping open the new building is one of my favorite memories of the Opry. We played "Hail to the Chief" like a hoedown. Vic Jordan played five-string banjo, and Joe Edwards played fiddle. And we made "Hail to the Chief" sound like a square dance number.

Me and Spider Wilson were standing off to the left of the upright piano when President Nixon walked over and started playing it. I couldn't believe it as the President played "Happy Birthday" and "My Wild Irish Rose".

Then we watched as Roy Acuff gave the President tips on doing the yoyo. And just when it couldn't have gotten any greater… it did. President Nixon went back to the piano and played "God Bless America", as everyone sang. It was pretty awesome to be so close to the President of the United States. It was a night I will never forget.

A few months after the Opry move, my career was also moving, as an all-Jimmy Capps guitar instrumental album was released. The album was called "Truck Drivers Instrumental", and there are some pretty interesting stories about that album.

The idea for the album came from Jerry Smith and his brother Walter. They had a publishing company and record label called Papa Joe Records. Jerry Smith was a popular session piano player, who had gotten very hot and did tons of sessions. He played on a bunch of Bill Anderson and Mel Tillis songs. His brother, Walter, ran their publishing company.

Jerry did some albums for the Lawrence Welk company. He recorded an instrumental album called "The Magic Organ", wherein he did all the keyboard on it. He told me that his entire budget for the album was $40! He recorded everything in his home for free, but it had cost him forty dollars for one hour at Hilltop Studios so they could transfer the tracks for him.

He turned in the album to the Welk company, and they sold it. Jerry's first residual check from the Welk company was for $90,000! He called them and asked if there had been a mistake, and the person who answered said, "Jerry, we are sorry, but it will be more next time."

He said, "Are you kidding me? I was afraid to cash this check because I thought you'd made a mistake."

And they said, "Your albums are selling as fast as we can print them!"

Jerry and Walter thought that we could have similar success with a guitar instrumental album, so he told me he would produce

145

the album, but that he wanted to gear it toward truck drivers. Truckers were buying a lot of Red Sovine and Del Reeves trucker records at the time. So I played every song, and each instrumental was given a truck-driving-themed name, like "Truck Stop", "Detour", and "Overdrive".

They released a couple 45 singles from the album, and one of those got to be number one on a radio station in Louisiana. The song was called "Road Hog", an original piece that Jerry Smith had written. And it sold a lot of records! I have no idea why or how it got so popular in that part of the country.

That album contained some nice music. But probably the most interesting thing about the entire record was the cover. They put my name on the front of the album, and my picture is on the back... but they chose to use somebody else's photo for the front cover! They used a photo of a girl in a bikini standing on a big truck! I'm pretty sure they thought she would sell more albums to truckers than I would!

I had no idea who the girl in the bikini was. I had never met her, and I still have never met her. It wasn't until I started writing this book that we decided to look her up. I guess I should have tried to get to know her back then, because that girl in the bikini grew up to be one of the most powerful women in television!

Her name is Carole Black. At the time of the album cover, she was writing articles for the trucker's magazine "Overdrive". But just a short time later, she got into TV news. She started working her way up in TV, and she never stopped! Carole ended up being the President and CEO of the Lifetime Television Networks. "Ladies Home Journal" magazine named her one of America's 100 Most Important Women of 1999.

Two years later, Fortune Magazine said she was one of the Most Powerful Women in Business. And she owes it all to me! Ha! Little did Carole know what her future held, as she stood on top of that big rig wearing that little bikini for my album cover.

Opry Staff Band, 2002. (L-R) Tim Atwood, Tommy White, Billy Linneman, Hoot Hester, Spider Wilson, Kerry Marx, Jimmy, John Gardner

Michele and I the day before our wedding. Our Opry Dog joined us for the photo.

Going' to the chapel...

My bride and I, cheek to cheek

Mr. and Mrs. Jimmy Capps

In our limo, headed to our wedding reception

*Arriving
for our
reception*

*We were
so touched when
Porter Wagoner
came to our
reception*

A signed photo from my friend Jimmy Fortune

T. Graham Brown joins the Diner cast

The Sheriff

The Diner crew, 2011

My Long Leaf Pine Award

State of North Carolina

James B. Hunt, Jr.
Governor

Reposing special confidence in the integrity, learning and zeal of

Jimmy Capps

I do by these presents confer

The Order of the Long Leaf Pine

With the rank of Ambassador Extraordinary privileged
to enjoy fully all rights granted to members of this exalted order, among which
is the special privilege to propose the following North Carolina
Toast in select company anywhere in the free world:

Here's to the land
of the long leaf pine,
The summer land
where the sun doth shine,
Where the weak grow strong
and the strong grow great,
Here's to "down home,"
the Old North State!

By the Governor

Date: August 10, 1996

Michele and I visit with Connie Smith and Marty Stuart

The Sheriff gets casual as Michele and I perform on the CFR, Diner Cruise

Oh yeah! Thumbs up with Michele and Buck Trent

A special moment with my long time friend George Hamilton IV

Anita Stapleton, Michele, Jimmy, Steve Wariner, Jan Howard.
Courtesy Ron Harman

The Malpass Brothers join us on the Diner

Visiting backstage with the Malpass Brothers

My son Mark's wedding day.
(L-R) Jimmy, Michele, Tara, Mark, Summer, Jeff

My sons Mark and Jeff

Playing with Vince Gill and Paul Franklin

Michele and I with Vince Gill and Paul Franklin

Michele and I become honorary Riders in the Sky

My Grammy certificate from my work with Riders in the Sky

presents this certificate to

Jimmy Capps

in recognition of your participation as a

Musician

on the GRAMMY®Award-winning album

"Monsters, Inc. – Scream Factory Favorites"
(Riders In The Sky)

in the category

Best Musical Album For Children

45th GRAMMY® Awards Year 2002

I will never be able to thank Phil Johnson enough for capturing this moment with Jean Shepard.

Sharing another big laugh with Jean Shepard and Larry Black

With Joey and
Rory

A moment with Dailey
and Vincent

With my pal Charlie Daniels

Playing with Mandy Barnett for Jack Greene's memorial service.
Courtesy Jerry Overcast

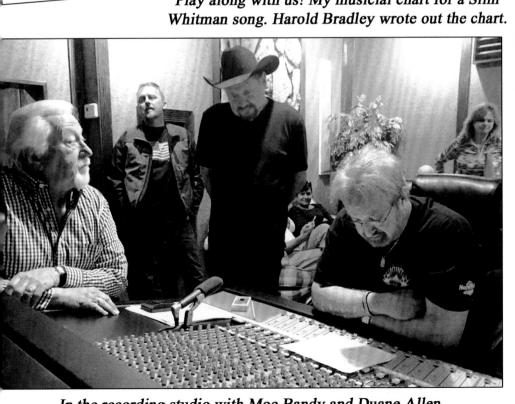

Play along with us! My musicial chart for a Slim Whitman song. Harold Bradley wrote out the chart.

In the recording studio with Moe Bandy and Duane Allen

*Gene Watson sings
on the Diner*

*Gus Arrendale's
boots match the
dress of Michele's
mom Jean.*

John Conlee visits the Diner

Michele and I visit with Harold Bradley

Tuning Little Jimmy Dickens' guitar before he goes on the Opry

Playing the Opry behind the great Little Jimmy Dickens

Senator Jack Johnson
and John Greenwood
announce that I will be
honored by the State
Senate.

Tennessee Lt. Gov. Ron
Ramsey listens as I
address the Tennessee
Senate

(L-R) Jan Howard, Jimmy, Michele, Lt. Gov. Ron Ramsey, Tami Bandy, Moe Bandy, John Greenwood, Ray Pillow

Resolution from the Tennessee Senate honoring my career

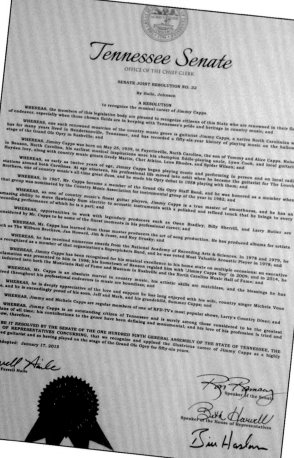

Playing for Connie Smith at Little Jimmy Dickens memorial service.

The Country's Family Reunion Band (L-R) Mike Johnson, Dirk Johnson, Hank Singer, David Smith, John Gardner, Les Singer

The day Moe Bandy and
wore the exact same shi
to a CFR taping!

My Larry's Count
Diner family

Ben Isaacs (my number 3 son) showing me some love

Playing with Doyle Dykes on the Diner

A bad hair day! On vacation with Bill and Jeanine Walker

With Michele, Jan Howard, Keith and Emy Joe Bilbrey, Jimmy and Nina Fortune

Always a wonderful greeting from Charley Pride backstage at the Opry

Where you could find me for the past 60 years.

Playing behind my buddy Darrell McCall on CFR. His brother Dennis and
Norah Lee Allen are in the back

Bobby and Jeannie Bare, Michele, Jimmy and Keith and Emy Joe Bilbrey

With Michele's parents Dean and Jean on the CFR cruise

Playing for my pal Ray Pillow

Pretending we a
Roy and Dal

With Brenda Lee,
backstage at the
Opry

Our dear friend Lorrie Morgan visits the Diner

Charlie McCoy, Jimmy, Gene Chrisman, Hoot Hester, Dennis Crouch, Joey Miskulin

With my son Ma

With D.J.
Fontana, Ray
Stevens and
Scotty Moore

The end of the night after the Opry Birthday Bash

Arletta Voan, Paul Voan, Jimmy, Michele, Jean Voan, Dean Voan at my
induction into the Musicians Hall of Fame

Giving my speech after being inducted into the Musician's Hall of Fame

Playing as The Oak Ridge Boys perform for my induction into the Musician's
Hall of Fame

William Lee Golden listens as I give my Musician's Hall of Fame
acceptance speech. *Courtesy Roxane Atwood*

George Hamilton IV announcing I will be inducted into the North Carolina
Music Hall of Fame

My induction into the North Carolina Music Hall of Fame

Trying to remember the words as we perform at the wedding with Jeannie Seely and Gene Ward

On the set of a Country's Family Reunion Christmas show

(L-R) Reggie and Jenny Young, Jimmy, Michele, Lea Jane Berinati, Harold Bradley

Playing on the CFR Alaska cruise

Our last visit with Merle Haggard. Jesse McReynolds, Connie Smith and
Michele all on Merle's bus.

Our dear Opry Dog

Ray Edenton, Jimmy Fortune, Jimmy

The Man in Back
in black and whi

With my Don Warden Fender
Deluxe. See Page 62 for the
story about this special gift.

With my favorite cowgirl
in the Opry circle

Current Opry Staff Band (L-R) Eamon McLoughlin, Tommy White, Mike Noble, Eddie Bayers, Kerry Marx, (Opry background singer, Tony King), Randy Hart, Jimmy Capps, Larry Paxton. Not pictured – Mark Beckett

Phil Johnson wearing the shirt he made in my honor. Phil took all of the Larry's Country Diner photos you see in this book.

With my great frier Jimmy Wayne

Visiting with Larry Black and Mandy Barnett

(L-R) Michele, Jimmy, Johnny Carver, Lisa Carver, Brandon Carver

Thanking Kenny Rogers for letting me play on his classics The Gambler a
Coward of the County

Buddy Miller, Mandy Barnett, Duane Eddy, Jimmy Capps

Steve Chapman, Scotty Moore. Jimmy

With Mark Wills. You can read the story behind this crazy photo in the
Larry's Country Diner chapter.

Billy Yeargin announces that May 2019 will be Jimmy Capps Month in Benson NC.

Showing off my Tennessee Ambassador of Goodwill Award

The Sheriff's next campaign photo.

Good for another 60 years.

While Carole Black went on to make it big in TV, in 1975 I ended up on the big screen. The movie was called, simply, "Nashville". They shot a lot of it inside the Opry House, and I was in the movie, along with the rest of the Opry staff band. We just basically played ourselves. But some thought "Nashville" showed a caricature of country stars and fans.

There were many people, many in the business, who thought that the movie didn't paint a good picture of Nashville and of Country Music, but I thought it was pretty true to life! None of us had any idea how popular that movie would become, and I still get residuals from it. I also get residuals from music I played in movies, including "Apollo 13", "Coal Miner's Daughter", "Five Easy Pieces", "Smokey and the Bandit 2", "The Gambler", "Sweet Dreams", "Four Weddings and a Funeral", and quite a few others.

In 2002, I was part of "Monsters, Inc." I did that with the Riders in the Sky. The Riders won a Grammy award for it, and the Grammys gave me and all the musicians a certificate of credit. I had no idea it was going to turn out like it did.

And we recently did some more stuff for Disney. They're using it at an amusement park in China. If you happen to go there, you'll hear our music on one of the rides. Joey, the Riders accordion player, produced all of that, and he did a great job. The Riders have included me in a lot of great things, so I thought it only fair that I include them in my book.

"I hired Jimmy to play with the Riders in the Sky on a number of recordings for the Walt Disney Corporation. We created some music that's played at Disney's park in Shanghai, China. Jimmy is also on our music which plays in the Cars attraction at Disneyland in California.

Jimmy played guitar for the Riders when we did an animated short film for Pixar called "For the Birds". Jimmy played his butt off on that, and his work also helped us win a Grammy award as we did the music for "Monsters, Inc.". He was a huge part of that.

One of the highlights of my career was when Jimmy asked me to play on his "In Time for Dinner" album. Charlie McCoy, Hoot Hester and some other great musicians were on that album, and I was so honored that he let me be a part of it as well.

When I found out that Jimmy would celebrate his 60th anniversary on the Opry in December 2018, I was just in awe. But I really wish that it was just his 10th anniversary... because then we could have 50 or 60 more years with him."

– Joey, The Cow Polka King, Riders in the Sky

"When you think of classy musicians, and the way they ought to play, and look and behave on and off stage, you should think of Jimmy Capps. He is the gold standard.

I sometimes have to miss the Opry when I'm playing with the Time Jumpers group, and Jimmy fills in for me. He becomes a Rider in the Sky for the night, and he always does a masterful job. When he's taking my place, he trades his usual guitar for his Gibson archtop, and on those occasions, you can see Jimmy wearing a cowboy hat. He has such beautiful hair, and he doesn't cover it up with a hat very often.

Jimmy produced a record for Stu Phillips, and he had us come in a sing a few songs with Stu. We also sang on a couple songs on Moe Bandy's 'Lucky Me' album, which Jimmy was also the producer on. Jimmy is just a great guy to work with. He's always so complimentary of everyone.

Jimmy has been a joy to be around and to work with. I have admired him forever. He is a first-class gentleman. When I grow up, I want to be Jimmy Capps."

– Ranger Doug, the Riders in the Sky

The Opry Staff Band got some attention from the "Nashville" movie. We were also showcased on two albums recorded by the

Opry Staff Band and Singers, and if you can find one of those, you can actually hear me sing!

On our first album, Spider Wilson and I sang a song called, "You're a Real Good Friend". It's a great tune, in spite of my singing, and I'm now trying to talk Gene Watson and Moe Bandy into recording that song.

I also did an album with Weldon Myrick, who was a member of the Opry band. You can hear his steel guitar on so many classic country songs. His steel was on every Connie Smith hit, especially her signature, "Once a Day". Weldon also played on landmark songs, including Jesse Coulter's "I'm Not Lisa", Jeannie C. Riley's "Harper Valley PTA", and Cal Smith's "Country Bumpkin".

Name a country standard, and there's a good chance that Weldon Myrick was playing steel guitar on it.

In 1990, Weldon told me he wanted to do an instrumental album that would feature me and him, and we would use the Opry Staff Band. We recorded the album we called "Grand Ole Steel and Guitar" in Ben Hall's garage, which he had turned into a really nice studio. Ben was an excellent engineer, and the sound on that album still amazes me.

The Opry Staff Band was a really great band. Weldon played so good on the album. He always played good on everything, but he was extra good on our album. And it was fun to cut it with all the band. Weldon Myrick passed away in 2014. He was 76 years old. He was one of the greats.

Losing our friends and our musical heroes is not easy… but in 2010, we almost lost the Opry House itself.

One day, on May 1st, it started raining in Nashville. No one thought anything of it. But it kept raining. All day, and all night. And on May 2nd, it was still raining, again, all day and all night. And when it finally stopped, more than 13 inches had fallen on Music City.

That once-in-a-lifetime flood destroyed homes and businesses throughout Nashville, causing more than two billion dollars' worth of damage. And worst of all, twenty-six people lost their lives in the flood.

Some of the worst flooding came when the Cumberland River turned into a raging ocean of water that devastated the entire Opry Mills Mall. Hundreds of cars in the parking lot were submerged. Raging water overflowed into the Opryland Hotel, as 1,500 guests were being evacuated. The Opry Museum was destroyed, and then the water came for the Grand Ole Opry House itself.

When it finally stopped, the Opry stage was under six feet of water. They had to row a canoe inside the Opry House just to get up to the stage. As I watched the local news coverage, I thought, "That's it. It's over. The Opry House is gone."

But even the most devastating flood was not enough to stop the Opry. The show continued to go on, as we took the show on the road. For the next five months, we did the Opry from different locations around Nashville, including the Ryman Auditorium, the War Memorial and Municipal Auditoriums, Allen Arena at Lipscomb University, and even Two Rivers Baptist Church!

After the flood waters started to recede, my mind started racing. I thought, "What did I leave in the Opry House when the rain came? Oh my Lord! Our instruments! They were all there."

I had left some instruments in the Opry band room. If they hadn't been hanging on guitar hooks, they were now all under water. Hoot Hester always left his fiddle under a little computer desk. Hoot always kept that fiddle in a real cheap Styrofoam case. When they finally got into the band room, his fiddle was floating on the water! But when they opened it up, there was not a drop of water on that fiddle, because it had been in that Styrofoam case! While some of the other musician's instruments in more expensive cases were destroyed, Hoot's was totally saved, thanks to his cheap case!

I had one guitar, a Fender Stratocaster, sitting on the floor when the flood hit, and it ended up underwater. But it was zipped up in a little case, just a tweed gig bag. We dried it out, and I took it out of the case, plugged it in, and it was fine! The only thing that was broken was the toggle switch. The screws had rusted a little bit. But that was it.

But they threw away tons and tons of electronic equipment. Peavey amps and so much other stuff. They threw it all into dumpsters. They threw away hundreds of thousands of dollars' worth of stuff.

And we found out later that all you needed to do was dry them out and plug 'em in, and that some of them would still work. I still have an amp in my garage that was in the flood. It had mud and slime on it. But I can plug it in today and it works fine.

The musical charts were all underwater. The band room was full of filing cabinets with charts from all the years of the Opry, and they were all underwater. It was heartbreaking. I didn't think there was any way to save those.

But they were somehow able to send them all to Dallas, Texas, where they were freeze dried. All the paper charts were sanitized by gamma rays, and we got them all back. We are still using those flooded charts today.

When I saw how bad the damage was, I wondered if the Gaylord company had enough insurance to cover the devastating loss. I figured that, even if they could put it all back together, when we walked in, we would still be able to smell the water and mud that had been in there.

As work on the Opry House continued, I began worrying about something else... I knew that there was different management leading the way now than what had been there when the Opry House was first built, so I thought that the new leaders might use this as a chance to make the Opry much more modern, and in turn it would not feel like the old place.

I shouldn't have worried. After a $20 million renovation, the Grand Ole Opry House was absolutely perfect. The moment I walked in, I was amazed at how they had been able to keep the nostalgia part of it, while making the new place even better. It had needed a facelift. And the cosmetic part of it is magic. It turned out so great that they started giving public tours backstage. It is just beautiful. Anyone who comes to Nashville needs to go to the Opry and take that tour. The dressing rooms each even have a theme and a title. It's just perfect.

Today, we have the very best of both worlds. We have the new and improved Opry House, and we have the greatest musical venue in the world with the now-renovated Ryman Auditorium.

When the Ryman fell into disrepair in the 1970s and 80s, many people thought that it should be torn down. It sat empty for years. And I was really scared. A lot of very historical buildings, studios and houses on Music Row in Nashville have been torn down. That's where history was made, and it's all gone.

One of the oldest studios in Nashville was torn down and they put a condominium up in its place. It seems like it's all about the money. They have sold off and torn down these important and historical places, just so someone can make a lot of money. It's very sad. The city of Nashville should have registered so many of those places so that they could have been saved. But it didn't happen.

One of the oldest studios in town, The Sound Shop, where so many hit songs were recorded, was torn down like it was nothing. And before it was even a recording studio, it had been the Grammer Guitar factory. That building had so much history, and it's gone. It baffles me.

And the Ryman Auditorium almost went, too. It was getting really rundown. But, through some miracle, it wasn't leveled. I don't know who was really responsible for saving it, but bless them, whoever it was.

Now we go back to do the Opry at the Ryman for more than three months out of the year. And to me, that really feels like home. The sound is so great in the Ryman. There is no better concert hall for sound. The Ryman is my favorite place to play. The audience is right on top of you. It can seat 2,200 people, and is so intimate.

The Ryman is my favorite place on earth. One day, before the audience came in, my wife Michele was walking up in the very last row of the balcony. I was on stage talking to someone; we didn't have any microphone at all, and Michele could hear every word we said. Then she said, "Hey guys," in her normal speaking voice, and we could hear her all the way from the balcony down to the stage. The acoustics are so impressive. I think the building is truly anointed, since it had originally been a church.

Bill Anderson has spent a lot of time in the Ryman. I respect Bill so much. He might be the greatest songwriter who has ever been in Nashville, and he has managed to stay up to date. He has kept his traditional sound, but he is still very current. His singing is so different, and the songs he's written are so great. He amazes me.

I've seen Bill follow Garth Brooks and other current artists on the Opry stage, and after that artist walks off, Bill has such a gift for bringing that audience back to him, and usually receives a standing ovation.

Many years ago, the Opry wanted to hire a new guitar player, and the manager asked me who I would recommend. I told him that Les Singer would be perfect. Les worked for Bill Anderson at the time, and just as Bill was getting ready to step out on the Opry stage, the manager walked up to him and said, "Bill, we're thinking about hiring your guitar player."

And that shook Bill up so much that, as he walked out to perform, all he could think about was that he was going to lose his long-time, great player, Les.

When he walked off, Bill came over to me. He said he didn't like that I had told the management they should hire his guitar player, and he asked me, "What about my needs?" He was really upset.

But a few days later, my phone rang. It was Bill, and he said, "Jimmy, I owe you an apology. I was wrong about trying to keep Les. I know it would be a good move for him, and it would be more money for him and his family." And then he added, "I'm praying that he gets the job."

For some reason, Les didn't get the job. But I got a deeper respect for Bill Anderson when I found out how he could admit it when he might be wrong about something. I have watched Bill Anderson entertain audiences for more than five decades, and I was so happy when Bill said he wanted to be a part of my book…

"Jimmy Capps has been on the Opry longer than I have. There's not many who have been around that long! I first met Jimmy when he was playing with the Louvin Brothers. I'd gotten to tour with them quite a bit, and I could see that he fit right into the style that the Louvins had. Jimmy also played on a couple songs I wrote that the Louvins recorded, and he always knew just what to play.

I'm so glad that I've gotten to know Jimmy over the years. He is a good friend. He is so capable, not only as a guitar player, but also as a record producer. He's been producing new records on Moe Bandy, and they are just fabulous.

Jimmy always has a big smile any time you go see him. And he just has an easy going way about him. As a player and as a person, he is very consistent. He never changes. He is always wonderful. I was always impressed by what a talented musician he was, but I was more impressed by what a nice guy he was."

Bill Anderson

Of course, Connie Smith also goes way back with Bill Anderson. Bill is the one who discovered Connie, and he invited her to sing with him on Ernest Tubb's Midnite Jamboree. Connie would return the favor when she turned Bill's "Once a Day" into a country classic.

I've known Connie Smith since 1964, and I still think she is so amazing. Connie lives the lyrics. She is always so good, and sings straight from the heart. I think she will go down in history as the favorite singer of thousands and thousands of people, and also of her peers.

I have played for Connie during a number of funerals for our Opry family members. It's always just me and my guitar, and her and her amazing voice. I don't know how she's able to get through some of those services. It's hard enough for me to play guitar when we're saying goodbye to one of our friends who is closer than a family member, so I don't know how Connie is able to sing. I am always honored when Connie calls me and asks me to play for her on one of those occasions.

After all of our years of friendship and of working together, I can only hope that Connie can come up with something positive to say about me!

"Jimmy Capps is a pure gentleman. It goes without saying that he's a great musician. Everyone knows that. But people might not know what a great person he is. He's a true friend. His heart is so big. I count him as one of my dear friends.

I sang 'How Great Thou Art' during the memorial service for Little Jimmy Dickens, and Jimmy accompanied me with his guitar. He did that for me several times. We also did the same thing for George Hamilton IV's service at the Ryman. I am always comfortable when I know I've got Jimmy playing behind me.

Jimmy plays my spots almost every time I'm on the Opry. I had a guitar player, Rick Wright, who had been with me for 17 years, but Rick was killed in a car wreck in 2016. And Jimmy helped fill in until we found another player.

Jimmy and his wife Michele are dear friends. My husband Marty Stuart and I both love them a lot. Any time we run into them, we love it. Jimmy is just the salt of the earth.

On October 17, 2015, Jimmy was with me for one of my all-time favorite Opry moments, which actually took place off stage. Merle Haggard always loved me. He was just a big fan of mine, and he would do anything for me.

My booking agent also booked Merle Haggard, and he told me that Merle was in town. I asked if he was going to come to the Opry, and he said, 'No. I tried to get him to, but he won't do it.'

I said, 'Shucks! I'm hosting the Opry this week,' and he said, 'If you called him, he might do it.'

So I called Merle, and I was so thrilled when he said he would come play the Opry. It was the first time he'd done it with his band, the Strangers, in over twenty years, and it turned out to be the last time he would get to do it.

After Merle's part of the Opry, I went out to his bus, and Jimmy and his wife Michele also went with me. We all had such a wonderful time as we visited with him for a few minutes.

I call my band the Sundowners, but for a short time, my bass player came up with the name 'the Men in Back'. I used that occasionally, but it was never their official name. But Jimmy had heard it, and when he wanted to name this book 'The Man in Back', he didn't want me to think he stole it from me. So he actually called me, and asked if it would be OK to name his book 'The Man in Back'. It was not necessary, but I thought it was so nice for him to ask. It should be his. That title is meant for him."

– Connie Smith

Connie mentioned the last night that Merle Haggard played the Opry. I'd like to add a few more things about that magical night.

I was always a Merle Haggard fan. I had heard that Merle watched Larry's Country Diner, but I didn't really know if it was true. During Merle's part of the Opry, I stood over on the side of the stage so that I could watch him and his band play. I didn't know that it would be his last time on the Opry, but I did know that I was watching history.

Merle's son, Ben, played guitar with him. But as I watched, I was so touched when Merle called MY name and said that he'd enjoyed working with me and the staff band the last time he was there. That really touched my heart. I couldn't believe that he mentioned my name.

After he sang his final song, Merle went to his bus, and I went over to Ben and said, "Ben, you played so good. You are a great player."

Ben asked if I had talked to his dad. I told him I didn't get to. "Let's go to the bus," he replied. "I know he will want to talk to you."

When my wife Michele and I walked on, Merle was there with his wife. He had already changed from his stage clothes into a t-shirt, and was now sitting at a dinette in the middle of the bus. We sat and talked, and he loved visiting with Connie Smith.

Then Merle said, "I've been watching you on the Diner." And he watched the show very closely. He said, "I can tell, when you finish a lick, if it's what you wanted to play and it came out just right. And I can also tell when it doesn't come out like you want it to." It just knocked me out that he watched it that close!

Jesse McReynolds came onto the bus, and Michele and I said goodbye to Merle. Then, as we got ready to leave, I told him, "You ought to come in and do Larry's Country Diner."

And he said, "I just might do that."

Can you imagine Merle Haggard sitting at the Diner counter with just me playing guitar for him? That would have really been something. Unfortunately, Merle never got to visit the Diner. He died less than six months later.

It was such a huge loss for our business when Haggard died. He sang so good, right up to the end. He was such a stylist, and his songwriting was so great. He wrote for the working man and the average person. I don't think there will ever be a honky-tonk or club that doesn't play at least one Merle Haggard song every night. Every local band has to know some Merle Haggard.

One of my dearest Opry friends is Jan Howard. Not many people know that Jan is the female voice you hear on Johnny Cash's big hit "Daddy Sang Bass". The woman singing the real high line "Mama sang tenor!" is Jan Howard. Most people think its June Carter Cash. It's not. It's Jan Howard. She never got public credit for it, but she has a gold record hanging on her wall that Johnny Cash gave to her.

It reads, "To Jan Howard, as a small token of my appreciation."

Jan had some big hits on her own, and some big duets with Bill Anderson. Jan is just a sweet lady. She asked me to be the leader for all of her Opry spots, and we got real close. She has always been there for me. Jan wrote a truly amazing autobiography called "Sunshine and Shadow". And I'm so grateful that she also took the time to write a few words for my book. If mine turns out half as good as hers, I know it will be great.

"I came to the Opry in 1960. And Capps had already been there. I call him Capps. To last that long on the Opry, you have to have talent and professionalism, and he has both. Capps is the most talented person I've ever seen. I've worked with a lot of people, but he is one who has everybody's respect. I respect him tremendously.

After my son Jimmy was killed in Vietnam, I've done a lot of work with the military over the years. I was asked to do an appearance for the Wounded Warriors, and I asked Capps to go with me; and he played 'Wind Beneath My Wings' as I sang it for that group. I did another event for the MIA/POWs, and he played guitar for me there, too.

Capps has always been there for me, for anything I ask. And I would do anything for him. We have had a lasting friendship that has grown over the years. And I never take that for granted."

Jan Howard

Of course, I've talked a lot about the singers and musicians who play on the Grand Ole Opry... but the Opry engineers are equal with the staff band. They don't get a run through. They haven't heard anything. They don't get a sound check. There's so many artists on each show, there's no way they could do a sound check with everyone.

But today's technology helps the engineers. They're able to program an artist who is on the Opry quite often. For example, they can program the Ricky Skaggs band into the sound board so that their mix is the same every week. But the engineer must have a musical ear. They have to know who is going to be doing the solos so that they can push them up in the mix. And they might have six or seven mixes that they're listening to. The engineer needs to be musical, even if they're not playing an instrument.

When I started out, there was no mixing board. They only had a few microphones on stage. There were no stage monitors. There were no amplifiers, except for the bass player. The electric guitar players and steel player had a speaker that was hung up in the air, which they tilted to the side of the stage so that it wouldn't get into the vocal mic. We plugged into a junction box that had four inputs.

A lot has changed over the last six decades at the Opry, but my excitement about coming to work has not changed. I don't take many days off. I still enjoy doing the Opry... as much as I did sixty years ago.

Chapter Twelve

MICHELE

I started enjoying the Opry even more than usual when I got to know the Opry's "Chart Chick".

I met Michele Voan in 1995 when she came to Nashville to record her first album.

Kevin McManus, the owner of Oak Valley Studio, called me and said that a girl from Texas was coming in, and she wanted to do an album of old Pop songs.

Kevin asked me to be leader on the CD, and to also play guitar on it. I asked Beegie Adair to help me on the sessions. Beegie is one of the best Jazz players I have ever heard. Even though Michele's album featured Pop songs, I hired Country players for the session. I knew that Country players can adapt to almost anything. Country players can play Jazz music lots easier than most Jazz players can adapt to Country... but Beegie Adair could do either one.

At the time, Michele was married to a man named Clayton Hedge. They lived in Texas and both worked for Lowes, doing setup work for stores all across the southeastern part of the country. They traveled from town to town, helping to get new Lowes stores ready to open. But in 1996, they moved to Nashville.

Michele never really wanted to be a big star. She just liked to sing. She never tried to record songs that she thought might make it to the radio, but after her first CD turned out so well, she asked me to help her with another one.

It was a Christmas album, and it was great. While we were working on those albums, Billy Linneman, who played bass on the Opry, and I, became very good friends with Michele. Any time Michele and her husband wanted to come to the Opry, either Billy or I would get them in backstage; and they would come to the Opry quite often.

At the time, the Opry staff band needed someone to be in charge of our musical charts. Harold Weakley had that job, but after he died in 1990, no one took his place, so all of the musicians were in charge of getting all the musical charts ready. It was a big job, and if an artist wanted to change or add a song at the last minute while they were performing, it was very hard for the musicians to get the right charts.

One night, Michele was backstage and she saw what a hassle it was for all the players, so she offered to go and get the charts. Then she started volunteering to do that for each Opry show that she could get to. The band got to where they really relied on Michele's work. She knew the music, and she was very dependable, and she was doing it all for free!

After a while, she was doing it so much and was doing such a great job that our drummer, John Gardner, said, "Guys, we need to start paying that girl." He asked all of the staff band to give her a little money each week. John would take up a collection and give it to Michele.

A short time later, the musician's union was renegotiating with the Opry. Pete Fisher, the Opry manager, and Steve Buchanan, who was Vice President, wanted to put Michele in our contract as Music Librarian. And while that move made Michele an official employee, it also led to a cut in pay for her! The donations that the staff band had taken up each week for her were actually more than the Opry paid her!

When the band members found out about the pay cut, Spider Wilson and guitarist Kerry Marx continued to pay Michele out of their pockets. They would hide money in her purse, or in charts. One weekend, Kerry wrapped a twenty dollar bill around a hot dog and he put it in Michele's purse. Since her job was to pass out all the charts that have the musical number system we use, all of the musicians nicknamed her "the Chart Chick". She still answers to that today!

My wife Anne died in 2005. By then, Michele was divorced. After a while, we found out that our friendship was growing into something more. I was so comfortable when we talked. We could easily talk about anything.

I was attracted to Michele's honesty, and also to her talent. She was much different than most other female singers. I loved her music, and we could talk to each other. I could talk to her about anything. She had such a great personality. She's a Texan, and she will tell you what she thinks. If you don't want to hear the truth, don't ask her a question!

Michele was raised in Tarkington Prairie and Shepherd, Texas. Her mom and dad had a country music show, and she sang on the show. She also played upright bass in a bluegrass band when she was a little girl. She sang solos, and was featured in her church choir at Shepherd United Pentecostal Church. Michele's mom has a beautiful voice, and you can hear that on Michele's Christmas album, "Christmas At Home with Michele", on the song "O Holy Night". It brings me to tears every time I hear her mother sing.

When she was in her twenties, Michele worked as a letter carrier for the U.S. Postal Service for eight years, and she was known as the Singing Letter Carrier! She walked ten miles every day, and she would sing as she walked her route. Everyone could tell when their mail lady was getting close! She even took requests from them! It's a wonder she ever got all her mail delivered.

One unique thing about Michele and I is that we have the same birthday. We were both born on May 25th. I like to say we were born under the same sign... a neon sign. We share the same birthday, but of course, we weren't born during the same year. I am quite a bit older than Michele. But neither one of us ever questioned it. I was very comfortable with it. I knew I could overlook the fact that she was younger and more beautiful than I was!

Michele and I were married on July 15, 2007. Guess what we did on July 14th? The night before our wedding, we played the Opry, just like always. Bill Anderson announced it to the crowd, and when he told everyone that we were getting married the next day, Michele whispered to me, "There's no turning back now."

Our wedding was held at the River of Life Church in Smyrna, Tennessee. Johnny Minick was the minister of that church, and he also sang and played piano for the Happy Goodman Family.

He'd hired me to do a couple songs he was doing for his father. It was a personal project for him. And when I told him that I didn't want to charge him anything, Johnny said, "Well, I'm going to let you have our church for your wedding." He also officiated our wedding!

Michele and I had a small, very intimate wedding. We only invited a few close friends and family members. Ricky Skaggs and Sharon White Skaggs surprised me, with Michele's help, and came to sing a beautiful song for us. Our ceremony was small, but we had planned for a huge reception at the Grand Ole Opry Museum. On our way there, I asked Michele, "What if no one shows up?"

She said, "Don't worry. They will."

She was right. We had so many Opry members and musicians and friends there.

We spent most of our honeymoon in Charlie McCoy's condo in Fort Myers, Florida. Charlie had a beautiful condo right on the ocean. As a wedding gift, he and his wife Pat gave us a week stay at their condo on the beach.

As I was writing this, I got to wondering what it was that attracted Michele to me. I guess I'll find out when I read this next part along with you!

"I loved Jimmy's eyes. I fell in love with his blue eyes. But then I got to know his heart. I found out that he's got a heart as big as he is. The way he treated me when I came to Nashville, he was so kind. I watched him as he was so kind with everyone he came into contact with. We became really good friends over a lot of years.

We were drawn to each other as friends first. As we got to know each other, I knew that, if I was having a bad day, I could call Jimmy up and I would always feel better just by talking with him. He always lifted me up. We were friends for a dozen years before we got married.

Many years before we ever started dating, Jimmy was the band leader on a record for me. He also played on the CD. We were in the studio, doing a song called 'Love Walked In'. A couple seconds after I sang the last line and the song ended, the tape was still rolling when Jimmy said, 'There's your record Hoss!' I kept that part of him saying that, and put it on my CD. We played that song at our wedding ceremony, and everyone loved it when the song ended and then they heard Jimmy say, 'There's your record Hoss!'

After I became the Opry Music Librarian, most of the guys in the band started calling me the Opry Chart Chick. I just call myself the Opry Staff Band Babysitter. That's what I really do!

I often get asked how much younger I am than Jimmy. I never tell my age! But Jimmy does keep me young.

When people ask him if he's a real sheriff, I tell them that he would make a horrible sheriff. He's too loving and too kind. He'd let everybody out of jail! Jimmy is the most loving and caring human being that I've ever met. He is a rock. He is my rock, and I love him more than I can ever put into words."

– Michele Capps

I thank my wife for the appearance and look I have right now. I had stayed clean shaven for most of my career. I did have a goatee for a short time, but a few years ago, Michele talked me into growing my goatee back. She had seen a picture of me with a goatee while I was touring with Ferlin Husky, and she'd really liked it. Of course, when it came in this time, it was not dark brown! At the time I met Michele, I was also coloring my hair brown. My hair started turning grey when I was just 27 years old. So I colored it for decades, and I hate to say it, but I was also perming my hair! Michele told me to stop all that. She turned out to be right, since people seem to like my natural silver hair that matches my silver goatee.

Chapter Thirteen

MY TV LIFE BEFORE THE DINER

Most people reading this book may know me from my appearances on the Larry's Country Diner and Country's Family Reunion TV series, and I will talk a lot about those in just a bit. I have been blessed to get quite a bit of television exposure throughout my career.

Besides the local TV shows in North Carolina and Nashville that I've already mentioned, I have also been able to play in front of a national audience on many programs.

In the late 60s, I did the Jim and Jesse Show. Grand Ole Opry members Jim and Jesse McReynolds had started their syndicated show in Lexington, Kentucky.

I met Carl Jackson for the first time when we taped a show in Lexington. He was only 14 years old! But he was already playing great. He was on the show for five years, and then got a job playing in Glen Campbell's band.

We did twenty-six Jim and Jesse shows in Lexington, and then they brought it to Channel 2 in Nashville. Jim and Jesse were known for their bluegrass music, but their TV show was more country than bluegrass. I think Jesse McReynolds still owns the show. I don't know why he hasn't done anything with it. I don't know how expensive it would be to get it transferred from tape to digital. Jesse is still an amazing musician. He has always been such a great player.

Jim and Jesse were never afraid to branch out and try different things. In 1965, they did a whole album of Chuck Berry songs, called "Berry Pickin' in the Country", and it got a lot of airplay.

In the early 1970s, I did the Wilburn Brothers Show for a couple years, which we also filmed at Channel 2 in Nashville. Hal Rugg played steel guitar on a lot of those shows. Buddy Spicher played fiddle, Leslie and Lester Wilburn, Doyle and Teddy's older brothers, were also on the show. The drummer was Buddy Rogers, who later owned Uncle Bud's Catfish.

But Hal Rugg and Buddy Spicher quit the show. Doyle came to me when I was working the Wilburn's spots on the Opry, and asked me if I'd like to play on their TV show. I said I would love to, and they hired me and Curly Chalker at the same time. Curly took Hal Rugg's place.

Loretta Lynn had been with the show from 1963 to 1971. The Wilburn Brothers Show is really what launched Loretta's career. She also toured with Doyle and Teddy during that time, and they are the ones who helped get Loretta seen by millions of people.

I always thought that the Wilburn Brothers were unsung heroes of Nashville. If it had not been for the Wilburns, there might not have been a Loretta. They kind of put their own career on the back burner so that they could help push her.

When Loretta was trying to get started, Doyle Wilburn took one of her songs to Owen Bradley. He wanted Owen to sign Loretta to his record label.

After Owen listened to it, he said, "Boy, that is a great song!" But then he said, "I've already got Patsy Cline and Brenda Lee. I don't need another female singer. But I would like this song for Brenda Lee."

"You can't have the song if you don't sign Loretta," Doyle said back.

Owen finally gave in and said he'd sign Loretta. He gave Loretta's song to Brenda Lee and she took it to number one. And then, once he'd started recording Loretta, of course she had one hit after another.

Since all the big songs she wrote were with their company, the Wilburns reaped a lot financially from her. But they helped her just as much. By the time I joined them, Loretta had already left the show and was on her way to becoming a superstar.

Here's a funny story about Curly Chalker, who played steel for the Wilburn Brothers TV show, a great player who had come to Nashville from Las Vegas and went on to play on Hee Haw for 25 years.

When Curly passed away, Leon Rhodes, Spider Wilson and me all went to the visitation. We were all standing next to the casket, when another steel guitar player named Howard White walked up.

Howard had a drinking problem, and he had been drinking before the visitation. And when he walked up to Curly's casket, I met him and said, "Howard, we have lost one of the best."

But loudly, Howard said back, "Well, to be honest, I never did like the S.O.B." (except, he used all the words in S.O.B.). Curly's family was standing right next to us, and they were shocked. But Howard kept on talking real loud, saying, "You know what really ticks me off? I never got to tell the S.O.B. how much I hated him!"

I tried to calm him down, as I whispered, "Howard, that is not nice to say."

But he kept on, with "I guess I'll just have to wait until I get to Heaven to tell him."

"What if he didn't make it to Heaven?" I asked.

"Then YOU tell him!" he yelled.

In the late 70s, I played on the Marty Robbins Spotlight series. That was such a great show. Marty would always have one guest on each show. They were all country music legends.

I did a bunch of the "Pop Goes the Country" shows. Jerry Whitehurst was the musical director, and when he needed an acoustic guitar player, he would call me. They used a lot of the Opry Staff Band on that show.

I also played on a lot of the "That Good Ole Nashville Music" shows. It was a real popular show. They eventually changed the name to "That Nashville Music", and all totaled, it was in syndication from 1970 to 1985. They still rerun it and "Pop Goes the Country" on RFD TV.

I wasn't on the original Johnny Cash TV series on the ABC network, but I did play on all the Johnny Cash network specials. Johnny did Christmas specials for CBS from 1976 to 1979, along with many other network shows through 1985. And any time Johnny hosted something on TV, he wanted the Bill Walker Orchestra there. Bill had been his musical director on the original Johnny Cash TV Show, and since I was part of Bill's orchestra, I was blessed to be on most of Johnny's television shows.

My work with the Bill Walker Orchestra led me to some great opportunities. It basically put me on just about every major country music TV show there was. We did the CMA Award shows for more than 20 years. We did the Music City News Awards for another 20 years. Those awards were huge productions, and Bill Walker always used a full orchestra with strings, horns, background vocals and a country rhythm section.

I am thankful to Bill Walker for giving me so many wonderful experiences, and I'm also thankful that he took the time to say a few words for my book...

"I started using Jimmy Capps when I was working on all the Johnny Cash television specials. From there, we did hundreds of different TV shows over three or four decades. We played on almost every country music award show, and on some non-country music award programs. We were part of more than 160 one-hour Statler Brothers TV shows.

Jimmy was always my first call for acoustic guitar, and if I needed an extra electric guitar, I would also call him. He was my most important guitar player for many, many years. He was just so good.

Jimmy and Hal Rugg were a great team. If you signed both them up for a project, then you were already halfway home. I could throw anything at them, and they could get it done. I once asked Jimmy and Hal to play on a recording of 'Send In The Clowns'. It was far from country. One of them said, 'Bill, I think you've sent in the wrong clowns to play this!' But they played it great.

As a musician, Jimmy has no equal. He is a great guitar player, in all types of music, not just country. I never had any worry when I knew Jimmy was in my rhythm section. As a person, he's fun, always with a good attitude, always on time. He is just a wonderful guy."

– Bill Walker

I played in Bill Walker's rhythm section on May 16, 1989, when the orchestra went with Loretta Lynn and Crystal Gayle to play with the famous Boston Pops. We filmed the PBS special "Evening at Pops with Loretta and Crystal".

The Boston Pops is known around the world, but Loretta was more comfortable with the Bill Walker Orchestra, so she requested that his rhythm section also come along and play with the Boston Pops!

And that's just what we did. Bill Walker played piano for the show, Hal Rugg played pedal steel, Bill Harris was on drums, and Bruce Watkins and I played guitar. The Pops was conducted by the legendary John Williams.

Our regular rhythm guitar player, Mark Casstevens, couldn't make the trip, so on my recommendation, Bruce Watkins took his place. But before we got there, the man in charge told all of us musicians, "Under no circumstance do you bother the conductor John Williams. You are not allowed to approach or talk to Mr. Williams!"

As soon as the man walked away, Bruce Watkins turned to me and said, "I'm having my picture made with Mr. Williams!"

Sure enough, as soon as John Williams walked in, Bruce walked up to him and said, "John, we are the rhythm section from Nashville. And we would like to have our picture with you."

John Williams said, "Man, I would be honored." He shook all of our hands, and couldn't have been nicer.

I was honored when Crystal Gayle offered to say a few words about that night...

"The Boston Pops show was incredible. I worked with symphonies all the time, but it was not as easy for Loretta to sing with the big orchestras. She was much more comfortable when she could look over and see a few familiar musicians from Nashville. She wanted Jimmy and that core group of players she was used to working with, and she took her cues from them.

Jimmy is one of the greatest session musicians ever. But he has such a horrible temper, just a terrible temper! Of course I am joking! He is such a great person, and it seems like he has always been a part of my life.

I know that I could do a full show out on the road with just Jimmy as my band. All you need is him and his guitar. He plays so tastefully, and he puts his heart and soul into a song. Jimmy is a very special person and I am honored to call him my friend."

– Crystal Gayle

In 1991, the Bill Walker Orchestra was chosen to handle all of the music on a brand new TV show. And that would lead to seven of the most fun years of my life. The Statler Brothers Show ran on The Nashville Network from 1991 to 1998, and during that time the show become one the most popular programs, not only on TNN, but on all of cable TV.

Harold and Don Reid wrote all the scripts for those shows. They wrote a lot of funny stuff. You never knew what the Statlers were going to pull on the show. The band laughed the entire way through.

Those guys were so good to work for. They had great guests. But the show could have been just as much a success without any guests, featuring just the Statlers. It was a variety show. They would have magicians on. They'd have jugglers. It was a little bit of everything, kind of like shows were back when TV was just getting started.

Janie Fricke was the featured female vocalist on the show for the first few seasons before Crystal Gayle joined the show. They were both great singers. Rex Allen, Jr. was also on the show.

Any time I would get a solo in one of the Statler Brothers songs, Harold, the bass singer, would turn to me and say, "Here's Eddie Capps!" or "Here's Jerry Capps!" He intentionally never got my name right. He did it so much that they got mail from people asking if I had a twin brother named Eddie or Jerry!

The Statler Brothers was one of the best shows I've ever worked. It was also one of the best-produced shows, and one of my favorite parts about it was the food! A company called McConnell's was the caterer, and they were the very best.

One week though, the show changed caterers. A woman named Frances was handling the job, and the new caterer brought in fish that had bones still in it. Harold was eating, and when he got some bones in his mouth, he got up and went to Frances and said, "Frances, in the mornin', I either want to read McConnell's name in the obituaries, or I want to see them here catering our food!"

McConnell's was back the next day.

After the show was cancelled, I called Harold and said, "I don't miss you. But I sure miss McConnell's Catering!"

The Statler Brothers show could have lasted forever. Whoever cancelled it made a big mistake. They had such a huge viewing audience. We were all shocked when TNN cancelled it. Of course, TNN itself was also gone only a short time later.

Jimmy Fortune joined the Statler Brothers in 1982, after Lew Dewitt became ill. At that time, they had already had a huge career, but when he came on, that really gave them a second wind. He breathed new life into the group, giving them a whole new career with the hit songs he wrote and the great songs he sang. The new guy ended up being with them 21 years until they retired!

I didn't think the Statlers would ever retire. I thought entertaining was in their blood so much that they would never get out. But since then, Jimmy Fortune has gone on to have a great solo career. He is amazing. I'm wearing a Jimmy Fortune cap as I write this! I am a big fan of Jimmy. He is one of my closest and dearest friends. I was so touched when Jimmy agreed to write the foreword for my book. He may be the nicest man on earth.

Chapter Fourteen

COUNTRY'S FAMILY REUNION

Larry Black came up with the idea for Country's Family Reunion after he saw one of Bill Gaither's Homecoming Gospel Shows. Larry met with Bill and told him he wanted to do something similar using the legends of country music. Bill gave him his blessing to do it "Country Style," and I am so glad he did.

Thanks to Country's Family Reunion, Larry has been able to save a very important part of country music history. He's been able to capture on film the songs, the stories and memories that would have all been lost if it weren't for that show. In addition to that, he's also been able to help so many country artists. He has put those performers back in the spotlight, on national TV.

In some cases, the CFR show has totally resurrected the careers of a few of the artists. They found out that yes, indeed, they still had fans! And their fans were able to find them again, long after radio and other TV shows had forgotten about them.

I have been doing Country's Family Reunion since the first show. Larry had hired Mike Johnson to be the band leader and play steel guitar, and Mike brought me in to play guitar. As we filmed the first show back in 1997, I thought it was magic. We all did. As I listened to the stories all these legendary artists were telling, I turned to one of the other musicians and said, "Man, I ought to be buying a ticket to this!" I just enjoyed it so much.

Bill Anderson is the host of CFR, and he is one of the greatest hosts there has ever been. He is the very best. He has such a gift.

He's hosted the show since it began. Bill was also there during the most embarrassing moment of my entire career. I'll let him give his version, and then I'll tell the rest of the story...

> "Jimmy is such a bedrock for the Country's Family Reunion Band. He is always perfect. Always perfect... except once. And Jean Shepard never let him live it down. It was during one of the early Family Reunions. Jean was singing one of her biggest hits, a song that I wrote called 'Slippin' Away', and there was a modulation change in the middle of the song. Everyone modulated the right way, except Capps! He went out somewhere in left field, and it embarrassed him so bad. He kept begging Larry Black to let them do it over, but Larry insisted, 'No, we are putting it out just like it happened!'
>
> But he took it in good fun. He was able to laugh at himself."
>
> Bill Anderson

What Bill didn't tell you is that, before the show, I asked her, "Jean, on that modulation change, is that a half tone or whole tone?"

She told me one thing, but then I went to Mike Johnson, who was the band leader, and he told me something else. When we did the song, I listened to Jean and played it the way she'd told me... but she was wrong. The rest of the band went one way, and I went another. They went to C-Sharp and I modulated to D, and it was bad. I was so embarrassed!

I asked Larry Black if we could do the song over, but Jeannie Seely started hollering, saying, "Don't touch that! Let it stay in the show."

I said, "That's all I'm going to be remembered for! For the rest of my life, people will remember me for goofing up Jean Shepard's song."

Jean shouted back, "Don't touch it! Leave it the way it is. He deserves it for goofing up my song!"

I begged Larry to let me fix it. But he explained, "No. That's what this show is all about. When stuff like that happens, it is magic."

And he was right.

I was also right when I predicted that I would be remembered for the screw up. I've had dozens of people come up to me since and say, "You are the guy who messed up Jean Shepard's song."

Jean never let me live it down. Years later, any time I would start to play for her, she'd say, "Capps, you think you can play this right?". She liked to kid people she loved. So I always knew she must have loved me a lot!

All the artists are so nice to always compliment the band on Country's Family Reunion. When he assembled the band, Mike Johnson picked some really good players: John Gardner on drums and Les Singer on acoustic guitar. Les and Mike had worked together in Mel Street's band, and here they both wound up working for Bill Anderson, as did Dirk Johnson, the wonderful piano player on the shows. David Smith is on bass, and Hank Singer plays fiddle (Randy Hardison, deceased, originally played drums, Glen Duncan played fiddle, and Billy Linneman played on some of the shows).

They are all a bunch of guys who love traditional music, and we love each other. We are all friends. There is no jealousy among the musicians. Mike picked everyone for their ability, but he also ended up picking a group of musicians that all got along, and we all grew to respect and love each other. We owe it all to Mike for putting together the band.

On most of the shows, they sit me and Les Singer side by side. Many years ago, before I had my goatee and silver hair, Les looked a little like me. Some people even thought we were related, and I would jokingly tell people that he was my "illegitimate son". Les still calls me "Pops" to this day! And since he has aged a little, we now look more like brothers.

Les is a great guitar player. I don't know why I ended up on electric guitar and he ended up playing acoustic. When they did the tribute to Bill Anderson on CFR, I went to Les and told him he should be the one playing electric guitar, since he knew all the songs, but he said he wanted to keep it like it was. He is such a great player. He also plays a good five string banjo. He and all the guys in that band are very respected in Nashville.

Bobby Bare is one of the legendary artists who was part of the first Family Reunions. He has been on many of the different shows over the past twenty years. Bobby is also a member of the Grand Ole Opry, and I'm always honored to play on his Opry spots. I'm also humbled that Bobby told me he wanted to say a few words for my book.

"Jimmy Capps is like rain. He's always been here. I met Jimmy way back in the 60s. He was going on the road with Don Bowman; Don was a comedian, and he sang novelty country songs.

I have yet to meet a person who didn't love Jimmy Capps. Every single time I have ever walked in a room or studio and saw Jimmy, he's always had a huge smile on his face. He just warms your heart when you see him.

We were taping a Family Reunion when I started really paying attention to Jimmy's playing. The more I listened, the more I thought, 'That is the greatest sound I have ever heard come out of an acoustic guitar.'

As we go through life, if we're lucky, we collect lots of friends. But over the years, some of those friends can let you down or disappoint you, for one reason or another, but I have never been disappointed by Jimmy Capps.

The one thing Jimmy and I didn't get to do over the years is fish. I love to fish, but Jimmy was always playing sessions in the studio. He probably works more than anyone else, even today. Everyone knows he's one of the great ones, and they want him to be a part of what they are doing. He is still in demand, and I think staying busy keeps him young.

I loved Chet Atkins with all my heart. But Capps is right next to Chet Atkins in my book. I know it sounds syrupy, but Jimmy is just a great human being, the kind that you love forever."

– Bobby Bare

When I look back at a lot of the Family Reunions, it's so hard to believe that we have lost so many of those legendary stars. So many have passed over the last twenty years. I look at the Reunion shows, and I start counting all the people who have died. These were my heroes. Thank God... and Larry Black, that we got their stories and songs on tape.

While all of the veteran artists always knew how great the Family Reunion shows were, one of the first "current" artists to see how important the shows were was Vince Gill. I was really happy when Vince said he wanted to be on a Family Reunion. He has such respect for his peers, he actually cried during one of our tapings.

During one of the shows, I could see that he was staring at me and my grey goatee and hair. And when Bill Anderson asked him, "What brings you out, Vince?", he pointed at me and said, "I came out to see the Kenny Rogers lookalike."

Vince is such a good person. He has done so much for Nashville. He helps so many charities and causes.

I mentioned that so many artists have seen huge resurgences in their popularity thanks to CFR. Gene Watson was one of those who got a second wind to his career, and now he's as hot or hotter than he's ever been! T. Graham Brown is a regular guest on the Reunions, and T. Graham is amazing. He has such a big, strong voice. He and I have played Branson with just the two of us and Michele singing backup. He can blow the crowd away for an hour-and-a-half show, and they almost always sell out. When I told him I was writing a book, his exact words were, "Well, tell it like it used to be!" He also said he had a few things to add...

> "Jimmy played on my number one song 'Darlene'. He played on that entire album. Can you believe that was more than thirty years ago?! And Jimmy is still playing great today. I've played the Opry 300 times, and he's always there. It's always a joy to be around him. I've never heard him complain or whine about anything. He's always positive. He is such a sweet guy.
>
> We do a show in Branson, and it's just him and me. That's all we need! He does such a great job, and we also goof off during the show. I talk to him and joke around, and the audience gets to see him loosen up a little more than he ever does anywhere else.
>
> Everybody knows Jimmy from TV. He's played on thousands of songs and hundreds of classic hits. But no one outside of Nashville really knew him until he became the Sheriff on the Diner. Now he's got millions of fans.
>
> I love Jimmy very much. If I ever need him for anything, he will be right there, and the same is true going the other way. He knows if he ever needs me, he can pick up the phone and I'll be there."
>
> – T. Graham Brown

Johnny Lee got a huge boost from his appearances on the Family Reunions. And I love Johnny Lee. He is a talented joker. He is so much fun to be around. But you never know what will come out of his mouth.

One night, we went out to eat at a real nice steakhouse in Branson. Johnny and some other friends were there, and in the middle of the meal, he told a really off-color joke. I looked at Michele and started humming "Rock of Ages"!

Later, after we got home, Johnny called us and apologized. He could tell that Michele was uncomfortable. She is Pentecostal, and she practices what she preaches. When he apologized, I thought, "Wow, that is a big man. For Johnny to call us and say he was sorry, it meant a lot." Underneath his big, gruff outside, he is really a big teddy bear.

Moe Bandy also credits the show in helping keep him in the public eye. He is still drawing as many people to his concerts today as he did thirty years ago. Moe is a funny human being. A lot of people don't know that about him. They don't know how funny, and how clever and witty, he is. He is a great entertainer. He's very real and warm to the audience. I love him to pieces. He is a good man. I played on many of his hit songs, and I've produced the last couple of CDs he's done, including a brand new one, and he is singing so great!

Moe also had a lot to do with me doing this book. I really loved the autobiography he did, and I learned so much about him when I read his. I had no idea that he had done all the things he has. Moe and I are great friends, very close, and I could tell by the look in his eyes that he was very serious when he told me, "You need to do your book. You need to tell your story."

Michele had been on me for years to write one, but it took Moe's pushing for me to finally get it done. He promised me that if I did, he would say good things about me in it. I didn't believe him for a minute.

"From the very first time I met Jimmy, from the very beginning, I knew that I just didn't like the guy. As soon as we met, I just didn't like him, and I still don't like him! I'm just jokin', Jimmy!

I met Jimmy in 1974. He was booked to play on some of my first major sessions. Of course, he was a great guitar player, but he was also just a nice guy, and we really hit it off right off the bat. I noticed how nice he was to all of the singers he had to work with. I was scared to death, just starting out in Nashville. But Jimmy helped calm me down a little, and he made me much more comfortable in the studio.

181

Back then, Jimmy was one of the main guys who played on all of my hit songs. Jimmy, Weldon Myrick, Pig Robbins, Charlie McCoy and Bob Moore were some of the greatest musicians in Nashville, and I tried to have them play on as many of my songs as I could.

A few years ago, I asked Jimmy if he would produce a new album for me. We work together in the studio really well. He was the producer on my 'Lucky Me' album, and thanks to Jimmy, we had the Oak Ridge Boys, Ricky Skaggs, and Riders in the Sky all come in and sing with me. Jimmy's the guy who got that done.

'Lucky Me' was a great success, so I asked Jimmy if he would produce another CD for me. We worked on that throughout much of 2018. Jimmy found most of the songs for the album. Since he lives and works in Nashville, he knows most of the writers. He knows a great song when he hears it. I am so excited about that album. It's one of the best albums I have ever done.

My wife and I have gone on a number of the country music cruises with Jimmy and his wife Michele. We all really became close friends on those cruises, and I love to be around them.

Finally, for anyone reading this book... I want everyone to know that every time Jimmy and I go out to eat, I always have to pick up the tab. Jimmy always goes to the restroom right when the waiter is bringing the check!"

– Moe Bandy

Chapter Fifteen

ELECTED SHERIFF

Up until 2009, I had enjoyed a very successful, very busy and very full life. But I had no idea that was my life was about to change forever... thanks to the opening of a little diner. A diner that wasn't even real!

Terry Choate, who booked all the talent for the Country's Family Reunion series, called me and said that Larry Black was going to do a new TV show, and that they were needing someone to do all the music for it. A short time later, I met Larry for lunch at the Pie Wagon in Nashville, where he told me the concept of the show.

Larry had always liked Johnny Carson, and how he did his show. They wouldn't redo anything, even if Johnny or someone else had told a bad joke or screwed up something. Larry said that if he did a show, he wanted to turn the tape on and let it run. He didn't want to stop the show, even if there was a mess up.

Larry told me the show would be set in a make-believe restaurant in a make-believe town. They wanted to have artists drop in to have a cup of coffee, and then while they were there, he'd ask them if they wanted to sing a song or two. I would always be there, and I'd always just happen to have my guitar with me.

Larry said, "We need to give you a title. You can be either 'the Sheriff' or 'the Mayor'."

"I think I look more like a sheriff," I replied, "and I also like doughnuts!"

With that, Larry announced: "So, a sheriff you are!"

Larry also asked me, "Can you live with yourself, knowing that if you make a mistake, you can't fix it?"

I thought about it for a moment, and said, "Boy, that's a tough question." I had never been put in a situation like that. But then I thought about my work all those years on the Opry. When you make a mistake on the Opry, you have to live with it. There's no going back and redoing it, and that goes out live to everyone who's listening on the radio. So I told Larry that I thought I could do it.

When the premiere episode of Larry's Country Diner aired on RFD TV on August 3, 2009, we all thought it would run thirteen weeks and then be gone. But for some reason, that little show just caught on! I think the key to its success was Larry's original idea of turning the tape on and never stopping.

As the show's announcer, Keith Bilbrey, says at the end of every show: "Where the cameras are always rollin' and we don't care!"

And we didn't care. There was never any script for that show. On quite a few episodes during the first season, Keith Bilbrey couldn't even get the name of the show right. He called it "Larry's Country Café". He was just ad-libbing. Everyone was. When Larry messed up an artist's name, it stayed in the show. If Renae the waitress dropped a plate, it stayed, and the audience at home loved it.

As for the guitar player on the show… I did NOT want him to mess up! When I'm on the Diner, I try to look as cool and calm as I can, but most of the time I am a nervous wreck! I always want to do a good job. And since I am by myself most of the time, I know that any little mistake will be very noticeable. I know the artist is depending on me, and knowing the show will be taped live, with no retakes or stopping, there is always a lot of pressure.

We used to tape four Diner shows a day. We would do them one right after another, and I might get just ten or fifteen minutes to learn and run over four or five or songs with each artist. But I guess that's where all my years in the studio paid off. Session players, especially back in the day, always had to pick up the next song very quickly. You had to learn very fast.

I'll talk much more about the show, but first I thought I'd better let the man the Diner itself is named after say a few words:

"When we started planning the show, I told Terry Choate that I couldn't afford a full band. So Terry suggested that we ask Jimmy to be our entire band. He brought a prestige to our show. He had played on everyone's biggest hits. All the artists respected him, and they trusted him to be their full band. They knew they didn't have to bring in their own players, as long as Jimmy was there.

When I gave Jimmy the choice of being either a mayor or a sheriff on the show, if he had chosen mayor, he would have probably worn a dress suit as he played his guitar. If he'd chosen to be a mayor instead of a sheriff, that would have given the show an entirely different feel. I don't think it would have worked as well as it has if he had chosen to be a mayor. He made a wise decision.

The show brought a spotlight onto Jimmy, and he handles that light very well. He doesn't act like he's anyone special. He is so quiet and low-key. But he loves being a musician and making music. He has had to have great stamina to keep up the pace he has for more than sixty years!

Jimmy is such an important part of the show, and he is an important part of our family. We truly are a family. We share lots of meals together, and one thing I've noticed is that he and Michele very rarely sit apart from each other at a table. Usually, everyone sits with different people, but Jimmy and Michele are almost always side-by-side.

I wish I had more personal time with Jimmy. That's one of my regrets. We don't spend a lot of time together off the air. I wish we weren't so busy and we could be closer. But I know that he would be there any time I needed something, and I hope he knows that I am there for him."

– Larry Black

Many people think Larry's Country Diner is a real diner. They really did during the first few seasons of the show. But there was never a real diner. It was a set they had built in a TV studio in Nashville. Now, a decade after the show went onto the air, however, quite a few people are still searching for that real diner. And many even think I am a real sheriff!

One couple drove from Texas for one of our tapings, and the man said, "I'm in law enforcement also."

I said, "Well, I'm not really in law enforcement. I'm not smart enough for that. I'm just a guitar player."

People give me patches from their local sheriff's departments, police departments, etc. I've got about 200 patches that fans have given me, and they each mean a lot to me.

Larry's Country Diner has been so important to all of us. For Keith Bilbrey, it came just after he had been let go from WSM radio. He had been one of WSM's most important announcers for years, but the Diner helped make him more popular than he ever was in radio.

Keith and I worked for many, many years together on the Opry when he was announcing there, so we knew each other pretty well before they ever opened the Diner. I was so honored when Keith traveled to North Carolina to see me inducted into the North Carolina Music Hall of Fame, and I am honored that he would say a few words in this book.

"Larry Black called me and told me that he was putting together a new TV show. I had just been let go by WSM at the time. He told me he couldn't pay me very much, but he would like for me to be the announcer for the show. I said, 'Larry, you're talking to an unemployed man. Sure I will do it!'

I was happy to get the job, but when Larry told me that Jimmy Capps was going to be playing a Sheriff as he played his guitar, I was even more thrilled. I had admired Jimmy's playing for a long time, long before I'd ever met him. When I was a kid, listening to the Grand Ole Opry, I had no idea that I'd ever become best friends with Jimmy Capps. All of the pickers on the Opry were just an elite group of guys.

The cast of Larry's Country Diner is really a family. The biggest thrill of all, for me, was in getting to know Jimmy and growing closer to him than I had ever been before. When we took the show on the road to Branson, Jimmy and Michele shared a condo with me and my wife, Emy Joe. Jimmy and I always sat up late at night, and I'd try to stump him with song requests. We'd be up until two in the morning, and I could never come up with a song he couldn't play.

Also when we roomed together in Branson, Michele had Jimmy on a diet. She'd wanted him to lose weight, and she had bought a bunch of health food for him to eat. Of course, me and my wife had our usual junk food. We divided the cabinets in the kitchen of our condo. Half were ours, and half were Jimmy and Michele's. But a couple nights, I caught Jimmy going through our cabinets, trying to get a late night snack, and he didn't want anything healthy!

I was so glad when Jimmy and Michele got together. They came into each other's lives at the perfect time. I know there's no such thing as a perfect couple, but they are pretty darn close.

Jimmy always plays such tasteful licks. He wasn't a showoff; he does it with such ease and grace, but when he's playing, you have to listen just to hear what he is going to do next. He is always so solid. If someone turns to him and says, "Take it," he acts like that is an order and he takes it.

When he's playing on the Diner, Jimmy is the rock. The artists turn around and throw him any song and he can handle it, and Michele also adds so much to the show with her harmony vocals.

I can't believe we've done the Diner for more than ten years. Since we are such a family, any time any of us are going through a tough time, all the rest of us will go through it with them. They've always been there for me and I've been there for them.

A lot of guitar pickers idolize Jimmy. But he has a hard time taking compliments. He doesn't see himself as anything special. But he has a God-given talent. His talent with a guitar is just unbelievable. You'll never hear him brag about himself in any way, but I think that he truly is one of the greatest guitar players of all time. Jimmy has so many stories about the golden years of country music. He's told me some of them, but I'm looking forward to reading more of them in this book!"

– Keith Bilbrey

The show turned Nadine into a star. It was her first time in show business. Mona Brown is the woman behind the Nadine character. Mona is just a sweet lady and is so talented. She fits the show so good. Some people ask if Nadine is really a man dressed as a woman! I can't figure out why they ask that. She looks every bit female to me!

Off screen, Mona is such a classy, sweet person. She and her husband are just the tops. Her husband is an optometrist, and she is his receptionist. They are people you love to be around, who are always positive about everything.

By the way, Mona's husband is not really named Homer! I asked her if she wanted to say a few words for my book. She said she would, as soon she'd finished putting up the church sign.

"When I found out that Jimmy was going to be on the show, I went on the internet and looked him up. When I read about all the people he had worked with and all the hit songs he had played on, I was in awe of him! When I first met him, I was a little bit shy, because I knew what an important person he was in country music's history.

But when I got to know Jimmy, he became like my big brother. He is one of the most humble, quiet, gentle, even-keeled guys I have ever known. I love his laugh. He has such a great sense of humor. I have never heard Jimmy say one bad word about anyone. When he asked me to share some of my memories here, I honestly tried to think of something bad to say. I really did! And I could not think of one bad thing that he ever said or did.

When we started taking the show to Branson, we all traveled together in a big tour bus, and that's when I really got to know Jimmy and Michele. Those trips were quite an experience, and so much fun. Jimmy, Keith Bilbrey and his wife Emy Joe were all on those C-Pap machines, and they were running all night. It sounded like a Darth Vader convention.

Jimmy and Michele shared a condo in Branson with Keith and his wife, and Jimmy and Keith would stay up all night talking and having fun. They'd be going to bed at about the time the rest of us were getting ready for breakfast. I told them, 'You guys have seen dawn more times than Tony Orlando ever did!'

You can't be around somebody for more than ten years, and not see who they really are, especially when you travel with them. We all got to know Jimmy so well. The Diner cast really is a family. We miss each other when we're not taping.

As a musician, Jimmy is so dedicated and committed. When we're in-between taping shows for the Diner, while the rest of us are talking, relaxing, having fun and eating, Jimmy is always practicing his songs for the next show and going over everything with the artist.

Jimmy and Michele are so committed to each other. When we all go out to eat, Michele always says, 'I have to sit by Jimmy.' They want to be close all the time.

Of course, Nadine is known as 'The Church Lady', but when I look at Jimmy, I can see his faith. He doesn't have to talk about his faith. You can see it in his eyes, and in the way he acts. I told him that Nadine put up two church signs just for him. One said, 'Silence and smiles are two powerful tools. A smile is a way to solve problems. Silence is a way to avoid them.' And the other reads: 'If you're not doing what you love, you're wasting your time.'

Jimmy is an amazing man. He has had a life very well-lived. He is just a great guy. He is one of my favorites. God bless Jimmy Capps, because he sure has blessed us."

— Mona Brown/Nadine

On the Diner, Renae the Waitress is always there to serve everyone and keep Larry straight and on track. Off the show, Renae has also been Larry's right hand person for his company for many years. Renae always has a huge smile for everyone she meets. She makes you feel so good the moment she walks into the room. Hopefully I'll feel good after I read what she wrote about her favorite guitar-playing Sheriff!

"I met Jimmy when we started producing the Country's Family Reunion shows, but I didn't become close friends with him until we started doing the Diner. I look back at some of those first Reunion shows, and he looks totally different today. He is much more handsome now than he was twenty years ago. He's got his distinguished look down.

Jimmy is so quiet and shy. I'll say, 'Jimmy, there are some people out front who want your autograph,' and he'll ask, 'Me? They want my autograph?' He really doesn't realize how loved he is. He says he can't understand why people want to get their photo with him. He's just so humble.

Jimmy is very laidback. But he is also a lot funnier than most people might think, and he has so many great stories of country music's golden age. He has played for everybody. My husband Phil was a gospel music producer, and he hired Jimmy to play on a lot of sessions. Phil knew Jimmy a lot better than I did when we first started the Diner. I like to listen to them talk about their time in the recording studio.

You can tell that he and Michele love each other so much. We get a lot of questions from people wondering if Michele is his wife or his daughter! She has been very good for him. She always makes sure he puts his badge on the correct side of his shirt!

When we were planning the show, I went out and bought him a Sheriff's shirt. I'd gone to a place that sold clothes and uniforms for police and sheriffs' departments, bought the badge and a few shirts, and then when he put his shirt on for the first time, he asked, 'Where do I put the badge?'

We probably could not do the show without Jimmy. Our audience just loves him. Even though he doesn't talk very much on the show, the viewers can still feel his sweetness. Of course, all of us on the show love him so much. We have all really become a true family."

— Renae Johnson/Renae the Waitress

Renae mentioned that her husband Phil knew me long before the Diner ever went on the air. And Phil is the official photographer for the show; he took all of the Diner photos that you see in this book. But he is also a very successful record producer. Phil has hired me for a lot of recording sessions over the years. You might be surprised when he tells you about one of those first sessions.

"Of course Jimmy Capps is known for all of his country music work, but I actually hired Jimmy to play acoustic guitar on a Jimmy Swaggart gospel album. I was only 24 years old then when we first met, and now I'm 70! So Jimmy and I have known each other for a very long time.

I was producing Christian albums back then, and I'd hire Jimmy to play on the Rambos, the Lanny Wolfe Trio, and the Hemphills albums. Jimmy had made his reputation playing country music, but I found out very quickly that he could also play Christian music. He was quite versatile, and he has used that versatility to great effect on the Diner. It's also known for country music, but we also have bluegrass and Christian artists.

When I found out that he was going to be a part of the Diner, I thought that was just the absolute, most perfect choice they could have made. Terry Choate made the perfect call when he recommended Jimmy for the job. Jimmy is always a total professional. He always makes sure that he is as prepared as he can be, and he is just the nicest guy.

I co-produced Jimmy's 'In Time for Dinner' CD, and it was just incredible to be able to work with someone who has that much talent, ability and experience. He was always so open and willing to try anything I came up with. He'd listen to anything I suggested.

I think one thing that viewers of the Diner might be surprised at is how funny Jimmy is. He really loves to laugh. When we go to Branson, we like to eat at Landry's, and we both love their Cedar Plank Salmon. When they see us walk in, they know to get us a corner booth way in the back, so that we don't bother everyone else - because our meal always includes lots of loud laughter, as Jimmy tells one funny story after another.

One of the best compliments I've ever heard an artist give Jimmy came from Vince Gill, when we were taping the Songwriters Family Reunion. Vince and Jimmy were alone in the studio during a lunch break. I was a little ways off, taking pictures of the set, when I heard Vince say, 'Jimmy, I don't think you'll have any problem with my song. It's just a sweet, simple little ditty.'

And Jimmy said, 'Well, by the time I get through playing it, it might not be so sweet.'

Vince laughed, 'Yeah, you suck!'

One thing that people overlook with Jimmy is, he is a very good parent. He is a great dad. His sons love their dad, and he loves them. A lot of musicians of Jimmy's caliber have to spend so much time away from their family, and many of their children and wives will begin to resent them or feel that they are shortchanging them. But Jimmy's boys both know that their dad loves them.

Jimmy is admired by everybody. Every musician and every artist admires him. He is just a good guy. He is one of my favorite people in the world."

– Phil Johnson

My wife Michele also got involved on the show. She wasn't an official cast member, but since she was always on the set with me, she just started singing some harmony with a few of the artists. Then they let her sing a solo, and they got a lot of positive response from that, so she just became a part of the TV family.

One of the highlights of each year is the Larry's Country Diner and Country's Family Reunion Cruise. Before those started, I had only cruised one time. I enjoy the LCD cruises, even though it's a lot of work. I do the Family Reunion show, and I also do the Diner shows, and then we do autograph sessions, and those often last longer than the shows do.

The cruises are a lot of work, but the fans are so loyal to that show. Larry books artists who know how to mingle with the fans. They don't go to their room and hide, and I think that is important. All of the artists and musicians are regular folks; we just happen to make a livin' playing music. And I think that's a big reason the cruises are such a success. The entertainers don't hide out in their rooms, away from the fans.

Mark Wills is one of my favorite Diner guests. Mark has also gone on many of our Diner cruises with us. We really became great friends during those cruises. I'm pretty sure Mark thinks we're even more than friends, since he almost always greets me with a big kiss! I never knew why he did that, so I thought this would be a good time to ask him.

"I don't know where or why it started, but one night, we were on the Larry's Country Diner cruise and everyone was getting their fancy photos taken. All the couples were in their dress clothes, posing for the ship photographer. But when Jimmy and Michele walked over near me, I grabbed Jimmy and we had our photo taken like we were a couple! I bought two 8x10s of it! After we had posed, I gave him a big kiss on the cheek. And now whenever we see other, I think Jimmy kind of expects a kiss. I think he likes it.

I've played the Grand Ole Opry for twenty years. I knew Jimmy was there when I started, but I had no idea he had started there forty years earlier! I really didn't know about his history and how important he was.

But then I found out he had played on almost every country record I was listening to as I grew up. Now, when I go back and listen to "The Gambler" and some of those great Kenny Rogers songs, I can always pick out Jimmy's acoustic guitar.

My relationship with Jimmy is a little bit different than most, because he has never played on any of my records. So we have more of a friendship than a working relationship. I know that if I ever need anything, I can call Jimmy. He is always willing to help anyone with anything. He answers any guitar questions from everyone, and he shares his knowledge and experience.

I also love Michele. She is a doll, and Jimmy has always been as sweet as he can be. I've never heard him say a bad word about anybody. There are very few people in the world as wonderful as Jimmy Capps. I think the world of him."

– Mark Wills

One of the first times I realized how very popular the show was getting came when Michele and I were out at a Cracker Barrel near Houston. After we had eaten, we went to the gift shop, and I was looking at the DVDs there.

This man came walking up to me and said, "Aren't you the sheriff?"

I said, "I might be."

"I watch the Diner on RFD TV," he replied, "and you look just like the Sheriff."

I said: "Yes, you got me."

A short time later, I called Earl Dunn Pontiac in Nashville, asking for the service manager, and when he got on the phone, I said, "I would like to get my oil changed."

When he asked me my name, I said, "Jimmy Capps," and he asked, "The Sheriff?!"

The Opry gives tours backstage before and after the show, and Michele and I are usually among the last people to leave. When the backstage tours go by us in the band room, there are always a half dozen people or more who will leave the tour and come talk to me and Michele. They always say, "Hey Sheriff!"

It knocks me out that they are willing to lose their place on the tour just to come say hi to us. That's a high compliment.

I should be the poster boy for the power of TV. After playing on hit songs, after all the legendary artists I've recorded with; after traveling the country, working road shows with big stars; and after sixty years on the Grand Ole Opry... I am known as The Sheriff. All because of a little TV show. If you are on a successful TV show, more people see you in one week than have ever seen you through your entire career.

I sometimes wonder what my life would be like, if I had not said "yes" to Larry Black when he asked me to be a part of Larry's Country Diner and Country's Family Reunion. I know I would have a lot more free time today. But I wouldn't be having near as much fun.

Chapter Sixteen

A GIFT FROM CHET

Merle Travis was a huge hero of mine. He invented the thumb style guitar playing. He was such a nice guy, and was also extremely intelligent. In 1966, I drew Merle Travis' name in a Christmas gift exchange. That entire week of Christmas, Merle was a guest on the Eddie Hill TV show on Channel 5, so we included him as the cast drew names from a hat, and I happened to get his name.

I had no idea what to buy Merle, but I knew that he was very close friends with Grandpa Jones. Those two were almost like brothers. So I went to Grandpa and asked him what I should buy, and he told me, "Give him a screwdriver. He's queer for screwdrivers! He can't go in a hardware store without buying one. He loves any kind of screwdriver."

So I bought Merle a little screwdriver that he could adjust his guitar with. When he opened his gift, he loved it. Nine years later, in 1975, Merle was booked to play a guest spot on the Opry. He was in his dressing room, and as I walked by, he hollered, "Hey Jimmy! Come here."

When I stepped into his room, he opened up a pocket in his guitar case, and pulled out the little screwdriver that I had bought him in 1966! He had kept that screwdriver, and he always remembered that I had given it to him.

Merle never forgot that little gift I gave him, and I will always remember a gift I received from another one of my guitar heroes...

Every person who has ever picked up a guitar has dreamed of playing like Chet Atkins. Me included. Like everyone else, I was never in Chet's league. We all tried to learn from and copy Chet. But when he was starting out, he had no one to listen to. He had no one to emulate. He did hear Merle Travis playing in Cincinnati, but other than that, Chet was the creator of everything. He was the creator of his sound.

Chet had such a smooth touch. The first thing I noticed about his playing was the tone of his guitar. It just flowed like honey. He played directly from the heart, and it was a gift that came from God.

The few times that I worked with him when he was a producer, I noticed that he was in total control of what was going on. He wasn't power hungry, though. He never had the attitude that he was the boss and that everyone had to do what he said. He gave you all the freedom in the world.

It seemed like Chet never quit learning and creating stuff, and he learned from anyone. Hopefully he noticed something that I did. I hope that he liked something from my playing. I sure stole a lot from him that I will never be able to pay back!

Every time I hear Chet play on a CD or record, it takes me back to when I was just a kid and I was hearing that sound for the first time. Chet Atkins was, and always will be, my hero. This is the story of a special gift that my hero gave me.

Bob Whitaker was the manager of the Grand Ole Opry. The Opry was going to do a special Christmas show. Chet was scheduled to be on the show, and Bob asked me to meet with Chet to see what songs he wanted to do.

When I got to Chet's, he was in the kitchen of his office, sitting at a 1950s chrome dinette table, and playing his guitar, always practicing. I told him that we needed to make a chord chart for what he wanted to play with the Opry band.

Since he was holding his guitar, he told me he would just play me what he had in mind, and I could write it all out as he played. I told him that I didn't bring a pencil or paper, and Chet reached up over his desk and pulled out a pencil. He was so excited, as he told me, "These are the best chart-making pencils I've ever seen! They write real dark with a soft lead."

I asked him where he got them, and he said, "Bergen White gave me a whole gross of these pencils." Bergen is a great musical arranger.

Then Chet gave me the pencil he had been using for quite a while. It had been sharpened down to the point where it was only about two inches long. I used it to write down his chart, and when we had finished, I handed the pencil back to him. We visited a little more, and then finally I said, "Chet, I guess I need to mosey on."

Very excitedly, he said back, "Wait a minute! I have a gift for you!"

My mind started racing. I just knew that my guitar hero was going to give me an amazing gift! It was probably the new Bear Family box set, with his complete recordings. Or maybe he was going to present me with one of his very own old gut string guitars that he had stopped playing. No matter what it was, I knew it was going to be good!

Then I watched Chet reach up into the big gross of pencils. He said, "Man, I want to give you one of these pencils."

I said, "Chet that is great." (I was already thinking, "Well, it's no Chet Atkins guitar, but I guess it's the thought that counts!")

He was still holding the used pencil I had been writing his chart out with. And when he started to hand me the new pencil, instead he ended up giving me the old, short one. As I looked at this used pencil, I again said, "Chet this is great. Thank you so much." Then I said, "I wonder where Bergen got these pencils?"

Chet answered, "The phone number for the company is on it."

I held out my short, used up pencil, and said, "Not on mine."

"You S.O.B. Give me that pencil back!"

"No way," I said. "This is too great of a story."

I still have that pencil today.

Since I didn't get a guitar from Chet that day, I guess this would be a good place to talk about some of the guitars I do have.

I own about 120 guitars right now, and I can tell you exactly how many I owned when I started out… one!

I have had some great guitars, though, that I was unable to keep. I had a 1953 Fender Telecaster that would be worth $40,000 today! But the guy I was working with at the time told me, "That is just a board. You need to get a real guitar if you're gonna work for me."

But I loved that guitar. My dad and I paid $125 for it and the case. We bought it at E.R. Pool Music in Raleigh, North Carolina. The store got the franchise for Fender because of me ordering that guitar.

When I was a kid, I had a cousin named Roy Cook who lived in Oregon. He had written a letter to his mom in North Carolina, and I read the letter. It said, "I traded my amp for a Fender." I thought he was talking about a fender for his car! I had never heard of the Fender company. But when I talked to him, he told me that they had a new amp. He said it was great, and that I should get one when I could. So I ordered an amp when I ordered my Fender guitar. I loved them both, but the guys I worked for wanted me to get a different guitar. They let me keep the amp, but I ordered an ES-5 Gibson, a big-bodied guitar.

My favorite guitar to play today is a hybrid. I was doing the Statler Brothers TV show, and Chuck Davis, one of the engineers, came to me and said, "Jimmy, you have to see this guitar that the Peavey company is making now. They are $125!" (Artist price.)

He got out his guitar and said, "Why don't you play it on the show and see what you think about it?"

As soon as I'd played it the first time, I told him, "You ain't gettin' this guitar back!"

I bought it from him right then and there. I played it for two years, and the neck went bad on it. I called up Peavey to buy a new neck, and they told me they didn't sell parts.

So I went over to Fender, and told them my problem. I loved the guitar, and I wanted to keep it, but it needed a new neck. They said, "The neck is the only place the guitar name is. We'd be glad to put a Fender neck on your guitar!"

I ordered an Eric Clapton neck, and now I call it my "Peaver" guitar, because the body and all the electronics are Peavey, but the neck is a Fender. That's the red guitar that you always see me playing on all the Country's Family Reunion shows. I've played it on everything since the 90s. It's my favorite guitar, and it cost me $125!

Another of my favorite guitars was a Gibson ES-335. I got it when I came out of the service. It was THE guitar, at the time. Everybody who played on sessions used the 335. I paid $200 for it, brand new. It was one of Gibson's greatest guitars. It was just perfect. But it was stolen one night, backstage at the Opry.

I was working at the Ryman Auditorium, and I always sat my guitar back behind the backdrop. Everyone would open their guitar cases and leave them sitting on the floor during the Opry. During intermission, the band all went over to Tootsies, which was right across the alley from the Ryman. We'd all go there to have a cool one.

But when I came back, my guitar was gone. I said, "OK guys, who's got my guitar?" Everybody said they hadn't seen it. I kept looking for it, and I got more and more upset as the time for us to get back on stage got closer.

I said, "Man, if someone's joking with me, you need to stop it." I thought that Weldon Myrick or Hal Rugg had taken it as a joke. But as the second half of the Opry began, and I still didn't have a guitar, I got more and more frantic.

I had to borrow someone else's guitar to finish the night. I knew none of my musician friends would have done that to me, and I was right. During our break, a guy had gotten backstage and stolen my guitar. He just left the empty case there. I didn't find out the entire truth until more than ten years later.

I was getting an eye exam, and the nurse said, "Can I tell you something?"

I said, "Yeah."

She continued, "My husband stole your guitar, and he sold it to buy drugs." I sure wish I had that guitar today. I never could find one to replace it.

That was one of three thefts I've had occur in my career. The first one happened on a tour I was on with the Louvin Brothers in 1959. We were at the Flame Club in Minneapolis, Minnesota when someone stole my 6120 Gretsch. It was a Chet Atkins model. For some stupid reason, when I'd ordered the guitar, I'd had them remove Chet's name from the pick guard, and my first name in its place. Of course, that destroyed a lot of its value, but maybe whoever stole it was named Jimmy! Either that, or they had to take the pick guard off.

One of the worst thefts happened when I was playing on a Merle Haggard session in Nashville. It was for Merle's Christmas album, and we were at the Quonset Hut on 16th Avenue. I had a little Subaru station wagon, which I'd had tinted the windows so that no one could see inside, because I always had it loaded up with instruments.

After I had been in the studio all afternoon though, I came out to my car and every single instrument I had in there was gone.

Someone had stolen my 1938 Gibson L 5 that I had bought from Ray Edenton.

The Gallagher Guitar Company had built me a guitar. It was stolen, too.

They took a 6 string tic-tac bass. It would be a collector's item today.

I called the cops and reported it, and they said there was no way I would ever get them back. But today, it's easier to find instruments that are stolen. You can notify all the pawn shops immediately, and with the internet, people can keep an eye out for your stolen stuff a lot better. Today, if someone tried to sell a 6120 Gretsch that had the name "Jimmy" on the pickguard, you'd probably hear about it.

I never got those stolen guitars back... but I did get a very special replacement. The Gretsch company was doing a tribute to Chet Atkins, and during that, Michele started talking to Joe Carducci from the company. She told him about my Gretsch being stolen, and a short time later, the company gave me a brand new Chet Atkins model 6120. It was a total surprise.

I also received a very special guitar from my dear friend, Gene Watson. He had it made by Summey Guitars just for me. The framework, body and neck are all hand-made. Gene designed all the electronics configuration, and the GW guitar gives you the sound of four or five different guitars. It can be an acoustic guitar. It can also sound like a Gibson 335, or it will sound like a Fender Stratocaster. It will do so many things.

I was so honored when Gene presented that guitar to me on one of the Country's Family Reunion TV shows. I'm also honored that Gene wanted to say a few words in my book...

> "I've known Jimmy Capps just about as long as I have been coming to Nashville. It's like we grew up together. He played on so many of my songs. He was on a whole lot of those hits that I had. If you go through my albums and look at the credits, you will see his name on so many of them. He was always a great player, and it was always a great privilege to have him working on my sessions.
>
> I've also worked with Jimmy for so many years on the Grand Ole Opry. Even when I've got my own band with me, I still get Jimmy to sit in with us to play acoustic guitar. He is such a fantastic guitar player. Of course, he is a member of the Musician's Hall of Fame, and that right there says it all.
>
> Jimmy is like a clock that keeps perfect time. He is the exact same, every time you see him. He always asks me what I'm driving. We always talk about the latest car or truck that I've bought, and we call each other quite often. We'll call and not even talk about music at all. We are just the best of friends.
>
> It would be impossible to say just how much Jimmy Capps has meant to me and to my music. He is just a large part of it. I think the world of Jimmy, not only as a musician, but I love him as a person. He is one of the nicest, kindest people I've ever known. His wife, Michele, is the same way. They are just good people. I love them."
>
> – Gene Watson

There is one guitar in our house that has more sentimental value than all the others. It actually belongs to Michele. It's a J 45 Gibson, and it was Michele's dad's guitar. He paid $125 when he bought it new in 1956, and that included the case. He paid ten dollars a month until he'd gotten it all paid off.

Over the years, that guitar meant so much to Michele's family. It was the first guitar she ever heard, and it was the first one she ever held. She had always wanted it, and she had planned to keep the guitar forever.

But five years ago, her dad sold it without telling anybody. Her mom called her and said, "Michele, I just thought I ought to tell you that your dad sold the guitar." When she found out he had sold it, she just cried and cried.

Michele asked her dad why he sold it, and he told her, "Your mom wanted a screened-in back porch on our house. We'll enjoy that back porch every day. I only took that old guitar out of its case two or three times a year." Michele and I would have been happy to help them pay for a porch, but he had too much pride to ask us for any money.

A couple nights later, when we went to the Opry, Vince Gill was sitting backstage playing an old Gibson. Michele walked over to him, and told him how her dad had sold his Gibson guitar. Vince was as heartbroken as Michele was. He said, "You have got to get that guitar back."

She told him that she had just gotten the phone number of the man who'd bought it, and Vince said, "If you tell him how important that guitar is to you and your family, I bet he will sell it back to you. But if he won't, then tell him that I will personally help him find another guitar just like that one."

She called the man the next day, and she just poured out her heart to him. She told him the offer that Vince Gill had made to help him get another guitar. Michele must have talked for ten minutes without even taking a breath. And when she finally let him say something, the man said, "I had no idea that it meant so much to your family. I will be glad to sell the guitar back to you for exactly what I paid for it."

Three months later, we went to her parents' home, and as soon as we got there, her dad started showing off his new porch. He bragged, "Can you believe what my old guitar bought? Look at this beautiful porch."

Then we got the guitar out of our truck. I had put it in one of my gig bags. When her dad unzipped that bag and pulled out that guitar, he was in total shock. He had to sit down, and he was just speechless! As he began strumming on it, he kept saying over and over, "This is MY guitar!" Everyone was crying.

Michele told her dad, "There is one catch: you can play it anytime you want to, but you've got to come to my house to play it." She will have it the rest of her life.

Chapter Seventeen

THE FUTURE OF COUNTRY…
AND OF JIMMY

I often get asked to compare today's artists with those from the 60s and 70s. I will say, there are some new artists who are pretty good. But I really don't think I'll be seeing the next George Jones, Waylon Jennings or Merle Haggard walk in any time soon.

Today's young musicians have access to so much great technology and equipment. Now, you don't have to be the greatest player or singer in the world. You can make it sound good thanks to Autotune and the technology. That makes it hard for the fans to know who is real. But those who are not real will not last.

But I love Chris Janson. Chris is very unique. He's great. You heard from him earlier in the book. I'm also a big fan of the Malpass Brothers. I was the producer on Chris' first CD. I played all the guitars on it, and led the sessions. Chris Malpass sang so good. He was just a young boy. Taylor was real little, and hadn't even started playing and singing.

The Malpass Brothers are different from anyone else that's out there today, but they are reminiscent of the old traditional country acts like the Louvin Brothers and Wilburn Brothers. I respect the Malpass Brothers so much for being true to what they are. They are not phony in any way. They are great people, and their mom and dad are so great. I can't say enough about them. But enough about them… let's see what they have to say about me!

"I was nine years old the first time I met Jimmy! I came to Nashville with Adam Barber to record an album. Jimmy's hometown of Benson is just 45 minutes from where we're from, so he was always a hero around North Carolina. But he would have been our hero no matter where he was from.

Jimmy was going to produce the album for me. I can't even imagine trying to produce a nine-year-old kid, but that's what he did! The first song I recorded with him was one called 'Peach Pickin' Time in Georgia'. I was so young and had never been in a studio before, and Jimmy was so kind to me.

When I came out to listen to the song, Jimmy asked me what I thought, and I said, 'I think I can do it better.'

He said, 'Well, let's try it again.'

I'm sure it was pretty bad, but he didn't say that. He was so gentle. He is a kind soul. They don't make people like him every day.

We are the world's biggest fans of the Louvin Brothers. Jimmy really helped shaped their career. He played on the Louvins song 'How's the World Treatin' You', and when he took over from Paul Yandell, it brought a whole new, fresh sound to the Louvins. Jimmy was the perfect fit for the Louvin Brothers. His playing fit their singing style perfectly, and they would not have been successful as they were without Jimmy.

The first time we played Larry's Country Diner, it was just magic. It was so natural playing with Jimmy. He just knew exactly what to do. If we could work with Jimmy all the time, we would. He truly is a legend."

— Christopher Malpass

"Chris was nine when he went into the studio with Jimmy, but I was so young that I wasn't even singing or playing yet. I was just a little boy. But I was there watching, and during the breaks, Jimmy sat with me in the lounge. He talked to me all day, and I was just in awe of him.

Jimmy is my biggest hero. Ever since I started playing guitar, I wanted to be Jimmy Capps. When I saw him play a Gretsch guitar, I bought one just like he had.

When we grew up, Chris and I ended up touring with Merle Haggard for seven years. We were very close to Merle. When Jimmy mentioned that he would like to say hi to him, I told Merle, and Merle was so excited! He asked, 'He wants to meet with me? Jimmy Capps is one of the greatest guitar players of all time.'

Everybody always asks me what Jimmy Capps is like. I tell them that he is one of the most genuine people I've ever known. He is a good, good man. I love him like a brother."

– Taylor Malpass

Next year, I will be producing a new album with the Malpass Brothers. I really think that they have the potential to be huge stars. They are so unique. No one else today is doing what they do.

Another one of my very favorite people is Mandy Barnett. She's still waiting for her first huge hit, but I can honestly say that I would put her talent and her voice up against any other female singer who's making music today.

I played behind Mandy at Jack Greene's service. It was a moving ceremony. Jack was such a friend to everyone, all of the artists and musicians. I have known Mandy almost her entire life, and my book wouldn't have been complete without me giving her a chance to tell you about our first meeting.

"I've known Jimmy Capps for over thirty years! Billy Strange produced a session for me at a studio in Brentwood, outside of Nashville. Tom T. Hall used to own the studio. I met Jimmy for the first time when he played on that session. Believe it or not, I was just 12 years old! I'm sure Jimmy was really excited as he played behind a 12-year-old girl. I say that very sarcastically. But he treated me like I was the biggest star in Nashville.

I worked with Jimmy again when I was 18. I had gotten signed by Asylum Records, and I really started to get know him when I was in my early twenties, when he began working on most of my sessions.

I consider Jimmy to me one of my dearest friends. He and Michele are two of the closest friends I've ever had in my life. Personally and professionally, I value them so much. Jimmy is kind and he's helpful in any way that he possibly can be. He was there for me when I sang at Don Gibson's funeral. Jimmy played behind me. It was such an honor for me, and I will never forget it.

Jimmy's level of professionalism is unlike anyone else I've ever met. He and Harold Bradley are similar in that way. They take every event, every session and every appearance very seriously. It doesn't matter if they are working with a superstar, or working with a 12-year-old girl who's never been to Nashville before.

Every time I play the Opry, Jimmy calls me a few days before and asks what I'm going to sing. He likes to practice everything so that he can do a great job. He would do a great job anyway - even if he phoned it in, he would still play better than anyone else could. But he always knows the material. He has gone over it at home, and he is just so reliable.

On the very rare occasion that he can't be at the Opry when I'm there, he will call and tell me how sorry he is. I feel so honored, and I'm very touched and flattered that he cares so much about me.

Here's a funny Jimmy story for you. Michele is always trying to get Jimmy to eat healthier. She doesn't want him to eat stuff that's bad for him. One day, my phone rang, and I saw that it was Michele. But when I picked it up, I could tell that she had rang me by mistake, butt-dialed me. I could tell that they were at a restaurant, and I heard her say, 'Now Jimmy, you don't need to be eatin' that! Your blood pressure and cholesterol will be bad.'

I knew Jimmy had a mouth full of something, as he said 'It's OK.' She just kept on him, but he just kept eating!

I felt kind of guilty sitting there listening, but I couldn't hang up. It was so entertaining! It went on for about five minutes. I used to go with them to Lorrie Morgan's hot chicken place, and Jimmy would always order the Atomic Chicken. It was so hot. He would just sit there and sweat as he ate that chicken.

The people who watch the Diner on TV can see how supremely talented Jimmy is. His style of rhythm guitar playing is very rare these days. People don't play like that anymore. I know so many players, and they don't know how to play like Jimmy does; and even if they know how, their wrists give out. I've taken some guys to the Opry and told them, 'You need to watch this man play rhythm guitar and he'll show you how it's done.' You don't see many of the younger generation play that way, because they can't.

Jimmy has influenced so many guitar players over the years. But he is so humble. He will not brag on himself. He is one of the most sweet, wonderful and endearing souls that I have ever known in my life. He really is."

Mandy Barnett

Jimmy Wayne is another young artist who I really love. Jimmy is known for hits like "Stay Gone" and "I Love You This Much". When I found out that he was another Jimmy from North Carolina, I wanted to cheer him on.

Jimmy recently wrote a children's book, and I was so surprised when he mentioned me in it! When I told him that I was now writing my autobiography, he said that he would like to explain why he included me in his book.

"When I was a kid, we didn't have anything. My mom was in and out of prison, and my dad was gone. I had a miserable life as a child. There was a lot of drugs, and a lot of abuse and violence. So listening to music was my escape from reality. The songs that Jimmy Capps played on brought me some of the only joy I had. It sounds funny for a kid to be listening to "The Gambler", but I can tell you exactly where I was when I listened to it. I loved "Elvira" and "Sleepin' Single in a Double Bed", and Jimmy played on all of those!

I don't have many photos from my childhood. Growing up in foster care, we weren't allowed to have a lot of photos taken. But when I hear songs from my childhood, they create images in my mind, and Jimmy played on so many of those songs. He was a part of my childhood through his music. My childhood photos are actually mental images that I put to those songs.

Jimmy is a North Carolina native, and so am I. He has always been very nice to me. I always like to watch him backstage at the Opry, and I saw very quickly that he was very nice to everybody.

I wrote a children's book called 'Ruby the Foster Dog', and I put Jimmy in it. I wanted kids to understand about foster care, and the story is about a dog that I adopted. In the book, I take my dog Ruby to the Opry, and I say, "Back there is Mr. Capps." Then Jimmy winks at Ruby. Jimmy had that much of a positive impact on me. He deserved to be in my book, and I'm so honored to be in his!"

– Jimmy Wayne

People ask me if there are any guitar players today who I really like or admire. There are many! But the one who is at the top of my list is Doyle Dykes. He plays so good. He was with

Grandpa Jones, but then Doyle became a pastor. He still spreads the gospel, but he uses his guitar to do it. The way he plays is like listening to a sermon on the guitar. He has the gift of being able to preach through his instrument.

Doyle really touches me when he plays. With one lone acoustic guitar, he can capture the entire audience at the Opry House. They are just spellbound as he plays.

When he started doing solo albums, Doyle asked me to come in and play on one. He told me that he had a Gibson archtop F-hole guitar. It's from the 1930s, and he asked me to play that guitar on a few of the songs. Once I'd played it, I told Doyle that I wanted to use it on the rest of the session.

At the end of the night, as I was loading my gear, Doyle came out to my car and said, "You forgot a guitar."

I counted my guitars and I said, "No, it must belong to someone else."

Doyle said, "No - I think it belongs to you." And he gave me that wonderful guitar. I still tear up when I think about that amazing gift.

Doyle does guest spots on the Opry as a solo artist, and he blows me away. I went to Terry Choate, who books "Larry's Country Diner", and asked if he would book Doyle for the show. I knew the audience would love him... and they did. Here's Doyle's version of how our friendship began.

"I met Jimmy in 1975, when I went to work with Grandpa Jones. Of course Grandpa played the Opry all the time, so I was able to get to know Jimmy during that time.

Jimmy was part of the iconic trio of Opry players - Spider Wilson and Leon Rhodes were also there. Those were the guys. Each one of those guys had a command. But Jimmy had such a sweetness to his playing. It was different from the other guys, but when you put all three of them on stage at the same time, they were better than a dozen of the other best players all put together.

You can't say 'Jimmy Capps' without getting a smile on your face. He has a very special personality and warmth about him. There is a spiritual side to Jimmy that many don't know about. He has such a heart. I have seen him with tears rolling down his cheeks as he plays his guitar on the Opry. He is easily moved, and he's a big enough man that he's not afraid to show that.

There have been a number of times when I've played a spiritual song on the Opry. I would play 'How Great Thou Art', 'The Lord's Prayer', or 'What a Friend We Have in Jesus'. I'd look back, and Jimmy would be sitting there behind me with tears in his eyes.

I've known him for 40 years. I have such a great respect for him. He has played with everybody, and he has such a knowledge of country music.

I never thought I'd get to meet and get to know anybody like Jimmy Capps. But once I did, he just made me feel like I was part of his family. He not only made me feel welcome, but he also made me feel that the music I made was important. He gave me more support and encouragement than anyone else on the Opry. When you are a guitar player, and you're going up on that Opry stage for the first time, or for the fiftieth time, you need all the encouragement and positive thoughts that you can get. He really made me feel like I belonged there.

I was very blessed that I met Jimmy at just the right moment, when I was needing the encouragement that he gave me. I needed someone of his stature telling me that I was good enough to be on that Opry stage. He always made me feel so special.

Jimmy always loved my daughter Haley, and when she got married, Jimmy came and played at her wedding. He wouldn't take any money for it. I will never forget him doing that for my daughter.

Jimmy played on a CD I did called 'Country Fried Pickin''. I wrote a song for it called 'Three Little Miracles', about a friend of mine who had triplets. I wrote the song with Duane Eddy in mind, and I wanted Duane to play on it. But I knew that if I was really going to get Duane's attention, I needed to find somebody who would make it a pleasure for him to go into the studio and work with. When I told him that Jimmy Capps was also on the session, that was all I needed to say! Dave Pomeroy and Paul Franklin were also on the session.

As a guitar player in Nashville, Jimmy has done more than I will ever do. I don't know anyone else who has even come close to doing what he has done. Of course he is a legendary musician, but as a person, he has a very tender heart. I just love him. He is a very special guy."

Doyle Dykes

I'm not in Doyle's league, but I have recorded a few instrumental CDs in recent years. I went for years and didn't record anything on my own, but I finally realized that I needed to get some of that music down. My son Mark was an engineer at The Soundshop, and he volunteered to work in the studio with me for free. Mike Bradley was the owner of the studio, and he let us record there for practically nothing.

We did an album called "Jimmy Capps - His Guitars & Old Friends Making New Memories", and that CD featured so many of my friends, including Jeannie Seely, The Carol Lee Singers, Steve Wariner, The Osborne Brothers, Charlie Louvin, Stu Phillips, Porter Wagoner, Billy Walker, George Hamilton IV, Darrell McCall, Ray Pillow, Bill Walker, Charlie Albertson, Charlie Walker, Sound, Inc., Johnny Carver, Steve Wariner, Clyde Mattocks, and my wife Michele.

I had an idea for the artist to come in and sing just a couple lines, and then I would play the rest of the song as an instrumental. All of those artists came in and did it for no pay at all. They all just volunteered. To have those big stars come in as a favor to me just totally humbled me. To think that Porter Wagner came in for me… I think Porter would have done it for anybody, but it sure made me feel good that he did it for me.

While we were recording Steve Wariner singing "I Walk the Line", I didn't know that Johnny Cash was just next door in a different studio. But my then-daughter-in-law brought Johnny over, and he sat and listened to Steve do the song; and Johnny really enjoyed it. I was honored that he would come over, and I was even more honored that he was proud of the way we did his song.

I have been blessed to receive a number of awards and honors in my career. I won the National Academy of Recording Arts and Science Super Picker award in 1977, 78 and 79.

On August 10, 1996, North Carolina Senator Charlie Albertson came on an episode of the Grand Ole Opry Live on The Nashville Network, and Senator Albertson surprised me by announcing that I was being given the prestigious "Order of the Long Leaf Pine" Award. That's North Carolina's highest civilian honor. I asked Senator Albertson if he had anything to say for my book - and like any good politician, he was not at a loss for words!

"Jimmy is one of my very best friends. I met him way back in 1952 at a local dance. Jimmy was playing guitar. I had just come out of the service, and I was also playing music on the weekend. Jimmy was one of the best, even after he had just started. You know when you're playing with him that you are playing with the very best.

Jimmy is just a good person. He is a lot like his mother. She was so humble, and was a God-fearing woman. His family were good people.

Jimmy helped get me on stage at the Ryman in 1974, just before the Opry moved to the new Opry house. I did a song that I had written, and I was so nervous. More than nervous, I was scared! And when they started the song, I messed up and started singing the chorus. Jimmy yelled at the band, 'He forgot the verse! Go right to the chorus!' It was one of the all-time thrills of my life.

Many years later, I was able to pay him back a little. I went to Governor Hunt and lobbied for him to give Jimmy the Long Leaf Pine Award. It's the biggest award given by the Governor of North Carolina. Not many people get it, but Jimmy was very deserving of that award. He has always represented the Tar Heel state very well.

Jimmy is a special person in my life. I love him dearly. He's like a brother to me. I admire the way Jimmy has lived his life. I have great respect for him as a person. He's got a good heart. He gets along so well with everyone, and is so humble. He always says, 'I don't need to be the star. I like supporting other people. I like being in the back,' so I wasn't surprised when I heard the title he had picked for this book. He nailed the title. It sums up how he sees himself."

Senator Charlie Albertson

My hometown of Benson celebrated "Jimmy Capps Appreciation Day" on May 25, 1998, at Johnston Community College. Helen Smith was the one responsible for helping to get me that honor. Helen was a friend of our family from back when I was a kid, and her husband, Ray, was the commander of the Benson American Legion. Ray rose to be the National Commander of the Legion. My parents looked at the Smith children, Anita, Gordon and Amy as their semi-grandchildren.

The Johnston County Heritage Center honored me in 2009 with another "Jimmy Capps Day", and they asked me to do a concert at the Barefoot Auditorium in Benson - the building that was originally my high school auditorium.

I kept telling Michele that we wouldn't have anybody come, but we ended up doing two nights, and they were both sold-out shows! It was weird and humbling to see people whom I hadn't seen in 30 or 40 years, and they all came out to support me.

In 2011, I won the R.O.P.E. Musician of the Year award. In January 2014, Bill Haslam, the Governor of Tennessee, appointed me as a "Tennessee Ambassador of Goodwill". I really didn't know what that title meant, but the proclamation says I am expected to "carry the message of Tennessee's hospitality to all people of other states and other lands".

That "other lands" sounds mighty impressive. Hope I'm up to it.

In 2012, the Country Music Hall of Fame named me one of its "Nashville Cats". A "Nashville Cat" is a session player or singer who the Hall of Fame thinks has played an important role in country music history. It is a very big deal. They choose you for what you've done through the years. It really made me feel good when they said I was worthy of that.

But the day of the ceremony just might have been the scariest moment of my life. I looked out over the audience and saw all of my peers sitting there, paying respect to me. I've never been as scared as I was then.

I looked out there and saw Jerry Kennedy, Weldon Myrick, Harold Bradley and Reggie Young. All of them were my heroes. That really got to me.

I asked them to let me do some music instead of talk. But they said the program was all an interview with no music. However, they finally agreed to let me do some songs. I got Michele to sing, while James Freeze played bass and Mark Beckett was on drums. The music made me more comfortable, and also made the program more entertaining. Since then, they have changed their program so that they have music on every show.

The highest honor for me is the fact that I was accepted by my peers. All the awards and recognition are great, and I appreciate it all so much. But when you are accepted by your peers, that is the highest honor there is. That is the top rung of the ladder for me. Speaking of top of the ladder…

On March 16, 2014, I was given an honor that was so huge, I had never even dreamed of getting it. I was inducted into the Musician's Hall of Fame, and I was so thrilled that my friend Barbara Mandrell was also inducted into the Hall on the same day. Since I had played with her on most of her hits, the occasion gave us a chance to celebrate our careers together.

During the ceremony, Kenny Rogers sent a video message. I was so humbled by the words he said, "Jimmy, congratulations on your Hall of Fame induction. I have done "The Gambler" with five hundred different orchestras and nobody can play that intro like you do. I'm glad you were part of my career and my success, and I'm glad to be a part of yours."

And just when I thought I couldn't get any more blessed, only two weeks later, George Hamilton IV announced to the crowd at the Grand Ole Opry house that I had been chosen to be inducted into the North Carolina Music Hall of Fame. That ceremony took place on Oct 16, 2014.

Luckily, I kept my best suit clean… because five months later, I was invited to the Tennessee State Capitol, where I was honored by the State Senate. I couldn't believe it, as I listened to them read the joint resolution that celebrated the life and career of Jimmy Capps! I was also touched that my friends Moe Bandy, Jan Howard, Ray Pillow, and Gus Arrendale were among many friends and family members who'd gone along to see me receive that honor.

As I was finishing up this book, I got word that, twenty years after the first "Jimmy Capps Day", I will be honored again in Benson. The month of May 2019 will be "Jimmy Capps Month", and Jerry Medlin, the mayor of Benson, says that they will put up a historical sign in front of the home where I grew up at 216 West Church Street. The street in front of my old home will be named "Honorary Jimmy Capps Blvd.".

I'm told the Sheriff of Johnston County will make me an honorary deputy, complete with my own official uniform!

Benson is located in Johnston County, which is known for producing more sweet potatoes than any other county in the world. And I'm sure that even after the big "Jimmy Capps Month" celebration, the town will still be known more for its sweet potatoes!

And I have now reached the milestone of being the longest tenured player in the history of the Opry. I am so honored and proud to have been there that long. That's a lot of years. If I was a real sheriff, I would have probably been voted out by now. If I had been working for Ford, or for some other company, they would have probably fired me and then hired me back with no perks.

But hopefully I have done a good job. I pray that I have done something right. I pray every day that I have earned my keep. I would hate to think that I had not done my very best for everyone I have worked with.

I have also done my best with the book that you are getting ready to close. I have tried to remember the things I needed to get down for history, and I've tried to keep it as entertaining as possible, while still telling the truth.

I have enjoyed the process of writing this book. I didn't think I would. But when I started going through all of our old pictures, so many memories came back to me. When I look at photos of me playing in the radio stations when I was 14, I can still smell the cigarette smoke that always filled those studios. I can actually smell that smoke right now.

I've enjoyed looking back and remembering things that I hadn't thought about for decades. I also enjoyed reading what my friends and other artists had to say about me. I was pleasantly surprised at their kind words! Many of them actually brought me to tears. It was kind of like being able to hear what people would say about you at your funeral, but they said it while I was still here! I like this way much better!

And just when I thought I had read everyone's comments, I was thrilled to learn that Vince Gill wanted to be part of my book!

"I am a musician at my core. I'm a singer and an artist, but I was a musician first. I say I'm a musician who wound up being a fairly good singer. I think I have more in common with guys like Jimmy who are musicians, than I do with performers who are stars.

I was one of those guys who studied the back of record jackets. I wanted to know who all the musicians were and who played what, and I saw Jimmy's name on so many of those records.

When I started performing on the Opry, I knew that I wanted him playing with me. He always plays all my Opry spots. Jimmy is one of a hand full of guys left that had all that history with the old guard, those great musicians who played on so many classic songs. There aren't many of those guys left who were part of that era. Not only is he still there, but he is still playing as great as ever, and he is probably as busy as he ever was.

The Opry is a cast of characters and I adore all of them. Jimmy is character, but he is a heck of a guitar player. I have a great deal of respect for Jimmy and always look forward to getting to hug his neck when I see him at the Opry. We have a great friendship.

In 2004, I did something on the Opry that upset Jimmy, and it really bothered me that he was not happy. I sang a song that I had written with Rodney Crowell. It was called, "It's Hard to Kiss the Lips at Night That Chew Your @ss Out All Day Long." It was a funny song, but I found out that it bothered Jimmy that I sang it on the Opry. Out of my respect for him, I never sang it again.

I live by the motto of "To get respect, it must be given." Jimmy has always given me respect and I've always wanted to give it to him in return. He is one of those guys who you are always glad to see. I'm grateful to have a friend like Jimmy Capps."

– Vince Gill

I was so surprised that Vince took the time to share his kind words, and then I was in disbelief when Marty Stuart yelled, "Stop the Presses! Don't print that book yet! I haven't given my two cents worth."

"Capps has been a part of my life since I was a little boy. I grew up in Mississippi and my favorite day of the week was Saturday. That's because each Saturday, they would air all the syndicated Country Music TV shows that came out of Nashville. My daddy and I would sit and watch those shows all afternoon. The first time I ever saw Capps, he was playing on the Jim and Jesse TV show.

When I was 13 years old, I met Jimmy in person, when I worked the Opry with Lester Flatt. I had watched him so much on TV, to me, he was so famous that he was almost unapproachable. His accomplishments before I ever got into town were just staggering.

Jimmy calls himself "The Man in Back," but he is a mighty important man in back. When Connie and I first got together, she didn't have a band anymore. When she performed, she didn't have that special Connie Smith sound behind her. So I called Capps and asked him to come over and have dinner. I asked him to help us get Connie's sound back. He did, starting with some who were playing on the Opry. And from there, we restarted her band and she got back to sounding like that classic Connie Smith that everyone has always loved.

I had Jimmy on my TV show and he played his heart out. He played a song called "What Was I Supposed to Do?" with the great bluegrass musician Paul Williams. I would put that performance in the top 5 out of 156 episodes of "The Marty Stuart Show." It was awesome.

If he had quit the day after he recorded with the Louvin Brothers, his legacy would have been set forever. But that was just the start for him! There hasn't been a decade in sixty years that he hasn't contributed in huge ways. He has innovated as he has hung onto tradition.

Capps has become the ultimate statesman for the entire Nashville picker society. He has a heart for all the old guys, but also for the new kids who are just starting out. He continues to play brilliantly. Any young musician wanting to come to Nashville, should study Jimmy Capps' life and career. They probably won't match his, but if they could be a tenth of the person and musician that he is, then they will be awesome. Jimmy is a great man."

– Marty Stuart

Marty has an amazing collection of Country Music memorabilia. He had Mother Maybelle Carter's high string guitar, and he asked me to re-string it. I was honored when he let me bring Mother Maybelle's guitar home, so I could work on it. It was such a valuable and historical instrument.

Marty and Connie Smith invited me to their home for dinner. At the end of the evening, Marty said, "Don't leave yet. I've got something for you." He was holding a couple checks that Hank Williams had written to his mother! Marty gave them to me as a gift and I will treasure them for the rest of my life.

Just as I was wrapping up my book, I got word that my dear friend Freddie Hart had passed away. One of the last interviews Freddie ever gave was for my book. I will always treasure the words he shared earlier in this book. Bless your heart Freddie.

With my book completed, to be honest, I'm a little relieved that I can put down my pencil. I'd much rather be holding my guitar! As I look back at my sixty years on the Opry, I can truthfully say, if you love what you do, time just flies. It does not seem like sixty years, and I want to play on the Opry for as long as I can. When I see that I can't do the job, as well as I need and want to, I will resign. But I'd like to do a few more years at least. I'm not quitting right now.

So I hope you'll come see us in Nashville sometime. When you come to the Opry, and they open the big red curtain… I'll be the man in back.

Chapter Eighteen

PARTING SONG

How do you convince someone that they need to write a book of their life story? I asked myself that question many times over a six-year period, as I tried to talk Jimmy Capps into doing that very thing.

When I moved to Nashville in 2001, I was already a huge fan of Larry's Country Diner, but I have to admit that when I first began watching it, I had no idea of just how important Jimmy Capps was in the history of Country Music.

But the more I learned about Jimmy, the more amazed I was that no one had ever written a book on him. So I thought, "Well, I guess I will have to be the person who does." I did a couple months of research, and the more I found, the more convinced I became that Jimmy Capps needed to have a book.

Then I approached Jimmy. His answer… "No. I don't want to do a book. No one would be interested."

I was heartbroken! But I don't give up easy… as you're about to find out.

In the next year, I helped write Ronnie McDowell's autobiography. It turned out to be a great success. Then I approached Jimmy Capps again. "Jimmy, I sure would like to write your book."

Again, he said, "Thanks, but no. No one would buy it."

A short time later, Johnny Lee asked me to help him write his autobiography, and it turned out even better than Ronnie's. And I knew that Jimmy was a friend of Johnny's, so I put a signed copy in his mailbox, along with a letter saying: "I sure would like to write your story." He totally ignored me. No response at all!

Before I had finished writing Johnny's book, his pal Moe Bandy asked if I could do a book with him. While we were working on it, Moe told me that Jimmy Capps was producing his latest album, and I asked if he would call Jimmy and ask him to do an interview with me for Moe's book. So Moe did, and Jimmy invited me over. At the end of our interview about Moe, I told Jimmy, "Ya know, I am having a lot of success with my books. But YOU are the person who I had always wanted to do a book with. All these other great artists are wanting me, but you always turn me down."

Jimmy responded, "Even if someone happened to buy my book, they would be bored reading about me. I'm no star, so thanks, but no thanks."

As soon as Moe's book came out (and it was a great one), I had him sign a copy for Jimmy and Michele, and I took it to their house. Unannounced. I didn't call ahead of time. It was about noon. I rang the door bell and waited... and waited. After about ten minutes, Jimmy came to door... wearing his pajamas.

Remember throughout this book when everyone said that "Jimmy has never said an unkind word to anyone"? Well, that may be true, but on the day that I got him out of bed, I am pretty sure that when I left, he was saying a few unkind words about me! I could tell that he was not happy. He didn't throw me off his front steps, but he didn't invite me in either! I gave him his signed copy of Moe's book and left.

I told Moe what had happened, and he promised that he "would work on Jimmy", to get him to do a book. From then on, every time Moe talked to him, he told him what a fun process it was and what a good guy Scot England was.

The next time I saw Jimmy, I quietly said, "You don't want to write a book, do you Jimmy?"

And he answered, "Ya know, I've been thinking about that. I love the books you've done with everyone. If you want to waste your time, we could try it."

I smiled and said, "I would love to waste my time!"

As I got to know Jimmy, I quickly found that he has amazing memory. He can remember names, years and details. I also found that he wears his emotions on his sleeve, and he's not afraid to show those emotions. He teared up many times throughout the writing of this book, as he talked about his parents, and as he heard what his friends had to say about him. The combination of a great memory and great emotion should make for a great book, especially after the incredible life that Jimmy has led.

Yes, Jimmy Capps is humble. He still doesn't believe that he "is worthy" enough for a book. He just does not realize how great he truly is. Hopefully this book will give him a little indication of that.

My sincere thanks to so many of Jimmy's friends who took the time to share their memories with me. I will always treasure my conversations with Barbara Mandrell, Ronnie Milsap, Steve Wariner, John Conlee, Charlie Daniels, Connie Smith, Bill Anderson, all the Larry's Country Diner cast, and so many, many more.

My thanks to Sylvia, Mandy Barnett and Moe Bandy, for sharing your memories as we shared a meal. When Jimmy Fortune comes over to your house for an afternoon to talk about his friend Jimmy Capps... well, it doesn't get any better than that.

Of course, I also want to thank Jimmy and Michele. You are such a wonderful couple. You know there is nothing I wouldn't do for you. Thank you Jimmy... for (finally) letting me come in off your front steps… and into your life. And thank you for allowing me to be the one to help you tell your amazing story.

– Scot England